My Love Affair with an Island

The History of the Jefferson Islands Club and St. Catherine's Island

Jefferson Glassie

My Love Affair with an Island
The History of the Jefferson Islands Club
and St. Catherine's Island
Jefferson Glassie

Published by:
Peace Evolutions, LLC
Post Office Box 458-51
Glen Echo, MD 20812-0458

Order books from: info@peace-evolutions.com
www.peace-evolutions.com

Printed in the United States.

Publishers Cataloging-in-Publication
(Provided by Quality Books, Inc.)

Glassie, Jefferson Caffery.
   My love affair with an island : the history of the Jefferson Islands Club and St. Catherine's Island / Jefferson Glassie.
   p. cm.
   LCCN 2006934505
   ISBN 0-9753837-5-2

   1. Saint Mary's County (Md.)--History, Local.
   2. Saint Catherine Island (Saint Mary's County, Md.)--History.
   3. Saint Catherine Island (Saint Mary's County, Md.)--Description and travel.
   4. Jefferson Islands Club--History.
   5. Glassie, Jefferson Caffery--Travel--Maryland--Saint Catherine Island (Saint Mary's County)
   I. Title. II. Title: History of the Jefferson Islands Club and St. Catherine's Island.

   F187.S2G54 2006   975.2'41
                            QBI06-600388

To a Clean and Healthy Chesapeake Bay

TABLE OF CONTENTS

INTRODUCTION 1

HISTORICAL SYNOPSIS.......................3

Part I - COLONIAL ST. MARY'S COUNTY

The Potomac River 5

The Voyage of the "Ark" and "Dove"........................... 6

Southern Maryland Native Americans...................... 8

Religious Toleration 9

Maryland Manors 10

Thomas Gerard and St. Clement's Manor...................11

Uprisings in Maryland (1634-1689) 13

St. Clement's Island 15

Part II - ST. CATHERINE'S ISLAND

The Island 29

Captain Jack and Other Owners of
St. Catherine's Island....................................30

Captain Charlie Beitzell....................................33

Local Commerce 35

Captain Sam....................................38

Boats and Builders 39

Ports 40

Doctor Jacobs and Mr. Forbes 41

Part III - THE JEFFERSON ISLANDS CLUB

The Club on Poplar Islands 55

Shang ri-La....................................58

The Transition 62

A Return to Poplar Island? 64

The New Club Improves 65

Uncle Don....................................69

Social Events 72

The 1960s 75

Part IV - MODERN HISTORY

Rejuvenation 87

Jeff and Terry....................................88

Erosion 92

Winter on the Island....................................94

Pleasant Summer Days 96

Late 1970s 99

The Early 1980s....................................101

The New Seawalls 103

The 1990s....................................105

An All-Season Visit to the Island....................................111

INTRODUCTION

I'm in love with an Island. Have been all my life.

Yep, it's true. Before I was old enough to know anything, I was in love with a body of land. It's not that pretty a body. No hills like breasts or streams like wet lips. The Island is really sorta rugged, but it's a beautiful ruggedness.

My parents first took me there on May 29, 1954, or at least that's what the big register book in the Clubhouse says. I was little more than a year old. I wish I could remember it, but then again I wish I could remember a lot of things. Now, in 2006, I've been going to the Jefferson Island Club on St. Catherine's Island for over fifty years. Sure makes you feel old to say that. And, all totaled, I figure I've spent maybe three years physically on that Island. It's home and it's where my heart is.

The initial reason for writing this was to provide Jefferson Island Club members (or even other interested persons, dubbed "off-islanders") with knowledge and appreciation of the history of the Club in all its social, political, local, geographical, environmental, mythical, and traditional aspects. In the 50th Anniversary year, I wrote the first version of this book: "The History of Jefferson Islands Club and St. Catherine's Island" as a historical and informational piece. For this version, although I have retained most of the original, I treat it more as a first person narrative and have woven in random thoughts and musings.

The book is divided into four parts; Colonial St. Mary's County, St. Catherine's Island, the Jefferson Islands Club, and Modern History. They combine to tell what I believe is a fascinating story of a very special and unique Island Club. Let me also mention here that many maps and records refer to St. Catherine's Island as St. Catherine, with no apostrophe 's.' But we've always said St. Catherine's, so that's what I'm going to continue to do.

Thanks and acknowledgements are due to many people and I shall attempt to list as many of them as I can remember here. Thanks to Joe and Rose and Bernie and Dot Wise, Flea Wise, Joe Oliver, Capt. Garner Gibson, George Beitzell, Bo Bailey, Jimmy (big and little) and Helen Oliver, Capt. Sam Bailey, Capt. Frank Fuqua, and Colleen and Darrell Wise. Special thanks to Edwin Beitzell, Robert Pogue and Frederick Tilp, from whom I learned much and used excellent material. Mrs. Mary Alice Palmer, Executive Secretary of the St. Mary's County Historical Society was very special because of her time and encouragement on the first edition. Also thanks to William Warner and James Michener for inspiration. I must also recognize Dante B. Fascell, Claude Pepper, Brooke Lee, and Bill Chappell for their help. Charlie Cromwell deserves special mention here, too. Douglas and Marie Gibson, Mrs. James White, Ed Terres, Jon Swindle, Dale Andrews and Pat Black, Judy Glassie Friis, "Little Henry" Glassie, Jim Somervell, Terry Cullen and Joe O'Malley also gave me assistance when I needed it. Of course, to my parents, Don and Claire Glassie, my brother Haywood, sister Claire, and to my wife, Julie (we got married on the Island) and my children Jay, Anne, and Max (who started going to the Island even younger than me). And also to the members of the Jefferson Islands Club, thank you. Rest well the souls no longer with us, who can't visit the Island anymore.

Jefferson Glassie
North of the Island, near the Potomac River 2006

HISTORICAL SYNOPSIS

In 1930, several Democratic Senators lead by Senator Harry B. Hawes of Missouri, Senator Key Pittman of Nevada, and Senator Joe Robinson of Arkansas sought an island retreat to escape the pressures of their hectic political lives where they could enjoy the beauty, peace, and quiet of the Chesapeake Bay. Compared to now, it probably wasn't so hectic back then. For Members of Congress in those days, travel back to their home states or districts was not as easy as by jet today. So, they tended to hang around Washington more on weekends, and actually spent time with each other, becoming friends with their colleagues across the aisle and even their families. They'd eat together, drink together, and hunt together. Nowadays, our representatives are only in Washington maybe two nights a week, and then fly home. So, they don't get to know one another as well and it seems they tend to hate their colleagues across the aisle. I think we'd be much better off if our elected representatives got drunk together like they used to in the old days.

Initially, the Senators had a difficult time finding the ideal spot for an exclusive retreat on the Chesapeake Bay. But they eventually arranged the purchase of two of the Poplar Islands off the eastern shore of the Bay and the Jefferson Islands Club began. The Club was incorporated as a Maryland stock corporation on January 5, 1931.

The founders decided to admit only "congenial Democrats" as members. In spite of what I just said about all this civility and bipartisanship, they probably wanted a place where they could get away from Republicans for a while. The Senators first contacted Franklin D. Roosevelt, then Governor of New York. A close friend of those who began the Club, he was solidly in favor of the venture. The list of Charter members assembled was pretty darn impressive and included Roosevelt, John Nance Garner, Vice President of the United States; William D. Bankhead, Speaker of the House of Representatives; Bernard M. Baruch, from New York; Royal S. Copland, Senator from New York; James A. Farley, Postmaster General; E. Brooke Lee, Speaker of the Maryland House of Delegates; Breckenridge Long, Ambassador to Italy; Millard E. Tydings, Senator from Maryland; Robert F. Wagner, Senator from New York; and, David I. Walsh, Senator from Massachusetts, to name a few. The complete list appears in a Club brochure dating back to the thirties, excerpts of which are reprinted in this book.

After Roosevelt was elected in 1932, the purpose of the Club expanded to provide a peaceful retreat for the President. The seclusion and solitude of the Poplar Islands in the Chesapeake Bay were treasured as a place where the President could enjoy privacy away from the White House. At least that was the idea. Governor Ritchie proposed an act to the Maryland Legislature to change the name of the islands to the "Jefferson Islands." The Legislature approved the proposal and, although the Club does not still own the islands, they still bear the names.

Under the leadership of Senator Key Pittman, the first President of the Jefferson Islands Club, the membership list was filled with the names of some of the most important and influential men in the country: Winthrop W. Aldridge, Chairman of the Board, Chase National Bank; Sosthenes Behn, Chairman, IT&T; Carle C. Conway, Chairman of the Board, Continental Can Company; Steven Early, Assistant Secretary to the President; Walcott H. Pitkin, General Counsel for IT&T; Louis Rosenstiel, Chairman of the Board, Shenley Distillers Corporation; Myron Taylor, Chairman of the Board, United States Steel Corporation; Gerard Swope, Chairman of the Board, General Electric Company; Thomas J. Watson, Chairman of the Board, IBM; and Owen D. Young, President, General Electric Company. They also had lots and lots of money, which was a good thing. This powerful group of men assembled as the first members of the Club - not too shabby. They initially constructed a large "cottage" or Clubhouse, which the members frequented to relax, hunt, fish, and in general promote the philosophy of "getting away from it all."

The Club enjoyed fifteen idyllic years on the Chesapeake Bay until a fire destroyed the entire Clubhouse on March 5, 1946. Drat. At that time, the Club moved to its present location on St. Catherine's Island in the Potomac River, about sixty miles as the fish swims from Washington, D.C. St. Catherine's Island sits at the confluence of the Potomac and the Wicomico Rivers. This site was much closer to Washington than

HISTORICAL SYNOPSIS

the Poplar Islands and did not require the hour-long boat ride from Annapolis they had to make at the time. The Bay Bridge had not yet been built.

Three miles to the east of St. Catherine's Island lies St. Clement's Island, the site of the landing of the "Ark" and "Dove," the ships that bore the first Maryland colonists. St. Catherine's Island was originally part of the Manor granted to Thomas Gerard in 1639 by Lord Baltimore. Both islands remain rich in history and native folklore. We'll talk a lot about the history of this area.

Today, after seventy five years, the Club has become a social, political, and fraternal organization that still provides a retreat for those weary of city life, but doesn't have enough rich members any more. Somehow, though, we manage to keep on keeping on.

PART I:
COLONIAL ST. MARY'S COUNTY

The Potomac River

I often wonder what the first colonists saw as they sailed up the Potomac River. After a long and hard voyage across the Atlantic, they must have been ready for some dry land. Though we don't have videotape of their arrival, we know one of the passengers on the first ships was Father Andrew White, S.J. He recalls what it was like in his popular book: "Relatio Itineris in Marylandium."

"On the 3rd of March 1634, we came into Chesapeake Bay, at the mouth of Patomecke. This baye is the most delightful water I ever saw, between two sweet landes, with the channel four, five, six, seven, and eight fathoms deepe, some ten leagues broad, at time of year full of fish, yet it doth yield to Patomecke, . . . this is the sweetest and greatest river I have seen, so that the Thames of England is but a little finger to it, but solid firme ground with great variety of woode, not choked up with undershrubs."

Obviously, Father White was impressed by the Potomac River as he sailed northward with the first Maryland colonists in the "Ark" and the "Dove." I have imagined these vessels sailing by the Island. I hail them, "Fare thee well," but they seem surprised to see me and don't wave back.

These colonists undoubtedly thanked "Divine Providence" that the land to which they had arrived was so pleasant. Lord Baltimore, who did not accompany these first settlers, also was grateful for the charter he'd received from the King of England to establish a colony where his fellow Roman Catholics would be free to worship God without religious persecution. Of course, none of them knew how Providence had created the Chesapeake Bay region. For that, we have to take you back, back in time.

During the Miocene Era, just some 10 to 25 million years ago, the level of the ancient seas rose and fell three times in the Chesapeake Bay area. Frozen water, locked in the huge glaciers of the Ice Ages, caused the sea to drop 300 feet below present levels. That seems hard to imagine, but apparently the remaining water in the area left a river that then cut a deep channel into the sea beds. This was the Susquehanna River, the mother of the Chesapeake Bay. The Susquehanna was the most ancient of the rivers that now form tributaries of the Bay. When the last glacier melted, the river valley flooded again and the Chesapeake Bay was formed.

These flooded river valleys are called estuaries, where the salt ocean water merges with fresh water. The Chesapeake Bay is one of the largest estuary systems in the world. Pretty cool, huh. Rivers bring the fresh water of the mountains and springs from the surrounding region and flow into the Bay, which washes back and forth with water from the ocean. A constant mix of the fresh and salt water in both horizontal and vertical directions is necessary for an estuary to be biologically productive. Large expanses of shallow water allow sunlight to penetrate to the bottom and promote rapid plant and animal growth. Many have claimed that the Chesapeake Bay breeds more species of plants and both land and water animals than any body of water in the world. That is, until they all die off from pollution and urban sprawl.

The identity of the first white men who explored the Chesapeake Bay and discovered this incredible ecosystem is not certain. The Vikings, who are known to have searched out and explored lands in the North American continent, may have been the first. Or, it might have been the explorers led by Giovanni da Verrazano from Florentine, Italy, who is reported to have sailed into the Chincoteague inlet in 1524. In 1588, Vincente Gonzales, Captain of a Spanish fort in St. Augustine, Florida, supposedly located the Potomac River and named it the "San Pedro." I think I like the word "Potomac" better, which is a Native American term basically meaning peaceful river.

No matter who the first explorers were, they found that the ancient river beds carved out millions of years ago were still quite deep and suitable for harbors. They were not as deep as they had once been, for the walls of these ancient river channels constantly erode and fill the bottom with sediment. Now, they're even more shallow, having been filled with man's trash and sediment from sewage and agricultural runoff for centuries.

Nonetheless, these explorers had discovered a veritable paradise. Who would not be overjoyed by the many different kinds of fish and seafood the first colonists found -- trout, mackerel, perch, sturgeon, shad, crabs, oysters, mussels, terrapin, toad fish, herring, hardhead, croakers, bass, and many other types that may now be extinct. One wonders whether these colonists were plagued by the sea nettles and jelly fish that now inhabit the waters of the Bay in summer.

On land, they found beautiful, tall forests, "with the goodliest trees for masts that may be found elsewhere in the world," according to Captain Henry Fleet. Fleet was a guide for Captain John Smith of Virginia, who was the first to record in detail the nature of the Potomac River and the Bay. Captain Smith sailed the entire Bay in 1607 and found the Potomac to be navigable for 140 miles. He chronicled the many different types of animals that lived on the land. With the additional information of Father White's accounts, it can be determined that elk, deer, mink, fox, bobcat, bear, wolf, martin and even buffalo roamed. Beaver, otter and muskrat abounded. The woods and forests sang with wild turkeys, pigeons, pheasants, partridges, squirrels, rabbits, woodcocks, snipe, crows, owls, hawks, buzzards and eagles, including the now nearly extinct bald eagle. The wild game proliferated to the extent that Father White wrote "deer exist in such quantity that they are an annoyance rather than an advantage." Funny, but some people would probably say that now.

One can hardly conceive of the numbers of geese, swan, and every type of duck imaginable that would visit the Bay area during the winter. These water fowl were attracted to the wild celery, widgeon grass, eel grass, and other kinds of sea weed and thick subaquatic vegetation that grew throughout the shallow water and marshes of the Bay and River. These marsh lands were ideal spots for many types of lizards and reptiles, but more importantly, provided breeding grounds for many types of fish. Unfortunately, champion mosquitoes found these marshes equally enjoyable. Many varieties of fruit and vegetables grew wild: asparagus and poke, chestnuts, walnuts, hickory nuts, strawberries, blackberries, huckleberries, elderberries and grapes. It certainly seems that it would be difficult to go hungry in such a region as this! The areas around Poplar Islands and St. Catherine's Island both proliferated with just such an abundance of wild fauna and flora. Lord Baltimore and the colonists had selected a virtually unspoiled paradise for their Maryland colony.

The Voyage of the "Ark" and "Dove"

George Calvert was the first Lord Baltimore, a member of Parliament and a secretary of state during the reigns of both Kings Charles I and James I. Imagine having your name include the title "Lord." That would be pretty neat. A member of both the London and Plymouth Companies and of the East India Company ("Exploration and exploitation are us!"), Calvert had interests in trade and colonization, demonstrated by his attempt to form a settlement in the 1620s in Avalon, New Foundland. This venture failed because New Foundland, though on the same degree of latitude as England, was much too cold. George Calvert had moved there with his family in 1627 only to return to England a year later. I can understand that.

Two years prior he had announced his conversion to Catholicism and the Avalon venture had been an attempt to find a location where he might settle and practice his religion freely. The announcement of his conversion nearly cost him his political career in London and created many enemies. He probably was viewed as a "radical" or "extremist" Catholic; you know how people don't like others who take a different faith just as seriously. With some stroke of "Providence," he was able to retain favor with King Charles I (imagine having a "I" after your name; that would make you pretty important, too). Shortly after his return to England he convinced the King to assign him a grant of land in North America. This land grant entitled him to an area Calvert called "Oceania" but was also named by the King "Terra Maria," or Maryland. The King prevailed, of course. Originally, the area specified in the grant was approximately twice the size of the State of Maryland today. Over the years, it was reduced -- some say stolen -- by Pennsylvania and Virginia.

For all practical purposes, this grant afforded George Calvert royal powers. Unfortunately, he passed away in 1632 and never saw the Maryland colony. The grant, however, was an inheritance possession and his son Cecilius Calvert became the second Lord Baltimore and took up the venture in the same determined manner as his father. Cecilius Calvert decided to stay in England and protect the Charter from some of his father's enemies in the Royal Court. He named his younger brother, Leonard Calvert, deputy governor of Maryland and sent him with the "Ark" and the "Dove" to the New World.

The Captain of the "Ark," Richard Low, planned to embark in the fall of 1633 so the ships could sail a warm weather course to Maryland and arrive in the New World for the spring planting season. Unfortunately, the voyage was not a pleasant one. On November 22, 1633, the "Ark" and "Dove" set sail. The "Ark" was a 400 ton ship approximately 72 feet long, while the "Dove" was tiny, only about 40 tons and 42 feet long. They set sail from Cowes on the Isle of Wight in England. Amazingly, over 150 people squeezed aboard these two ships. Seventeen "gentlemen" were aboard, including some of those who had invested in Lord Baltimore's plan to establish a colony in the New World; I suppose the rest of the men were unruly.

The "Ark" and the "Dove" set sail after having been detained by the decree of the government that the colonists take an oath of allegiance to the King and to the Church of England. Most of the individuals had complied, but some, including the Jesuit Priests Andrew White, John Altham and Brother Thomas Gervase, had hidden themselves on ship to avoid taking the oath. Good for them; I don't believe passengers should have to take an oath of allegiance to a King and a Church before taking off. Imagine the delays that would result at airports nowadays on top of security searches.

Immediately after departing, the ships encountered terrible weather and were forced to drop anchor in a close harbor. In the middle of the night, another ship was driven by gale winds upon the "Dove," which cut its anchor line to avoid collision and had to take to sea. The "Ark" pulled anchor and followed her so that the smaller "Dove" would not be separated so early in the voyage. The two ships survived that squall but on November 25, another fierce ocean storm developed. During the night of the storm, colonists on the "Ark" battled winds and raging seas, but in the morning the "Dove" was nowhere to be seen. Sorrowfully, the folks on the "Ark" assumed that the "Dove" had been lost and continued on the journey. Horrible weather still plagued the "Ark," which fought another storm so powerful that the main sail tore nearly in two. After repairs, the "Ark" enjoyed clear sailing the rest of the way to Barbados, where it anchored to take on fresh water and supplies.

Joyfully, the "Dove" appeared! Hooray! She had not been sunk on that unfortunate night in November, but had returned to England and waited out the weather in a safe harbor. That was really smart thinking; it was a weeny boat. She then had pressed on alone to rendezvous with the "Ark" in Barbados. The two ships together completed the voyage to the Chesapeake Bay.

The first stop in America was Virginia, where Leonard Calvert met with leaders of that colony and sought advice regarding the best site for a settlement. On the 3rd of March 1634, Calvert arrived at the mouth of the Potomac River. The colonists scouted the Potomac for 22 days and finally came upon an island considered safe to debark, which they named St. Clement's Island. This name was chosen because it had been on the feast day of St. Clement's in England when a plot to prevent the sailing of the "Ark" and the "Dove" had been discovered and quelled. Probably those radical Anglicans trying to keep the Catholics from the Promised Land.

March 25th commemorates the landing of the two vessels on St. Clement's Island, only three miles from St. Catherine's Island, and is now celebrated statewide as Maryland Day. The landing at this site points out the historic location enjoyed by the Jefferson Islands Club on St. Catherine's Island. In memory of this occasion in 1934, the 300th Anniversary of the landing, a 40 foot high concrete cross was constructed on St. Clement's Island. It can be seen by all those who sail by on the Potomac River. You can now even see it from the front porch of the Clubhouse. It used to be that you couldn't, but the land south of the Clubhouse eroded so much that it now provides a nice view.

A curious incident arose when Leonard Calvert sent the women ashore at St. Clement's Island with the dirty laundry. (I don't think he could have gotten away with that today.) Anyway, to the horror of Father White, the shallop (a small boat) that carried the maidens was overturned by a wave and not only were some of the women nearly drowned, but "the linen they went to wash was much of it lost, which is no small matter in these parts." Can you imagine arriving in the New World with no underwear!

The colonists quickly demonstrated thanks for the good fortune of finding such a peaceful, beautiful, and secure sight as this Island (in spite of the problem with the laundry). One of the first actions they took after dropping anchor and trying to wash their clothes was to construct a wooden cross on St. Clement's Island. Under this cross, Father White performed the Holy Sacrifice of the Mass, reportedly the first in the Maryland colony. This Mass celebrated their safe voyage and asked for blessings on the future of the colony. Very soon thereafter, Father White and several of the crew members sailed from St. Clement's past an island which they named St. Catherine's Island and into a creek. The good Father must have looked favorably on the snug harbor formed by the Island that is now the landing area for the Club, overlooked by the Farmhouse. He probably stopped and explored a bit of St. Catherine's Island before continuing up the Creek. White's Neck Creek (the good Father must have named the creek after his neck) now is the sight of the Jefferson Islands Club pier and parking lot. The creek was much wider at the neck than now, by local account.

Father White established a crude wooden missionary church on the banks of the Creek and began converting the Native Americans. He was very successful at convincing them that his god was better than their gods (probably because the Catholics had guns and clean clothes) and converted many of the Indians to Catholicism, both at this site and at other mission outposts he later established.

Meanwhile, Leonard Calvert left the crew with the "Ark" at St. Clement's Island and sailed up river with the aforementioned Captain Henry Fleet, who had joined the colonists to act as guide and interpreter. They sailed in the "Dove" to the village of the native Piscataway and Algonquin tribes. The Native American chief was very wary of the white men, as indeed he should have been. He reigned over a peaceful tribe that was even more afraid of the hostile and war-like Susequehannocks, who resided to the north, and also of the wrathful Iroquois and Senecas, who frequently raided his village. The Maryland colonists were granted permission by the chief to settle where they could. Governor Calvert returned to St. Clement's Island and, after discussions with the investors, decided on a sight for the new settlement down the river. Calvert and the colonists sailed south to the St. Mary's River (which had been originally named St. George's by Calvert) and upstream six miles to a small Yoacomico village. Henry Fleet had known of this village and also may have known that the Yoacomico chief was about to move his village because of his fear of raids by the Susequehannock Indians.

The Yoacomicos were very peaceful. They agreed to sell some of their land at the present site of St. Mary's City to Leonard Calvert in exchange for some of the supplies the colonists had brought with them. So it was that the first colony of Maryland was founded on the shores of the St. Mary's River, at a spot with a deep harbor and nearby high bluff to secure the colonists' fort. The site was named St. Mary's in honor of Henrietta Maria, Queen of England. St. Mary's was to be the capital of Maryland until 1695, at which time the government was moved to present day Annapolis.

Soon the colonists had built a large settlement stabilized by a fort 120 yards square with numerous houses and structures. There were gardens and fields both inside and outside the fort. Although the neighboring Natives were friendly, everyone living in both Maryland and Virginia were always afraid of the hostile Susequehannocks, Iroquois, and Senecas. Nonetheless, the settlers began to spread out and the city prospered. The first summer yielded a good crop, and a surplus shipment of corn was even sent back to England. Within the next few decades, the city included the Governor's House, the State House, the jail, several taverns, a mill, a chapel, several offices, shops and warehouse, and about 60 private residences.

Some buildings at St. Mary's City have been reconstructed as they were during the first days of the colony. A replica of the "Dove" sits at anchor and may be visited. Unfortunately, the original "Dove" was lost at sea on a return voyage from Maryland. She apparently had been neglected by her Captain in the year following the initial voyage. The "Ark" returned to England not too long after 1634, but no records of any further voyages have been found. I believe that names of these two ships should go down in history beside those of the "Nina," "Pinta," and "Santa Maria" of Christopher Columbus, and the "Mayflower" of the Pilgrims. It is a very pleasant experience to visit St. Mary's City and recall the beginning of the Maryland colony. One does wonder why St. Clement's Island or nearby Leonardtown was not chosen by Governor Calvert as the site for the first settlement. He might even have considered St. Catherine's Island!

Southern Maryland Native Americans

The reason most of the Natives in southern Maryland were peaceful was the bountiful supply of game, fish, and vegetables they enjoyed. They established villages at many different locations, but usually near the River and fresh water springs. At that time, and until recently, fresh water flowed and bubbled to the surface at many points in St. Mary's County. One of these points is River Springs, near St. Catherine's Island. Normally, many of the nomadic Natives subsisted at one fishing and hunting site until enough of a "trash pile" had accumulated and then they would move to another site. This accounts for the many piles of oyster shells and other Indian artifacts that have been found near the River.

Yours truly has observed one such large trash pile just north of the Island. It was high in a bank above the River. Erosion had caused the land to fall into the water, and the trash pile had been neatly dissected. It seemed to be about ten feet high, maybe twenty or thirty feet wide. Mostly oyster shells could be seen. Many local people and a few of the members of the Jefferson Islands

Club also have discovered Indian arrowheads along the shore of the River.

There were approximately 1,300 Native Americans in southern Maryland when the colonists arrived and they lived at many sites that now bear traditional names such as: Anacostia, Mattawoman, Piscataway, Nanjamoi, and Wicomico. They used small canoes or dugouts to travel over the rivers, creeks, and sounds. The Native Americans reportedly loved Father White and this accounted for his success in converting them to Christianity. A story is told by Robert Pogue of White's visit with the Piscataway tribe, located several miles north of St. Catherine's Island. The chief of the Piscataways, Kittamaquund, had listened for hours and hours to Father White tell the stories of the Bible and became convinced of its truth. When Kittamaquund decided to convert, Father White enlisted Leonard Calvert and some of the other gentlemen from the settlement to attend the baptism. Kittamaquund donned English clothing and was given the Christian name, Charles, during the ceremony. Kittamaquund was so devoted to Father White that seven years later he brought his little daughter to the priest. She was baptized as Mary Brent Kittamaquund and Leonard Calvert and the famous local landowner Margaret Brent agreed to become her guardians. Margaret Brent was one of the foremost lawyers in the Maryland colony and one of the first supporters of women's rights. After Leonard Calvert died, she became the girl's sole guardian and brought her up as one of her own. When this Native princess grew up she married Margaret's brother, Giles Brent. I myself have never understood trying to convince people that one religion is better than another.

The first years of St. Mary's City were peaceful, for the Yoacomicos were very friendly and brought the colonists much of their bounty, including wild turkeys, partridges, and cornbread. The Yoacomicos were different from many of the other southern Maryland tribes in that they were farmers who lived in permanent wood-barked houses. The Yoacomicos showed the colonists how to hunt and instructed them on the peculiarities of the area, including fishing for oysters and maninose clams. Leonard Calvert wrote to his brother Cecilius in England that the Native Americans were one of the main factors in the initial success of the colony.

It is sad to note, however, that within one hundred years there were only about eighty or ninety Natives left in southern Maryland. They had not warred with the white men, but their relationship with the men of the Calvert colony had put them in extremely bad standing with the Susequehannock and Iroquois Indians. The Marylanders and the Virginians had begun to have real trouble with the warlike Indians, who continually attacked both the peaceful southern Maryland Natives and the white men in Maryland and Virginia, murdering and pillaging. The weaker southern Maryland tribes had already started moving farther north along the Potomac River to avoid the destructive path of the Susequehannocks. Although a treaty was drawn in 1652 between the Susequehannocks and the whites, it was broken in 1676 when the Iroquois attacked the Susequehannocks and forced them south against the peaceful southern Maryland Natives. At this time, the Marylanders and the Virginians joined forces against the Iroquois and the Susequehannocks. Both of the hated tribes were defeated and almost wiped out by the whites under the command of Nathaniel Bacon in a bloody battle fought near Richmond.

An example of the friendship of the southern Maryland Natives to the Marylanders was given by Maquata, chief of the Mattawoman Indians, who volunteered his services against the Susequehannocks during this trouble. The Chapticos, Nanjemoys, and Piscataways also fought with the colonists against the Susequehannocks. From this time on, the southern Maryland Natives slowly dwindled away; their numbers diminished from years of raiding by their enemies; the Susequehannocks, Senecas and Iroquois. This is an unfortunate chapter in the history of southern Maryland, which initially had been blessed with good relationships with the Native Americans who lived along the peaceful Potomac near where St. Catherine's Island sits today.

Religious Toleration

In sixteenth century England, it was very difficult for a man or woman to practice his or her religion if that religion was not the Anglican Church. It was probably like modern day Islamic countries. A belief in the infallibility and supremacy of the Pope was certainly treasonous to the King, in the opinion of the good Anglicans, much like drawing cartoons of Mohammed are blasphemous to good Muslims. George Calvert, the first Lord Baltimore, realized that some sort of a retreat or haven was necessary for English Catholics to practice their religion. But he was practical enough to understand that he would never be successful in obtaining a charter from the King if he spoke too loudly of his goal.

Once he had regained the confidence of Charles I after declaring his Catholicism, and received the Maryland charter, he then faced the problem of attracting investors to finance the colony and men and women to inhabit it. He knew that most of those who might be eligible would be Protestants or members of the Anglican Church. This was proven correct, for those who had departed on the "Ark" and the "Dove" in 1633 had been required, as you will recall, to take an oath of allegiance to the King and to the Anglican Church.

Thus, the first Lord Baltimore had set out to achieve two goals for the Maryland colony. The first was to establish a colony in which any Christian, particularly of the Roman Catholic persuasion, would be allowed to live in peace without fear of retribution from the government; the second, that the venture be financially profitable and hopefully reap grand rewards. As stated previously, George Calvert died in 1632 before the voyage, to be succeeded in his quest by his son Cecilius Calvert, the second Lord Baltimore. Cecilius followed in his father's footsteps with the same purposeful energy. He proved to be a wise and strong leader, though he also was never able to see Maryland. Bummer.

In order to establish a political entity which would be stable and free from criticism by his father's enemies in England and that would still provide freedom of conscience for Roman Catholics, the second Lord Baltimore had to make it appear that Catholics did not control the new colony. He realized that the assistance of many Protestants would be necessary if his plans were to succeed. They obviously could not be expected to support him in a colony espousing a doctrine treasonous to the King. He thus decreed that all men should join together in the decisions affecting the common good of the colony. This could occur only if the Catholics were sure to avoid religious disagreements with the Protestants and were certain not to offend those who professed allegiance to the King, as ruler of the civil body.

The Catholics would have to endorse toleration of other religions as well as their own. Calvert believed religion was an individual concern and that only one's role as a citizen should be taken into account in civil affairs. He recognized that the only way to achieve this goal would be to end all discrimination and persecution on religious grounds. I'm all for that.

Thus, in his instructions to his brother Leonard, prior to the voyage of the "Ark" and the "Dove," Cecilius Calvert, the second Lord Baltimore, wrote that they must be "…. very careful to preserve the peace and unity throughout their voyage to Maryland amongst the passengers on shipboard and that they suffer no scandal nor offense to the Protestants, whereby any just complaint may here and after be made to them in Virginia or England and for that end to cause all acts of Roman Catholic religion to be done as privately as may be and that they instruct all the Roman Catholics to be silent, upon all occasions of discourse concerning matters of religion and that the said governor and commissioners treat the Protestants with as much mildness and favor as justice will permit. And this to be ordered on land and sea."

This decree may have been the first in the history of the world proclaiming religious toleration as a matter of law. The Catholics and Protestants were then able to work together to successfully settle the Maryland colony. This announcement of religious toleration was verified by an assembled group of individuals on April 2, 1649 at St. Mary's City, then the capital of Maryland. The General Assembly met and approved on April 21st the provincial bill entitled "An Act Concerning Religion," later to become known as the "Toleration Act." And while this is all well and good, the Act itself protected only believers in Jesus Christ from persecution. So, the Maryland Toleration Act was not as significant in my mind as the statue in Virginia penned by Thomas Jefferson, which provided broadly for religious freedom.

Maryland Manors

To accomplish his second goal of financial success, the first Lord Baltimore had needed a plan to finance and populate his new colony. Though the idea of a refuge for Roman Catholics loomed strong, George Calvert was forced to consider the practical applications of the success of the colony. He already had invested much of his fortune in the doomed New Foundland adventure and was hard pressed to support the Maryland colonization.

Due to the vast powers granted to Lord Baltimore in the charter, he essentially was free to develop any plan that would work. The charter from the King granted the proprietor of the colony the power to declare war, institute marshal law, legislate with the assent of an assembly elected among the colonists, establish courts, punish crimes, and appoint the officials necessary for the operation of the colony. In addition, the regulation of trade, the imposition of taxes and custom duties, and the creation of honors and titles were included in the powers given to the proprietor. For all intents and purposes, Calvert was "King of Maryland."

The plan which Lord Baltimore developed and his son Cecilius implemented enticed investors by offering them "manors" in Maryland, that is, large areas of land with all the titles and powers that went with the traditional European manor. In addition, the investors anticipated reaping great profits from the establishment of cities in the new colony and the expected lucrative trade from the New World, particularly the fur trade. I guess they planned to kill lots of animals, so that the gents and ladies back in England could have nice coats.

Lord Baltimore proposed to grant 2,000 acres of land to any adventurer who could transport five armed men between the ages of sixteen and fifty to the colony. The estimated cost of transporting and equipping a servant was twenty English pounds, thus for only one hundred pounds, a wealthy gentleman from England could purchase 2,000 acres of land in the New World. Not only that, but for each person brought to America, the financier would be promised ten acres of land in town, which Lord Baltimore predicted would increase rapidly in value as the towns grew larger. As an extra enticement, such adventurers were to be offered the possibility of titles and offices in the new colony.

Lord Baltimore planned to create a class of privileged gentry in the New World with the promise of social, political, and economic advantages that went along with the manor grant. He also anticipated that these gentlemen would maintain their loyalty to him, since their power in the new colony would be dependent upon his position as proprietor.

Because of his Roman Catholic inclinations, Calvert initially did have some difficulty securing investment. This proved to be a great drain on his already depleted finances but, to his credit, he pushed ahead. You know how those Catholics are! It may also not come as much of a surprise that the Jesuits were some of his chief early investors. The Society of Jesus financed the transportation of twenty men in the initial voyage and many others later. So that's how they got all their land! In addition to the Jesuits, there were several other individuals who became major supporters of the venture. Most well known of these were Thomas Cornwallis and Richard Gerard. Thomas Cornwallis was a devout Catholic and ancestor of Lord Cornwallis, familiar to those who have studied American history and remember the defeat of the British forces by George Washington in Yorktown in 1781. Richard Gerard was the son of Sir Thomas Gerard, a Roman Catholic in England, and of distant relation to the Thomas Gerard who was to receive the St. Clement's Manor grant.

While Lord Baltimore's manor plan ultimately provided finances for the initial colonization, the rewards were not quite as great as hoped. Revenue from the fur trade proved to be a disappointment (except to the animal lovers, if there were any back then). Not only were the colonists apparently uninterested in killing animals and trapping furs, but the first load of Maryland furs was lost at sea on the fatal return voyage of the "Dove."

Several other difficulties arose that reduced the effectiveness of the manor system. First of all, there was a great tendency of the colonists to spread out and settle away from the city. Many of those who journeyed to the new colony were indentured servants who soon gained their freedom. To many young men, the idea of continuing to rely on the proprietor seemed restrictive in such an unbounded territory. In addition, it has been argued that the ratio of five men to 2,000 acres was not sufficient to develop such a vast wilderness successfully and rapidly. Since the indentured servants were usually given the right to their own land after four or five years, the colony soon consisted of a majority of free land owners rather than one ruled absolutely by manor lords.

Nonetheless, the foundation of the manorial system led to the establishment of a viable, strong colony. Between 1634 and 1684, there were as many as eighty manors granted in the new Maryland. The so-called lords of these manors were influential in determining the areas where the colonists would settle. The manor houses or plantations themselves became bustling centers of activity and trade. This fact tended to disperse the population from the cities to the various manors rather than urbanize it as the Lords Baltimore had anticipated. George Calvert's plan was basically successful, but not in quite the way he would have hoped.

Thomas Gerard and St. Clement's Manor

The largest manor granted by Lord Baltimore was St. Clement's Manor, which was granted, in several parts. The original manor grant of 1,000 acres was issued to Thomas Gerard on November 3, 1639. This land grant included Colton's Point, bounded by St. Clement's Bay on the east and the Wicomico River to the west, and the three islands named by Father Andrew White -- St. Clement's, St. Catherine's, and St. Margaret's. Thus, Thomas Gerard was the first legal (English) owner of the Island now treasured by the members of the Jefferson Islands Club. Gerard continued to expand his holdings by bringing more colonists to Maryland. Additional grants later totaled the amount of land in St. Clement's Manor at over 11,400 acres. The King granted Gerard two other manors in Maryland: Bathsford Manor, to the north of St. Clement's, and Westwood Manor in what is now Charles County. In addition, he had been granted 3,500 acres of land in Westmoreland County, Virginia, directly across the Potomac from the St. Clement's estate.

At this point, it's appropriate to note for the record two gentlemen whose research brought to light the circumstances surrounding Thomas Gerard and much of the history of St. Mary's County. Edwin W. Beitzell, former Editor of the monthly Chronicles of the St. Mary's County Historical Society, was the pre-eminent historian of the area. Mr. Beitzell wrote many books, including "Life on the Potomac" a rich and valuable survey of the history of the area, including St. Catherine's Island. Mr. Beitzell's uncle, Charlie Beitzell, owned St. Catherine's Island from 1916 to 1927. More on that later. Mr. Beitzell was very helpful in assisting me with the initial writing of this book. He also is the man who researched most of the history of Thomas Gerard. I remember visiting wonderful old Edwin Beitzell in the late 1970's at his home in St. Mary's County. In addition, David Spaulding, a member of the Xaverian Brothers, wrote an excellent article on Thomas Gerard published in the Chronicles. Brother Spaulding's research has been a great benefit to those who study this facet of Maryland history. So, based on all this good research, let me tell you a little something about Thomas Gerard.

Dr. Thomas Gerard was baptized in Winwick, England, December 10, 1608, in the Gerard Chapel, now contained in the village church in Ashton in Lancashire. Thomas Gerard married Susanna Snow, the sister of three gentlemen who had become acquainted with Lord Baltimore and had supported and invested in the efforts of the Maryland colonization. Abel Snow held an important post in the Curator's Office in London. The other two brothers, Justinian and Marmaduke, traveled to Maryland but both encountered various difficulties and Gerard became the administrator of the Snow estate in Maryland. Evidently, Gerard had decided to throw his fate to the Maryland venture for several reasons: one, he was a Roman Catholic searching for a place to practice his faith; two, he was related to the Snow brothers who had already cast their lot with Lord Baltimore; and three, he saw the Maryland colony as an opportunity to win himself much power and land. For this vision he may be said to have been a very perceptive gentleman.

Thomas Gerard served for many years in the Maryland government. He was one of two Burgesses elected to the General Assembly in 1639. In March of 1640, he was commissioned by the Proprietor as Conservator of Peace for St. Clement's under the political division of the colony. (What a great title; I wish I could be the Conservator of Peace of Somewhere!) Ultimately, he was appointed to the Provincial Council, where he served for many years until 1660. Not only did Thomas Gerard claim credit in all of these positions, but he was also noted as a prominent practitioner of medicine, an able farmer, and a master at the manufacturing of liquor, "particularly peach brandy." In addition, he was responsible for the erection of an Anglican Chapel, probably before 1641, for his friends. This chapel was on Colton's Point, not far from the St. Clement's manor house that overlooked St. Clement's Island and Bay. Dr. Gerard constructed many other homes throughout the county.

As one of the largest landholders in Maryland, Gerard became more than just closely involved in the colony's political affairs. Several incidents had tremendous effects on the government of Lord Baltimore and the growth of the colony, including areas in the immediate vicinity of St. Catherine's Island, which became a hotbed of activity.

Gerard had a very large family and they reportedly were wild and unrestrained, for the St. Clement's manor house was sometimes referred to as "Bedlam Neck." He had ten children, seven of them daughters. Mary Gerard, the youngest of the ten children, married Kenelm Cheseldine, who was given St. Catherine's Island as a dowry, in addition to the land around White's Neck Creek, Westwood Lodge and Mattapany. The Cheseldine family held St. Catherine's Island for many years until it became the property of the Blackistone family. The actual land records only date back to 1831, when all previous information was lost in a fire that consumed the Leonardtown Courthouse.

Another of Thomas Gerard's children, Elizabeth, married Nehemiah Blackistone, who received St. Clement's Island, Colton's (Longworth) point, and Dare's Neck as her dowry. St. Clement's Island is still referred to as Blackistone's Island. This Blackistone is the same family as Zachariah "Demmie" Blackistone, the florist in Washington, D.C., who lived to 110 years of age. I remember visiting him, too, before he died. He was very old and did not remember much, but it was a privilege to meet him. Two of Gerard's other daughters married Colonel John Washington, an ancestor of George Washington. Yes, you read that right. Ann Gerard married John Washington first, and then when she died, her sister Frances married the Colonel. George Washington was born at Wakefield, Virginia right across the Potomac from St. Catherine's, where a national memorial now stands.

Uprisings in Maryland (1634-1689)

There were several instances after the initial founding of the Colony when the security of Lord Baltimore's government was severely threatened. These events oftentimes were affected by events in England, which underwent a very tumultuous period.

The earliest threat to the sovereignty of the Calverts came from the eastern shore of Maryland. Captain William Claiborne, a Puritan fur trader from Virginia, had settled on Kent Island in the Chesapeake Bay in 1631. This does, of course, undermine the credibility of St. Clement's Island claim-to-fame that it was the site of the first landing of colonists in Maryland in 1634. But the whole issue is sort of moot in that the Native Americans were already here and, if anyone had a claim to the land or sovereignty over it, they did.

Claiborne maintained that since he had settled prior to the signing of Calvert's charter, he was a citizen of Virginia and not Maryland. Claiborne actually possessed no legal right under English law to deny the authority granted by the Maryland charter, which included Kent Island, especially since the charter of the Virginia colony had expired in 1624. Nonetheless, Claiborne decided to fight the Second Lord Baltimore, Cecilius Calvert, and his younger brother, Governor Leonard Calvert. This eventually led to the "Battle of the Pocomoke," the first Maryland naval battle in which several men were killed. Claiborne's band was defeated by the Maryland forces, under the command of Thomas Cornwallis, and he was banished from the colony by Governor Calvert. Claiborne continued to cause dissension for Calvert for many years.

A man named Richard Thompson was one of Claiborne's henchmen. Thompson settled on Poplar Island just south of Claiborne's Kent Island. Poplar Island was the original site of the Jefferson Islands Club from 1931 to 1946, as we shall discuss in more detail later. Thompson accompanied Claiborne during the "Battle of the Pocomoke," but while he was away, the fierce Nanticoke Indians of the Eastern Shore attacked his home on Poplar Island and savagely murdered his wife, children and servants. Imagine, with so much land and abundant resources, humans have to be killing and fighting all the time. It's just so dumb.

Meanwhile, Governor Leonard Calvert returned to England in 1644 to visit his brother Lord Baltimore. During his stay, he married Ann Brent, sister of Margaret Brent, and spent several pleasant years in England. In his absence he had named Giles Brent, brother of Margaret Brent, acting Governor. At the time there was trouble in London and the Parliament was engaged in rather acrimonious debate with the King. Many horrible years in Maryland began with a single incident in St. Clement's Manor related to this debate.

In 1644, a Captain Richard Ingle of the English ship "Reformation" was visiting the Maryland colony. Ingle sympathized with the Parliament's position. While he was anchored near St. Clement's Island, Thomas Gerard and two future sons-in-law, William Harkwick and Walter Broadhurst, were invited to come aboard Ingle's ship. An argument ensued about the troubles in England and Gerard, a supporter of the King, and the two others later testified that Ingle had spoken words of treason against the King of England. Giles Brent promptly issued a warrant for Ingle's arrest. Perhaps because some of the Maryland leaders, including Thomas Cornwallis, argued that this might be a political mistake, Ingle was permitted to go free. Upon returning to England, Ingle complained vociferously to Parliament that his ship had been seized in the Maryland colony, which he accused of being a stronghold for supporters of the King against Parliament. Parliament gave Ingle a free hand to seek out and take appropriate action against those opposed to the Parliament. Ingle, taking advantage of this decree, set out for Maryland to punish Gerard, Cornwallis, and other supporters of the King.

On February 24, 1645, Ingle landed at St. Mary's City and proceeded to burn and plunder whatever he could find. The ships anchored there were no match against the "Reformation." Ingle's bloodthirsty crew ravaged the countryside and burned many fine houses along the River, including the St. Clement's Manor house of Thomas Gerard located on Colton Point, and robbed that of Thomas Cornwallis at St. Inigoes Creek. For two years, affectionately known as the "plundering years," Ingle wrecked havoc along the coast. During this time, Ingle also had Father White and another Jesuit, Father Copely, sent back to England in chains. Unfortunately, Father White was never to see Maryland again. Even though the charges against him were dismissed, his superiors would not let him return. He died several years later in 1656 at the age of seventy-seven.

Governor Leonard Calvert subsequently returned to Maryland and at great expense restored order to the colony by the summer of 1646. Calvert had only been able to regain power by receiving financial aid and assistance from the colonists in Virginia. Leonard Calvert then began the task of rebuilding the colony. The colonists suffered tremendously during these years of plundering. Many had left with family and friends to avoid the carnage wrought by Ingle, and there now were actually fewer English people in Maryland than had arrived with the first expedition. Calvert led the colony back on a progressive course and it prospered for several years.

In the 1650's, events in England again posed problems for the Maryland Colony of Cecilius Calvert. The King and Parliament were still arguing and vying for power, and Oliver Cromwell was about to make his move. Criticism of the Roman Catholic nature of the Maryland colony increased. In order to help alleviate some of this antagonism, Lord Baltimore appointed the protestant William Stone to be Governor of Baltimore. Robert Pogue in his book "Yesterday in Old St. Mary's County" relates the story of the events which next beset Lord Baltimore.

"A group of Puritans who had settled in Virginia were being persecuted and highly taxed because they were not welcome in Virginia. When Lord Baltimore heard of this he invited them to move to Maryland. They settled on the shores of the Severn River and named their town Providence. The name was later changed to Anne Arundel town, and later still to Annapolis. Maryland was never to be the same after the arrival of these Puritans. The Catholics and Anglicans had been living in harmony worshipping God in their own way. But these newcomers soon became dissatisfied. They liked neither the Catholics nor the Anglicans, and they wanted to run Maryland in their own narrow-minded way."

Lord Baltimore invited the Puritans to enjoy the religious toleration in Maryland, but also to dispel accusations that his was a Papist colony. After Cromwell took power in England and beheaded King Charles, who was Lord Baltimore's benefactor, the Puritans seized their opportunity. In 1654, they rebelled and rose up against the government. Governor Stone, nonetheless loyal to Baltimore, assembled a small group of ships and attacked their headquarters in Annapolis. Thomas Gerard fought alongside Governor Stone on this venture. Stone had not counted on the opposition of the English ship the "Golden Lion," which aided the Puritans. The Puritans not only repulsed Stone's force, but took many captives. The Puritans then proceeded to execute four of their captives, even though they had promised them safety during their imprisonment. More violence in the name of religion.

Next, the Puritans took control of the government and appointed two new commissioners to rule it, Richard Bennett and William Claiborne. This must have been particularly frustrating to Lord Baltimore because William Claiborne had been his enemy ever since the first days of the colony. The Puritans then proceeded to inflict the worst injury imaginable on Lord Baltimore and the colony. As Robert Pogue continued:

"In 1655-1656, they (the Puritans) succeeded in passing an act making loyalty to Lord Baltimore a criminal offense, and also nullified the Toleration Act. This, I think, was one of the most ungrateful acts in all history. This was the tribute Cecilius Calvert received after inviting these people to Maryland to enjoy freedom of religion. It makes me a little sick to write it here."

See what religious fundamentalism will do. And the Puritans are the same people we honor at Thanksgiving. There was a reason people didn't like them; they were convinced they knew what God wanted and were intolerant. I assume this sounds familiar to people today as being reminiscent of the extremists of many of the world's popular religious cults. Undaunted, Cecilius Calvert persisted and succeeded in winning the confidence of Oliver Cromwell, and on February 26, 1658, Cromwell restored Lord Baltimore's government and took it away from the Puritans. Thank goodness!

Within a year, more dissension - - referred to as "Fendall's Rebellion" - - arose in the Maryland government. Actually, it was led by two men, Josiah Fendall, who had been appointed Governor immediately after the Puritans were removed from power, and the influential Thomas Gerard. Gerard had been a loyal supporter of both the King and Lord Baltimore since his first manor grant was assigned in 1639. He had even fought against the Puritans in the uprising in Annapolis a few years earlier. Therefore, it is somewhat difficult to understand what prompted Gerard to rise up against Lord Baltimore's government.

Several Maryland scholars feel that taxation might have been the cause, for there was a sizable tax on many items exported from the colony, including tobacco, by then the staple crop of Maryland. However, Edwin Beitzell suggests that the real reason for Gerard's break with Lord Baltimore was over the matter of some land Gerard believed he should have inherited from his brother-in-law, Abel Snow, but which Calvert had repossessed. Due to the recent weakness and overthrow of the government by the Puritans, Gerard might have been concerned about the security of his land holdings and taken steps to guarantee the validity of his possessions. Gerard was very powerful within the government and he convinced the Assembly to meet at the home of his son-in-law, Robert Slye, who owned a home in Bushwood named "Ocean Hall," a few miles north of St. Catherine's Island on the Wicomico River. There he appealed to the Assembly to pass a law enabling the government to act without the assent of the Proprietor or Governor and thereby insure the lands of the colonists against seizure by Lord Baltimore.

Phillip Calvert, the secretary of the government, was the only Calvert now in Maryland. Leonard Calvert had passed away several years earlier, prior to the Puritan uprising. Governor Fendall and his partner Gerard controlled the armed forces and led a bloodless revolution in which the government was overthrown. However, circumstances back in England intervened when Oliver Cromwell died in 1660. King Charles II regained the throne and restored Lord Baltimore to his former position of power. This influenced the people of Maryland, who returned their support to Baltimore. At this time, Thomas Gerard was forced to flee for his life and took up residence at his lands in Virginia, named Wilton. He later returned to Maryland, but never was afforded the same powerful position he had held before his short-lived revolution.

In 1675, the second Lord Baltimore, the great Cecilius Calvert, died and Charles Calvert became the third Lord Baltimore. The contributions of Cecilius Calvert to the formation and foundation of the Maryland colony were immeasurable. He steadfastly refused to give up control of his government and survived several rebellions, even though he never set foot in Maryland.

Not long after this, the Orange Rebellion in England led to the ascension to the throne of King William and his Queen Mary and the ousting of the Catholic James II. This uprising affected events in Maryland. There was a Protestant named John Coode (pronounced "code"), who lived on the Slye Plantation where Gerard had assembled the legislatures during "Fendall's Rebellion" in 1659. Coode began spreading rumors that the Catholics and Indians were about to rise up against all Protestants and take over the government. Though this story was false, Coode convinced many prominent men of the time to throw in with him. Historical accounts relate that he was a very strong and persuasive leader. Important supporters reportedly included were Kenelm Cheseldine, owner of St. Catherine's Island who lived on the plantation "White Neck," and Nehemiah Blackistone, who owned St. Clement's Island and lived at the Manor house at Colton's Point.

In July 1689, Coode and eight hundred of his supporters, with Colonel Henry Jowles at the command of the Maryland Militia, marched on St. Mary's City and seized control of the government. Coode and Kenelm Cheseldine then proceeded to England to argue in the Court of King William and Queen Mary that the Baltimore government should be repudiated once and for all. The King and Queen agreed with Coode and Cheseldine and this sealed the fate of the reign of Lord Baltimore. In accordance with the wishes of the King and Queen, the Maryland Assembly revoked the Toleration Act and recognized the Church of England as the official religion of Maryland. This situation remained as such until the American Revolution, but the history of legal religious toleration permits Maryland to be known as the "Free State" forevermore. Gotta love being in a Free State.

St. Clement's Island

In the summer of 1934, Maryland celebrated its 300th anniversary, commemorating the arrival on March 25 of the "Ark" and the "Dove" at St. Clement's Island. St. Mary's County was appropriately honored as the Mother County of Maryland and St. Clement's Island was acclaimed for its contribution to Maryland history. A special fifty cent coin was issued by the United States government, with the pictures of Leonard Calvert, Father White and the "Ark" on one side and the Coat of Arms of Lord Baltimore and the image of Maryland Governor Albert C. Ritchie, a prominent member of the Jefferson Islands Club, on the other. A special stamp depicting the "Ark" and the "Dove" also was issued. Pretty cool stuff, huh?

In 1934, as previously noted, a memorial was constructed to remind anyone sailing the Potomac of the special historical value of St. Clement's Island. A 40-foot tall concrete cross was built and erected on the island by Eugene Morgan and Raynor Blair with a few helpers. Raynor Blair at that time was the caretaker of St. Catherine's Island just to the north. It can be seen plainly from the River, and now from the front porch of the Clubhouse. St. Clement's Island in 1634 was approximately 400 acres, according to Father White's estimate. Robert Pogue, author of "Yesterday in Old St. Mary's County," has noted that many of the early attempts to estimate acreage were low. Thus, it is likely that St. Clement's Island encompassed nearly 500 acres, which would have placed it even closer to St. Catherine's Island. Today, St. Clement's Island is only about 40 acres and, had it not been completely surrounded by rip-rap and bulkhead, it might not even exist.

Father White also had estimated St. Catherine's to be approximately 180 acres, from which one may surmise that the Island totaled over 200 acres. St. Catherine's is now estimated to be approximately 30 to 40 acres. These rates of erosion are horrifying. St. Clement's is now but one-tenth of its former size and St. Catherine's is approximately one-quarter of the area calculated by Father White nearly 350 years ago. The reason for the greater loss of St. Clement's is that it juts out into the River and is subject to the cruelest of the prevailing winter northwest winds, the summer south and south-west winds, and even Atlantic easterly and northeasterly winds. St. Catherine's Island is exposed to the winter winds, but not to the extent of St. Clement's, and is also protected by Colton's, formerly called Longworth's, Point the peninsula which separates St. Clement's Bay from St. Catherine's Sound. Given the effects of this erosion in the last three hundred and fifty years, one could even surmise that the two islands and Colton's Point were once united as one piece of land.

The history of St. Clement's Island is important because of its close proximity to St. Catherine's. One might say they are "sister" islands. With the help of information gathered by Edwin Beitzell, it will prove to be of interest to look further at the history of this island, only three miles south-east of St. Catherine's Island, as an indicator of some of the events that occurred in the area.

In 1669, Nehemiah Blackistone married Elizabeth Gerard and received as a dowry St. Clement's Island, Longworth Point, Colton Point, and Dare's Neck. The Blackistone family continued to own St. Clement's Island until 1831, when it was sold to a Richard H. Miles. It is difficult to find historical traces of many specific events during the early years and this effort is additionally hampered by the fact that the courthouse in Leonardtown, which may have offered some additional clues, burned in 1831. During the wars of the Revolution and of 1812, both St. Clement's Island and St. Catherine's Island were captured by the British and used as forts. The British also cut down many trees for masts and sunk wells on the islands. During each of these encounters, the British pillaged, plundered, and burned many of the homes in the area. The St. Clement's Manor House, then the Blackistone home, was burned during the Revolutionary War in June of 1781, and Nehemiah Herbert Blackistone was put in irons and taken prisoner by the British, though he later was returned unharmed. That was the second time the St. Clement's Manor House had been burned, the first having been during Richard Ingle's rebellion in 1645.

After John Blackistone sold St. Clement's Island in 1831, it changed owners a few times until it was purchased by Dr. Joseph L. McWilliams on March 7, 1850. McWilliams kept a very interesting and complete diary of his life on the island during the years 1868-1875, and the McWilliams family retained control until 1896.

About the time Dr. Joseph McWilliams first owned St. Clement's Island, the U.S. Congress erected a lighthouse on the Island to protect and guide ships traversing the River. The lighthouse had a fixed white light, was 46 feet high and visible for 12 miles. This lighthouse was in operation until 1932. There were at least 12 official operators of the lighthouse during this time, but the most interesting light keeper was Mrs. Josephine Freeman, one of Dr. McWilliams' eleven children. She was one of the very few women lighthouse keepers on the Potomac and maintained this important navigational light for 37 years. Shine on, baby!

During the Civil War, the lighthouse was operated by the Union forces. It was almost destroyed by the Confederates, so the story goes, were it not for the fact that the lighthouse keeper pleaded for his pregnant wife who was in the house and near her time, and thus the lighthouse was spared.

After the Civil War, Dr. McWilliams decided to make a commercial venture of the island and built a steamboat wharf. Conditions in the surrounding area were very poor due to the terrible havoc caused to the entire country by the war, but McWilliams seemed to fare quite well. Cottages were built and several families spent summers on the island away from their homes in Washington, D.C. Dr. McWilliams farmed the land and shipped produce to markets along the River. He kept a grove of fruit trees and these also yielded revenue. In the appropriate season, of course, he and his family would participate in whatever type of natural gaming was available, including duck and goose hunting, oystering, crabbing, and fishing. Between the years 1870 and 1910, Blackistone Island was famous for its bottled spring mineral water. Dr. A. C. Rauterberg, who owned a summer cottage on the island, marketed this healthful water as the "Diuretic Springs of Blackistone." This water was bottled in jugs encased in wickerware made by McWilliams and his family and shipped to Washington, D.C., Alexandria, VA, and Baltimore, MD.

Dr. McWilliams apparently thought that he would be able to capitalize on the island that so far had been beneficial for him and his family, and in 1883, according to Edwin Beitzell, he:

"subdivided the island in 34 sections of about 7 lots each and put them up for sale through Charles C. Lancaster, an attorney in Washington, D.C. The plan was quite pretentious -- streets were laid out running from west to east with such names as Dukehart, St. George, McWilliams, Lancaster, Plowden, Bretton, Morgan, and Phillips. The center of the island was designated as Washington Park, and the avenues, running from north to south, were named Wicomico, St. Clement's, Patuxent, St. Mary's, Potomac, and Patapsco. A brick hotel was built and run by a Mr. Belahay (who later lived on Bretton Bay), and more cottages were built and people from Baltimore and Washington flocked to the island for some years."

Unfortunately, this development plan ultimately failed and life continued much the same as it had been until Dr. McWilliams died and the property was mort-gaged and later sold in 1896. Several out-of-town own-ers possessed the island until it was purchased by the Butterfield's of Washington, D.C. in 1909. At this time, the island was approximately only 100 acres (remem-ber that it had been 400 or 500 acres in 1634). The Butterfield family lived on the island where they ran a machine shop for many years until 1928. The United States bought the island in 1919 to guard the approach to Washington, but did not take control of it until the Butterfield's left in 1928. During both World Wars, the Navy Department used St. Clement's Island. It was then leased by Mr. Robert D. Blackistone until sold in 1962 to the state of Maryland. Unfortunately, the old lighthouse had been destroyed by fire in 1956.

In 1963, through the efforts of the St. Mary's County Historical Society, twelve acres surrounding the con-crete cross were set aside as a memorial area. The Historical Society pressed the State for aid to stem the continuing erosion of the island, which by then was ap-proximately 40 acres. Between the years of 1964 to 1970 the state completed an erosion control program around the Island through the use of rock and bulkhead.

In 1968, the first annual Blessing of the Fleet was sponsored by the 7th District Optimist Club and held on the island. It is a festive occasion in which thousands of individuals and boat owners participate in the actual ceremony of the blessing of the fleet. For several years, the Jefferson Islands Club donated the services of its old 42 foot wooden boat, the "Seahawk," to help ferry visitors back and forth from Colton's Point to the Island on the day of the blessing. Recently, the St Clement's Island Museum was established on the shores of Colton's Point to serve as a landmark of the fascinating history of this island.

Senator Harry B. Hawes of Missouri,
Founder of the Jefferson Islands Club.

Roosevelt and his Cabinet
under the old Mulberry
tree on Poplar Islands,
left to right: Cordell Hull, Louis McHenry, Jim Farley, Sam Rayburn, Harry Woodring, Franklin D. Roosevelt,
Daniel Roper, Curtis Wilbur, Harry Hopkins, William Bankhead, and Marvin McIntyre.

Senator Key Pittman of Nevada, first President of the Jefferson Islands Club.

Sam Rayburn, Speaker of the House of Representatives

President Harry Truman "playing cards" at the old Clubhouse on Poplar Island.

The "Cottage" on
Poplar Island.

The long pier on
Poplar Island.

When Congress Meets

WITH THE ADVENT of the Democratic ascendency, the Club assumed a broader aspect than it had in the past. The Club has already been of service to the Party. It has served as a meeting place for conference and for serious work and, in addition, the companionable association of members, even outside of the Club property, has contributed to understandings of party policy, which have not been without their effect upon the destinies of the Party.

Beginning in January, with the congregation in Washington of leaders of the Party, an even larger field for the coordination of Party activities is presented.

It is hoped that members will feel they are part of the movement which has already contributed something and which may in the future contribute very largely to the welfare of the United States through the instrumentality of the Democratic Party, and that the obligations of membership constitute part of their contribution to the general welfare of an organization in which it is hoped they will actively participate and which offers the prospect of greater service.

Respectfully submitted to the members,

Jos. T. Robinson,
President.

Message from
Senator Joseph
T. Robinson of
Arkansas in old
Club brochure.

Sample JIC stock certificate April 3, 1934.

Club motto "Relax" from speech by Harry B. Hawes.

Relax

Extract from Speech

by

HARRY B. HAWES

President Emeritus of The Jefferson Islands Club
IN THE HOUSE OF REPRESENTATIVES, JANUARY 24, 1924

OUR forefathers came with the Bible in one hand and the rifle in the other.

Some of their descendants have lost the rifle; some the Bible; some both the Bible and the rifle.

Let us restore the confidence and strength that knowledge of the rifle brings. Let us restore the spiritual strength the Bible gives.

Let us help to bring back both by the purchase of a piece of the big "outdoors," where strong men and spiritual power find the best nourishment.

When we lose our "pep," when good food tastes bad, when friends do not satisfy, when life becomes a bore, when music seems out of tune, when the old dog annoys, when the doctor fails, and the good wife irritates, there is but one remedy for the "run down," and it is found in the forests or on the streams in the big "outdoors."

There we go to church and worship God by conversing with the things He made, listening to sermons from rocks and trees, choir music from the birds.

If you need a fresh start and want to lose the "run-down" feeling and get back your "pep," go fishing.

It is a notable fact that of the Twelve Apostles selected by Christ, four were fishermen.

They were natural philosophers who made their living in the big wide open, who knew the stars, the tempest, the sea, the sun, the moon, the winds, and the calm.

They were prepared for a campaign for men because they had first campaigned with the elements of nature.

Study of nature had prepared them for a study of men, and their thoughts and teachings were big, like the outdoors whence they came.

Departing from Naval Academy for JIC Party, June 25, 1937. (l to r) Rep. Sam Rayburn, Secretary of War Harry H. Woodring, Secretary of State Cordell Hall, Speaker of the House William Bankhead, Secretary of Agriculture Henry A. Wallace.

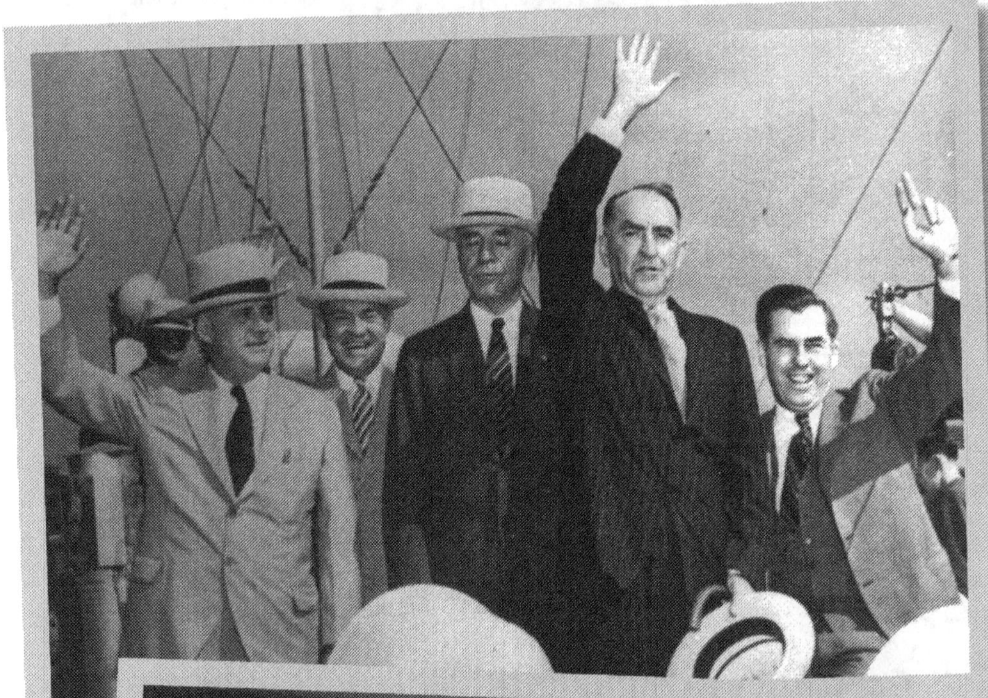

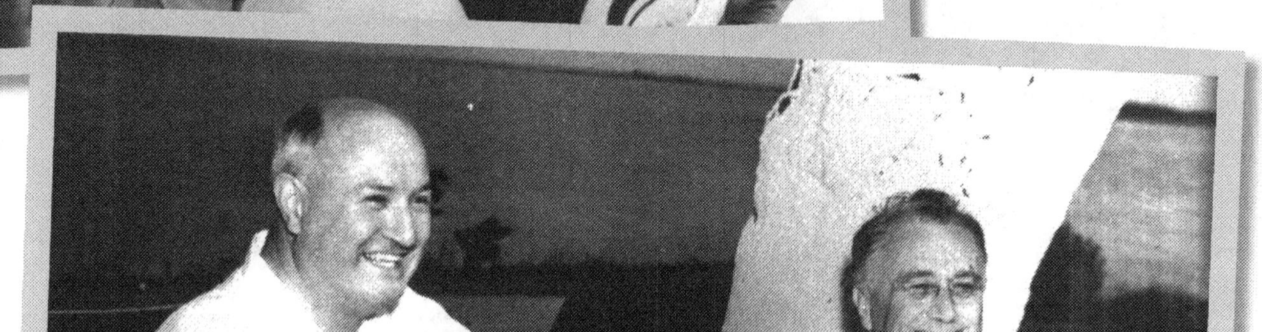

President Roosevelt and Postmaster James A. Farley on Poplar Island.

Committee on
Arrangements,
September 23, 1945.

President Truman
leaves for Poplar Island.

President Truman is
joined by then Rep.
Lyndon Johnson and other
distinguished guests on
arrival to JIC party in 1945.

Christine White gave
me these cards.

JEFFERSON ISLANDS CLUB
OFFICE OF THE PRESIDENT
Transportation Building
Washington 6, D. C.

OBJECTS
"For the purpose of supporting, defending and advancing the fundamental principles of government enunciated by Thomas Jefferson.
"To provide a Club House with suitable surroundings and comforts where members may assemble, discuss and promote Jeffersonian philosophies, to the end they may become controlling in Federal and State Governments."

OFFICERS

HARRY B. HAWES,
President

Vice Presidents
SAM RAYBURN
ALBEN W. BARKLEY
MILLARD E. TYDINGS
JESSE H. JONES
BERNARD M. BARUCH
BRECKINRIDGE LONG
HERBERT R. O'CONOR

JOHN B. GORDON,
Secretary
A. W. GILLIAM
Treasurer

BOARD OF
GOVERNORS

HORATIO H. ADAMS
RUSSELL M. ARUNDEL
ALBEN W. BARKLEY
BERNARD M. BARUCH
C. JASPER BELL
J. R. BELL
JAMES F. BYRNES
BENNETT C. CLARK
JOSEPH E. DAVIES
JAMES A. FARLEY
A. W. GILLIAM
WILLIAM E. GILLMORE
JOHN B. GORDON
ROBERT E. HANNEGAN
HARRY B. HAWES
THOMAS HUGHES
PETE JARMAN
JESSE H. JONES
ROBERT C. JONES
ALFONS B. LANDA
BRECKINRIDGE LONG
J. S. McDANIEL
H. MORT MERRIMAN
HERBERT R. O'CONOR
CLAUDE PEPPER
SAM RAYBURN
CARL D. SHOEMAKER
A. O. STANLEY
JOSEPH P. TUMULTY
MILLARD E. TYDINGS
JAMES A. WHITE

COMMITTEE
CHAIRMEN

House
JAMES A. WHITE
Barr Building
Washington, D. C.
('Phone: RE. 1544)

Game & Grounds
CARL D. SHOEMAKER
Transportation Bldg.
Washington, D. C.

Boats
J. R. BELL
Transportation Bldg.
Washington, D. C.

Memberships
CLAUDE PEPPER
PETE JARMAN
THOMAS HUGHES

C
O
P
Y

July 13, 1944.

My dear

     I spent a very pleasant evening with your
delightful book.

     Some 15 years ago, a group of Senators and
I started a club on one of the Islands in Chesapeake
Bay and I have spent the intervening years fishing
and duck-shooting there, so I know the country well,
which made your story doubly interesting.

     I have purchased 10 copies of the book and am
sending it to some of our officers on the Eastern
Shore and elsewhere.

     The next time you want to hide away a beautiful
young lady, send her out to our Club House. We will
find her a bed and something to eat and, if you come
with her, there may be a few drops of Scotch left at
that time.

                    Yours cordially,

Send her out to
the Club House?

The Club's purpose from the By-Laws.

By-Laws

★

Article I

NAME

The name of this Association shall be the "Jefferson Islands Club."

Article II

OBJECTS

The Club was formed for the purpose of supporting, defending and advancing the fundamental principles of government enunciated by Thomas Jefferson.

To provide a Club House with suitable surroundings and comforts where members may assemble, discuss and promote Jeffersonian philosophies, to the end they may become controlling in Federal and State governments.

To hold annual and special meetings for this purpose in surroundings that will provide recreation while pursuing this object.

Officers for 1944-1945

★

President
HARRY B. HAWES

Vice Presidents
SPEAKER SAM RAYBURN
SENATOR ALBEN W. BARKLEY
SENATOR MILLARD E. TYDINGS
HON. JESSE H. JONES
HON. BERNARD M. BARUCH
HON. BRECKINRIDGE LONG
GOVERNOR HERBERT R. O'CONOR

Secretary
JOHN B. GORDON

Treasurer
ARMISTEAD W. GILLIAM

BOARD OF GOVERNORS

HORATIO H. ADAMS	THOMAS HUGHES
RUSSELL M. ARUNDEL	HON. PETE JARMAN
SEN. ALBEN W. BARKLEY	HON. JESSE H. JONES
HON. BERNARD M. BARUCH	COL. ROBERT C. JONES
HON. C. JASPER BELL	ALFONS B. LANDA
J. R. BELL	HON. BRECKENRIDGE LONG
HON. JAMES F. BYRNES	H. MORTON MERRIMAN
SEN. BENNETT C. CLARK	J. S. McDANIEL
RENÉ F. CLERC	GOV. HERBERT R. O'CONOR
HON. JOSEPH E. DAVIES	SEN. CLAUDE PEPPER
WALTER E. EDMONDSON	SPEAKER SAM RAYBURN
HON. JAMES A. FARLEY	CARL D. SHOEMAKER
ARMISTEAD W. GILLIAM	JOHN P. STAFFORD
BRIG. GEN. W. E. GILLMORE	SEN. A. OWSLEY STANLEY
JOHN B. GORDON	HON. DAVID D. TERRY
HON. ROBERT E. HANNEGAN	HON. JOSEPH P. TUMULTY
HARRY B. HAWES	SEN. MILLARD E. TYDINGS
	JAMES A. WHITE

Club Officers and
Governors, 1944-45.

Officers for 1950-51

★

President
SENATOR MILLARD E. TYDINGS

Vice Presidents
HON. SAM RAYBURN
HON. ALBEN W. BARKLEY
SEN. VIRGIL CHAPMAN
HON. JESSE H. JONES
HON. BERNARD M. BARUCH
HON. LESLIE L. BIFFLE
HON. BRECKINRIDGE LONG

Secretary
JOHN B. GORDON

Treasurer
FELTON M. JOHNSTON

BOARD OF GOVERNORS

RUSSELL M. ARUNDEL	HON. JULIUS A. KRUG
F. GLOYD AWALT	HON. BRECKINRIDGE LONG
HON. ALBEN W. BARKLEY	J. S. McDANIEL
HON. BERNARD M. BARUCH	WALTER S. MACK, JR.
HON. LESLIE L. BIFFLE	LUCIEN H. MERCIER
HON. JAMES F. BYRNES	SEN. HERBERT R. O'CONOR
SEN. VIRGIL CHAPMAN	CLEMENT A. PARKER
HON. JOSEPH E. DAVIES	SEN. CLAUDE PEPPER
HON. HERMAN P. EBERHARTER	HON. ROBERT RAMSPECK
ARMISTEAD W. GILLIAM	HON. SAM RAYBURN
JOHN B. GORDON	HON. LANSDALE G. SASSCER
COL. M. ROBERT GUGGENHEIM	LT. GEN. JULIAN C. SMITH
HON. PETE JARMAN	SEN. A. O. STANLEY
FELTON M. JOHNSTON	HON. JOSEPH P. TUMULTY
HON. JESSE H. JONES	SEN. MILLARD E. TYDINGS
COL. ROBERT C. JONES	JAMES A. WHITE

Club Officers and
Governors, 1950-51.

Cottages and Lodge on Jefferson Island

POPLAR ISLANDS LODGE

Poplar and Jefferson Islands
"The Playground of Presidents"
IN THE CHESAPEAKE BAY

This historic Eastern Shore property consists of two islands, said to be the finest ducking and shooting site in Chesapeake Bay. Poplar and Jefferson Islands are 3 miles offshore from Sherwood, Maryland, and only 50 miles by air from Washington.

For many years Jefferson Island was the site of the Jefferson Islands Club, known as "The Playground of Presidents." In 1949 Poplar Islands Lodge was built on the site of the old club house, which had previously been the site of the Valliants' trading post.

The 17-room lodge is substantially built, with all modern comforts. Five big Heatilator fireplaces add a cheerful and sometimes welcome touch. The lodge is screened throughout, has ample closets, an exceptionally good heating system, six stall showers and plenty of modern baths. A large screened porch is as inviting when the weather is warm as is the big lounge with fireplace, picture windows facing south, and the heavy oak beamed ceiling. There are two cottages on the islands, as well as utility buildings and kennels.

Poplar Island is comprised of about 200 acres of good well-drained land, and a fine stand of marketable pine and oak timber. On it is a cleared air strip 2,500 feet long. Jefferson Island consists of 20 acres in timber and cleared land, with a pier running out to deep water for anchorage of good-sized boats.

The shallow waters around both islands have heavy growths of wild celery and other grasses which make them natural feeding grounds for canvasbacks, mallards and all kinds of game ducks. Miles of shoreline provide ample space for duck blinds. Poplar Island has good cover for quail, pheasant, wild turkey and small game. Striped bass and sea trout are so abundant in the area that the 1946 Fishing Derby was held just offshore, and good oyster and crabbing grounds lie in the straits between the islands and the mainland.

(OVER)

Lounge

Sitting Room

Advertising the sale of Poplar Islands Lodge in 1951.

Jefferson Island

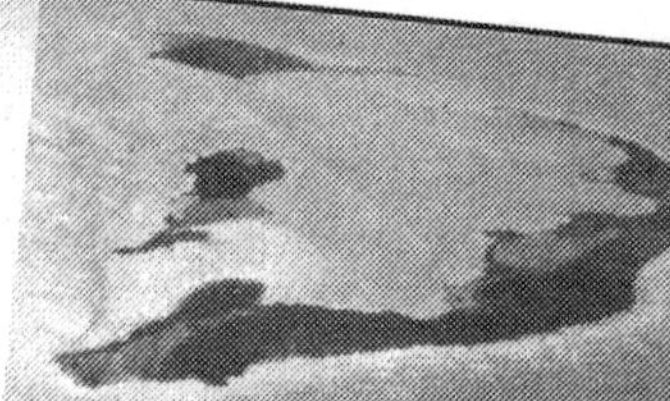

Poplar and Jefferson Islands

View to East

Skeet Range and Buildings

Poplar and Jefferson Islands

TABLE OF FACTS

LOCATION: Poplar Islands, Md., former site of Jefferson Islands Club, called "Playground of Presidents." Best duck-shooting site in the Chesapeake, 3 miles offshore from Sherwood (general store within ½ mile of landings), and Talbot County, well-known for bird and estates; near Tilghman, famous fishing center. School buses pass landing. Ferry service from Claiborne, connecting with ferries to Western Shore. Regular bus service to Easton (20 miles), county seat with good stores, churches, clubs, schools, RR; air service to all points (90 miles by air to Washington; 175 to New York). PROPERTY: Poplar and Jefferson Islands, total area about 254 acres, approx. 7 miles of waterfrontage. About 5 acres landscaped around houses, with lawn, shade trees, goldfish pool, skeet range and gardens, outdoor grill with roof. 16-acre cleared tillable field suitable for 2,500' landing field. Cleared walks through woods on smaller island. Remainder of acreage heavily wooded with fine stand of deciduous and pine timber, marshes, salt ponds where black ducks breed; sand beaches and coves. Lagoon between islands forms perfect harbor for boat anchorage and seaplane landing. New, exceptionally substantial Dock, 612' long, ended, 5½' of water last 130 feet (at Dock). LODGE: 17 Rooms (12 master bedrooms, 5 baths). 2-story, frame brick on concrete foundation, asphalt tile roof, built 1949. Screened throughout with plastic and copper screen. Tar paper insulation in walls. Ample closets throughout. Modern plumbing, with each bathroom and kitchen drained separately. 6 stall showers; 5 Heatilator fireplaces, interior woodboxes fed from outside. 2 oil furnaces, 3 separate gas-fired water heaters, 2 automatic Kohler electric plants (1 of 1,500 watts, 1 of 10,000 watts). Fuel gas (14 tanks). 360' artesian well. Septic tank. Radio marine telephone on boat. Everything brand new, in excellent condition. FIRST FLOOR: Large screened Porch, Lounge (34 x 18'), Heatilator fireplace each end, picture windows facing south, heavy oak beam ceiling, bar or recreation room, fireplace, pine paneling to plate rail. Pine-paneled Sitting Room, fireplace. Paneled Bedroom. Private hall to Bath with tub and stall shower. Linen and supply closets. 4 additional Bedrooms, Bath, stall shower. Kitchen (18' x 15') with Dining Area at one end. Modern kitchen equipment available for separate purchase. SECOND FLOOR: Sitting Room with fireplace connects with paneled Bedroom, adjoining Bath. 6 Bedrooms, 2 Baths, stall showers. Large supply closets. ATTIC, WATCH TOWER. OTHER BUILDINGS: 3-Room-and-Bath Cottage, 2-Room-and-Bath Cottage, both with screened porches, electricity, hot water. Engine and Pump House; Tool Shed; Chicken House; Dog House.

PRICE: $90,000   (OVER)

The Lodge

JEFFERSON ISLANDS CLUB

ADDRESS COMMUNICATIONS TO THE SECRETARY

Suite 1241-43 National Press Bldg., Washington 4, D. C. Tel. NATIONAL 6055

November 5, 1951

To All Members of the Jefferson Islands Club

Dear Member:

The old club site, Jefferson and Poplar Islands, located in the Chesapeake Bay, has been offered for sale in the settlement of the estate of George K. Bailey, who purchased it from the Jefferson Islands Club, after the clubhouse was destroyed by fire, and the club moved to its present location on St. Catherine's Island.

Mr. Bailey, in 1949, built Poplar Island Lodge, with 17 rooms (5 public rooms, 12 bedrooms and 5 baths) on the site of the old clubhouse, and replaced the wharf with one 612 feet long, running to 5 1/2 feet of water. He installed 12 duck blinds and purchased two excellent fishing boats, investing a total of approximately $90,000 (exclusive of boats) to develop an attractive resort for hunting and fishing parties. In addition to the Lodge there is a 5 room and bath cottage and a 3 room and bath cottage on Jefferson Island, and a small cottage on Poplar Island.

Jefferson and Poplar Islands are located about 3 miles off shore from Lowes landing at Sherwood, where the boats from the Lodge dock. This is 20 miles from the Eastern Shore town of Easton, Md., and some 95 miles by automobile from Washington, via the Sandy Point-Matapeake ferry. Crossing the new Bay Bridge - due for completion July 1, 1952 - the distance will be somewhat less and the travel time considerably reduced.

The present site, St. Catherine's Island, in the Potomac, near the mouth of the Wicomico river is 65 miles by road from Washington, travel time one hour and three quarters to two hours. Travel time from Washington to Jefferson Islands after the new bridge is completed will be three to three and one half hours, which may be shortened one hour by meeting the club boat at Deale, Maryland, on its weekly scheduled trips. The bridge toll will be $1.75 each way.

The duck shooting on both islands is good. Which has better shooting will depend upon conditions, varying from season to season. Early season probably better at Jefferson Islands, with greater variety of ducks; late season probably better at St. Catherine's.

Letter to Club members from John Gordon discussing possible return to Poplar Island. (Continued on next page).

The fishing recently has been so abnormally poor in both the Bay and the Potomac River that it is difficult to make a comparison, but in parts of the Bay accessible to the Jefferson Islands, the fishing is generally better than in the Potomac in the vicinity of St. Catherine's.

The accommodations at Poplar Lodge are better than those at the clubhouse and farmhouse at St. Catherine's, though the latter are usually satisfactory to the members when on hunting or fishing trips. There are sleeping accommodations at St. Catherine's for 18. The Lodge at Jefferson Island accommodates 24. St. Catherine's contains 60 acres of land, Jefferson Island 37, and Poplar Island 200. Both have good harbors for small boats.

The price to the Club for the Jefferson and Poplar Islands is $60,000, subject to prior sale. Sufficient furniture and equipment to carry on with, (though more would probably be needed) now in the Lodge and cottages, including 3 skiffs and 218 decoys, can be purchased for $2500.

The Lodge is now heated by hot air oil burners and fireplaces. Should it be deemed advisable, steam or hot water heat can be installed for an estimated cost of $3500. One of the fishing party boats can be bought for $4,000 to replace the "Houn Dog" which has reached the age where it is no longer economical to keep it in safe running condition.

It is believed that operating expenses at Jefferson Islands will approximate those at St. Catherine's. It is also believed that there will be a ready sale for St. Catherine's Island and that satisfactory arrangements can be made to finance the purchase of the Jefferson Islands. A loan will be necessary, with carrying charges in addition to the operating expenses.

Since it is the desire of the Executive Committee to ascertain whether the majority of the members prefer to return to the old site or to continue to operate the club at the present site it is requested that you express your preference on the enclosed card and forward it to the Secretary by return mail in enclosed, addressed and stamped envelope.

We enclose, herewith, a prospectus which was issued when the property was first offered for sale which will give you more detailed information.

Very truly yours,

John B. Gordon,
By Direction of the Executive Committee.

Enclosures: 1. Prospectus
2. Stamped, addressed envelope
3. Ballot

The Island

At the confluence of the Potomac River and the Wicomico, its largest tributary, there lies a beautiful island jewel called St. Catherine's. It was named by Father Andrew White, one of the first white men to see it. St. Catherine's Island now covers about 30-40 acres in size though, as stated previously, records indicate that the Island was approximately 180-200 acres when Father White established his first mission at White Neck's Creek, immediately northeast on St. Catherine's Sound.

The Island truly must have been paradise. Covered by tall trees, there was probably little undergrowth. The cove was much deeper than now and afforded a snug, safe harbor for passing ships. Certainly, the Island abounded with game, for even within recent years it is known to have been a home for diamondback terrapin, muskrat, mink, and otter. All of these animals have been hunted and trapped so extensively, however, that today there are hardly any left.

The Island was practically a jungle, with trees that blanketed out the sunlight, yet provided nesting sights for an infinite number of birds. The Island may be best known for its ducks, geese, and swan. Fresh water springs used to bubble up through the ground. In the past fifty years, the springs that used to flow continuously have been depleted. When I was a youngster, there were artesian wells both on the Island near the Farmhouse and on the mainland near the site of the present Club dock, where cold sweet water ran continuously. You just had to bend down to the short pipe in the ground to get a drink. The water was so full of energy that the site directly across the Sound to the east is known as "River Springs." Over the years, men have extravagantly used the water resources for development. The Club has had to dig deeper and deeper wells just to have running water, with the current well over a thousand feet deep. Progress.

Still, the Island sparkles with life and may evolve again to its former state. The ducks still return, though fewer than before. Bright white swan visit in the winter and Canadian geese fill the air with their characteristic honk in the fall. Deer continue to swim to the Island to escape the dangers on the mainland. Thousands of species of insects (most not man-eating) and many dif-ferent types of plants, trees, flowers, weeds, and seagrass adorn the area. The Jefferson Islands Club is simply the current custodian entrusted with the task of preserving the Island while enjoying its splendors.

To better understand and appreciate the Island and its surroundings, it behooves one to study its history and environment and the people who live nearby. As we have seen, the Island was originally part of the St. Clement's Manor granted to Thomas Gerard. Kenelm Cheseldine received the Island and other property as a dowry for his marriage to Mary Gerard. Though these first landholders may not have lived on the Island, it most certainly would have supported a tenant and been under cultivation. Most probably, the Cheseldines held the property until 1772 when Nehemiah Herbert Blackistone married Mary Cheseldine and took possession. However, the records are incomplete. For example, one unvalidated piece of written evidence states that a Thomas Mudd owned the Island in 1680. This Thomas Mudd had left Bristol, England on August 14, 1665 when he was 18 years old. He later owned much other land in the Maryland colony. He was an ancestor of Dr. Samuel Mudd, who set the broken leg of John Wilkes Booth the night after he murdered Abraham Lincoln. There is no way to prove or disprove the fact that Thomas Mudd once owned St. Catherine's Island, but it seems probable.

The first recorded land deed available in the St. Mary's County Courthouse in Leonardtown states that a Morris Shanks of St. Mary's County purchased the Island (referred to as "Saint Catharine's Island" in the deed; that is, with an "a") on March 14, 1831 from the estate of Kenelm Blackistone, who had just passed away. His estate was settled by Dent Blackistone, Kenelm's brother, and Nathaniel Blackistone, Kenelm's son. Kenelm and Dent were sons of Nehemiah Herbert Blackistone, the same imprisoned by the British during the Revolutionary War of 1812. The deed refers to "Morris Shanks as complainant and Dent Blackistone and Nathaniel Blackistone were defendants." This nurtures speculation that Morris Shanks had sued the estate of Kenelm Blackistone for what may have been an old gambling debt. This type of occurrence was prevalent in those days, for one gentleman might put a particular piece of property up to match or raise his opponent's wager.

Whatever the reason for transfer, Morris Shanks and his wife Elizabeth continued to own the Island, though one can only surmise to what purpose it was put. It may have been used as a summer vacation spot. In 1854, the Shanks sold the Island for $4,000 to George Wetherd of Baltimore City. The deed states this transaction in somewhat more legalistic and specific language:

"The said Morris Shanks and Elizabeth E. Shanks, his wife, have bargained and Sold, aliened and enfeoffed, and by these presence, to give, grant, bargain and sell, alien, enfeoff, release, convey and confirm unto the said George T. Wetherd, his heirs and assigns, all that tract or parcel of land, called "St. Catherine's Island" situate and lying in St. Mary's county aforesaid and bounded around by the waters of the Potomac and Wicomico Rivers, and St. Catherine's Bay containing 100 acres of land more or less together with all singular, the buildings, improvements, ways, water, water courses, rights, members, privileges, advantages and appurtenances thereto belonging or in any wise appertaining."

It is important to note that the Island at that time encompassed some 100 acres. So, in the 200 years since the arrival of the colonists it would be estimated that more than 80 acres had been lost due to erosion. Again, it is not known for what specific purpose the Wetherds used the Island, but possibly they visited it as a summer home and may have employed a local caretaker and placed it under cultivation . Since the Wetherds must have been wealthy individuals from Baltimore, it is unlikely that they lived on the Island.

In October of 1871, the Island was sold to James Etchberger, also of Baltimore. The deed shows that the Island was purchased by Etchberger for $2,300, which $1,700 less than the Wetherds had paid only 15 years earlier. This seems to make sense, due to the fact that real estate values were certain to have declined after the Civil War. What does not seem so logical is the fact that James Etchberger sold the Island only six days later to a Benjamin W. Jenkins and his wife, Fanny H., for an undisclosed sum. In any case, the Jenkins family sold the Island five years later to Andrew Jackson Cheseldine, a direct descendant of the Cheseldines who originally owned the Island.

Captain Jack and Other Owners of St. Catherine's Island

Andrew Jackson Cheseldine was born in 1834. He was a native of the area surrounding St. Catherine's Island and spent a good deal of his time on the River; working it, fishing it, and living by it. Many miles were sailed in his schooner, the "Harvester." A well-respected man, he lived to be over 80 years old. Rather small, intelligent, and energetic, Cheseldine normally sported highly polished boots and was a meticulous dresser. A long white beard framed his blue eyes, which looked fiery red from a distance because his eyelids were a hot pink color, almost deformed. Captain Jack, as he was called, and his wife, Maria, purchased St. Catherine's Island in March of 1876.

Captain Jack had served on a gun boat during the Civil War for the Confederate forces. Most southern Marylanders were sympathetic to the rebel cause and one still hears them speak of the "damn Yankees." Incidentally, the state song "Maryland, My Maryland" is actually an anti-Union song. It was adopted as the state song in 1939. The nine-stanza poem was written by James Ryder Randall in April 1861. A native of Maryland, Randall was teaching in Louisiana in the early days of the Civil War and was outraged at the news of Union troops being marched through Baltimore. The poem articulated Randall's Confederate sympathies. Set to the traditional tune of "O, Tannenbaum," the song achieved wide popularity in Maryland and throughout the South.

"I hear the distant thunder-hum, Maryland!
The Old Line bugle, fife, and drum, Maryland!
She is not dead, nor deaf, nor dumb-
Huzza! She spurns the Northern scum!"

If you asked me, I think Maryland should pick another state song that isn't so divisive and judgmental.

Anyway, Captain Jack Cheseldine couldn't read or write, like most of the other watermen of that era, but he knew the River well. He had previously owned a 120-acre farm on Canoe Neck Creek, about a mile north of Blackistone Island off St. Clement's Bay. He purchased St. Catherine's Island to pursue a very profitable "occupation"-- market gunning, i.e., wholesale duck hunting.

St. Catherine's Island had always been one of the best sites for duck and goose shooting in the Potomac River. The large cove provides a beautiful spot for ducks and geese to feed, while sheltered from the rough River. The bottom traditionally has been covered with eel grass, widgeon grass, and other types of vegetation and roots ducks love. The seaweed was so thick when I was a kid that a power boat couldn't enter the cove without fouling the engine or the propeller with thick grass. Cursed in those days, now these grasses are recognized as being beneficial as a water purifier, a breeding area for crabs and fish, and a soil retainer as well as excellent duck feed.

When Captain Jack lived on the Island, practically every type of duck that ever existed could be found in or around St. Catherine's Sound. Well, that might be a bit of an exaggeration, but you get the picture. The most "lucrative" types of water fowl were Canada geese, whistling swan, brant, canvas-back, and redhead. One could fetch up to a dollar a pair, which in those days was good money. In addition to the swan and geese, it was not uncommon to find hundreds of mallards, gadwalls, black ducks, pintails, pigeons, shovelers, scaup, golden-eye, buffle-head, old squaw, ruddy duck, merganser, and more. And a good hunter could kill two or three hundred a week with only two or three shots.

It boggles the imagination to think that a man could kill 100 ducks with one shot, but not when you realize that the guns used by these market hunters were about 9 feet long and 1-1/4 inches in diameter. The hunter would fill three fingers of black powder and five fingers of shot, which resembled b-b's. These guns were not smokeless and when detonated it sometimes took several minutes for the air to clear. To achieve the best results, these long barreled guns were mounted on boats called "sneak boats," which were long and narrow, about 16 feet fore to aft and 3 feet wide. The hunters used "sneak paddles," only a foot and a half long and tied together with a leather strap. An expert sneak paddler would situate himself low in the boat and could move silently, oh, so silently, and position himself almost as close to the ducks as he wanted. Close enough to reach out and pluck a tail feather.

These boats were so quiet that a story is told of how one hunter was out one night and spotted a friend of his on the shore of St. Catherine's Island. The man on shore was standing at the water's edge on the beach, facing inland. The man in the sneak boat paddled silently right up behind the one on shore, slowly eased up and slid the boat smack dab between the standing man's legs, who jumped about four or five feet in the air and hollered bloody murder!

These sneak hunters worked at night so they couldn't be seen by the ducks. They would kneel on sheepskin in the boat, paddle up to the best position, and fire. The tremendous explosion would knock the boat back about 40 or 50 feet in the water. Of course, with such a weapon it would be an easy task to kill 100 ducks at a time. St. Catherine's Island was such a perfect spot for hunting that Captain Jack may not have even needed to use a sneak boat. He probably could have shot from a chair in front of his house, the original structure of the present Farmhouse.

There were many other market hunters practicing their profitable trade in the late 1800s. Captain Jack's brother Kenelm (Kelly) Cheseldine, a master boat builder, hunted ducks for market, as did Walter Cheseldine, a relative, and Willy Husemann. Undoubtedly, there were many more and the locals know who they were. It's rumored that several of these old ducking guns are still in the possession of some of the natives of the area. I heard Walter Cheseldine's gun and skiff were owned by Capt. Fred Cheseldine, his son. Husemann's gun was inherited by his grandson, Billy. This type of market hunting continued for many years and at the end of its era, the first few decades of the 20th century, ducks could be sold for $3.00 to $5.00 a pair. Most of these ducks were transported by steamboat to Baltimore or Washington and many of them even were shipped to New York City.

Captain Jack also farmed on the Island and probably raised livestock. Another business for him was shipping goods up and down the River. Prior to the 1920s, practically everything moved by water and ships were needed to carry the goods. The schooners were the most beautiful of these boats and a good number of them called St. Catherine's Sound their home port. The River steamboats were also transporters of a large amount of heavy supplies, goods, and livestock. Captain Jack owned many boats, including a 39 ton pungy, the "L. B. Platt," built in Dorchester County in 1873. Pungys, or oyster boats, were fairly large keel vessels like schooners rigged with two tall masts and a main top mast. Pungys drew about nine feet of water.

Captain Jack's last boat was the pungy "Capitol." His son Robert was sailing "Capitol" one day in October, 1896 just off Sandy Point with another pungy, "Dove." The "Dove" was sailed by two of his cousins John and George Cheseldine. The boats were caught in a bad storm and wrecked. John and George Cheseldine were able to swim to shore and save themselves, but Captain Jack's son Robert was caught in the rigging and drowned.

Captain Jack often used a favorite 20-foot canoe with only a main sail. Edwin Beitzell relates a story about Captain Jack, his great uncle, in his book, "Life on the Potomac River:"

"After his retirement and when he was in his late 80's, Captain Jack continued to sail out on the narrows (St. Catherine's Sound) to fish almost every summer day. As both his hearing and eyesight were getting poor, he could neither hear nor see the thunderstorms as they were coming up. On one particular summer's day, a real bad one began to make up in the south-west and there were great rolls of thunder in the distance but the captain fished serenely on. His daughter, Ida, who lived on St. Catherine's Island, became more and more worried and finally prevailed upon her husband, Charlie Beitzell, (who owned the Island at the time) to go out in the motor boat and give her father a tow to White's Neck. By the time Charlie reached him the storm was even more threatening and promised to break loose any moment. Charlie came along side and hollered a warning about the storm and grabbed the anchor rope. Captain Jack said that he could take care of himself and for Charlie to go back home if he were worried about the storm. With the storm becoming more and more threatening by the minute, Charlie stopped arguing and pulled up the anchor, dropped it into his boat and started his engine and began towing the Captain in. Captain Jack grabbed this bait knife, cut the painter, got his sail up and with his dignity complete, he beat the storm home by a hair breath and informed all his women folk who were clucking around that by all that was good and holy he had sailed that river, man and boy for over 70 years and he wasn't through yet, and if any of them sent Charlie Beitzell or any other upstart to tow him anywhere they were going to wish they hadn't -- or words to that effect. Captain Jack died some years later."

Andrew Jackson Cheseldine was an indication of the independent nature of the people who lived nearby on St. Catherine's Sound. The local people only bestow the title Captain upon those who are deserving of such high regard and Captain Jack truly was. In 1888, Captain Jack and his wife sold the Island and moved to Foster Neck Farm, just off White's Neck Creek. The Island was then purchased by a gentleman named E. Gray Pendleton of the District of Columbia.

Many people have asked the question whether the present Bullock Island just northwest was once a part of St. Catherine's. The 1888 deed between Captain Jack and Pendleton provides an answer. It states that Cheseldine would transfer St. Catherine's Island to Pendleton ". . . less three acres of land more or less which have been separated from said island by water flowing between, and, which separated three acres of land more or less, is known as Bullock's Point, and is reserved by said Cheseldine and said Cheseldine reserves the right to use one-half of the 'swash' between said St. Catherine's Island and said Bullock's Point, for the purpose of planting oysters there on, said Pendleton said to have the same right in respect to the other half of said swash."

This section answers several questions. First of all, we know that Captain Jack also owned Bullock Island. We also can see quite clearly that at one time Bullock Island adjoined and was part St. Catherine's. What the deed does not answer is the question, when did the islands separate? It's easy to imagine that a swampy marsh could have adjoined the two islands and then broken through. Since the deed written in 1888 is the first to mention this break, it might be surmised that the separation occurred just prior in the 1870's or 80's. Indeed, a chart dated 1907 shows the north-east point of the northern leg of St. Catherine's Island quite close to Bullock Island and curving more in that direction than it now does. It then pointed more toward the south for many years, but speculation contends that this was caused by the water flow of the channel dredged between St. Margaret's Island and the mainland, just to the north of St. Catherine's

Within a short time, the distance between the islands grew to over one-half mile. However, the great grandfather of Bernie Wise (who, with his brother Joe, managed the Jefferson Islands Club for nearly 30 years, as we will discuss in great detail later on) remembered when there was only a ditch between the two islands and one could jump across it. This would date the break as having occurred around 1850 or earlier. Until conclusive evidence is discovered, this information indicates that erosion caused the northeastern point of the northern leg of St. Catherine's Island, a segment perhaps three or four acres in size, to separate from the main Island approximately 1850-70.

It is not clear what Pendleton did with the Island, but he held it for 17 years. In 1905, St. Catherine's Island again returned to the hands of the Cheseldine family. Freeman Cheseldine, son of Captain Jack, purchased it from E. Gray Pendleton on November 4 of that year. The deed also speaks of the "swash," but indicates that Andrew Jackson Cheseldine retained control of Bullock's Point and also half of the swash between the islands. Freeman, of course, gained ownership of the other half nearest St. Catherine's.

Andrew Freeman Cheseldine reportedly was a tall, slender and high strung individual, with a family of three girls and one boy. As meticulous a dresser as his father Captain Jack, he was somewhat of a loner, yet a determined man. He also was a market gunner and owned a long skiff. In addition, Freeman owned several schooners and was an excellent sailor. His first, schooner was named the "Annie L," and his second a 28-ton schooner, was the "Bessie Reed." In 1896, he acquired the "George B. Faunce" from Captain Matt Bailey in a trade for a store on White Neck Creek. Like his father, he used these large boats to trade and transport goods up and down the Potomac River and in the Chesapeake Bay. Before the dawn of automobiles and trucks, an island such as St. Catherine's would have been right in the thick of things. With myriad vessels transporting produce and supplies, the man on the Island would know the comings and goings of everything on land. This was a significant value of owing the Island.

Local lore suggests Andrew Freeman Cheseldine was a caretaker for several years for Mr. Pendleton and decided to purchase the Island when Pendleton sold. Freeman and his family farmed the Island and grew several types of crops, including corn, tobacco, and wheat as well as maintaining a small garden. Andrew Cheseldine's mother-in-law and her husband, Mary and Ollie Long, also lived in the Farmhouse for several years between 1905 and 1910. In 1916, after eleven years on the Island, Freeman Cheseldine and his wife Maude, sold the Island to Charles H. Beitzell.

Captain Charlie Beitzell

Between the years 1916 and 1926 when Charlie Beitzell owned St. Catherine's Island, his son George became the last person to be born on the island. He might not say it quite that way though. He might say, "Well, I was born, quite a natural thing as far as I was concerned. Just so happened that I was born out on the Island."

Nevertheless, George does carry that distinction and because of it, he knows a great deal about the Island as it was when his father owned it in the early twentieth century. George is extremely good natured and gregarious, and probably one of the most talkative individuals you will find. He laughs and smiles constantly, so much so that he talks right through his teeth as he smiles with a face that seems locked in a permanent squint. He speaks so quickly that sometimes it's hard to tell which story you're listening to. Last time I talked with him, many years ago, he lived in a house a short distance off White Neck's Creek. Most of the information I know about Captain Charlie Beitzell and his years on the Island comes from George and his cousin, Edwin Beitzell, the premier historian of St. Mary's County.

Captain Charlie was an adventurer. He had no qualms about picking up and leaving everything, and he did. He first left home at age 15. When he was just a young man he set out to join the Coast Guard and later turned west to make his fortune in the Klondike gold rush. A story is told of the reason he left. He was supposed to marry a girl who lived on Canoe Neck Creek. Unexpectedly, she jilted him for a red-headed fellow with only one arm, even though Charlie had already bought the wedding ring. Charlie took the ring, threw it as far as he could into the creek and left the next day for Alaska. He didn't make much money out there in the Gold Rush and drifted south to the Imperial Valley in California. He unexpectedly returned home for a pretty girl named Lelia Cheseldine, and took her back to the West Coast with him. To his sorrow, she and one of his two children contracted and died of tuberculosis. He brought the remaining child back to St. Mary's County and purchased St. Catherine's Island in 1916.

Soon he married Mary Ida Cheseldine, Lelia's sister. Together they made many improvements on St. Catherine's Island. The Farmhouse had only three rooms at the time and during the years 1917-18, Charlie enlarged the house so that there were three bedrooms upstairs. Of course, the house wasn't insulated, but George "guarandamntees" big goose feather beds and down quilts kept a person warm enough, indeed. A wooden barn southeast of the house was used to store farm implements and the like and also as a cattle barn for the half-dozen cows Captain Charlie owned. George remembers well his morning task of milking the cows. There were some hogs and two or three horses used to plow the fields. Large, thirsty mosquitoes were present in prodigious numbers, which made it difficult to get workers on the Island. The horses had to be covered at night to keep the blood-sucking insects away.

The land was excellent for farming mostly because of the thick grass that still abounds today. It feels so sharp, it could cut your feet. This tough grass covered very fertile soil. Captain Charlie planted two or three acres of alfalfa, five or six acres of corn, Irish potatoes and another five or six acres of tobacco, the main cash crop of the day. The barn was used to cure the tobacco, which was then taken to Bushwood for sale. There was a double posted fence all around the Island, which set the boundaries of the different fields and kept the cows from falling down the banks into the river. Captain Charlie took much of the crop himself in a dory boat to Washington for sale. The Beitzells kept a small garden with vegetables for their own use. An artesian well flowed cold water into the Farmhouse to chill milk, butter, and other items for the family.

Captain Charlie did not farm the southeast end of the Island, which has never been under cultivation. A forest of tall trees grew in that area, including pine, cedar, persimmon, and mulberry trees. A great many of these are gone today. The cattle used to stray away and get lost in this area, for George Beitzell remembers rounding them up there. Thousands of large birds roosted in the trees, including osprey (or fish hawks), egrets, heron, and eagles.

Several bald eagles nested on the Island, which the local people didn't appreciate, because they killed many ducks. The eagles scared up rafts of ducks to look for weak or crippled ones, or if there were none, singled out a healthy one and chased it down. These bald eagles also were expert at stealing fish away from osprey. If an eagle saw an osprey catch a fish, he would position himself under the osprey and chase it up very high and practically out of sight. At that point, the eagle would attack the osprey and make him drop the fish. From there it was simply a matter for the eagle to catch the fish on the way down.

The deed that transferred the land from Freeman Cheseldine to Captain Charlie in 1916 contained an unusual stipulation. There was a portion of the Island excepted from the transaction. According to the deed, this portion, "... lies nearest to Bullock Island and north of the line drawn straight in a westerly direction across said St. Catherine's Island from a cedar stake now set on the north shore of a cove, generally called "the House Cove" to another cedar post now set at a cove generally called "Roger's Cove." The House Cove is the large cove where the dock is now located and which is overlooked by the Farmhouse. Roger's Cove was the small cove on the northern leg of the Island formed by what used to be a long northwest point and the leg itself. This segment of land was excepted from the deed of sale because a man named William Cheseldine lived on the point, which was called "Captain William's Point."

Captain William was the son of Andrew Jackson Cheseldine by his first marriage. He lived in a small two room house, which had a well and a brick foundation. The bricks could be found there years ago, but I think are now either covered over or may have eroded away. There also used to be a half-acre brackish pond in this area.

Captain William was a rather strange man, according to the local folks; some say he was "half-simple." When Edwin Beitzell visited his Uncle Charlie in the summers, he was always told not to bother William. Ed

says they used to see him rummaging around the shore like a beachcomber. William had a wife and one or two children and made a living oystering and following the water. He had no regard for the law or anyone else. Captain Plowden of the Maryland Marine Police was always after him for illegally tonging oysters on Sundays.

When confronted, William always replied, "You take care of your business, Captain, I'll take care of mine." During the bitter cold winters, William walked off the Island on the ice without any fear whatsoever. He strode nonchalantly across even the deepest parts of the Sound saying, "the deepest water makes the strongest ice." Captain William lived on the Island unbothered from about 1910 until 1930.

One of the most famous events to occur on the Island was the annual summer rabbit round-up to which Captain Charlie would invite local friends and many people from Washington. There were hundreds, if not thousands, of rabbits on St. Catherine's Island then. This is no exaggeration, for I remember looking out on the field between the Clubhouse and the Farmhouse when I was a little boy and seeing hundreds sitting in the grass at one time. One time, Joe Wise caught a small baby rabbit and put it in my hands. Unfortunately, in the mid 1960s, a disease spread through the rabbit population and killed all of them in one summer. I also remember seeing some of the rabbits at that time, sitting on the grass immobile from the disease. It was very sad.

The Island back in the early Twentieth Century reportedly was cleared except for the trees at the lower southeast point. For the rabbit round-up, the men would walk in a line and force the rabbits into a V-shaped pen down by the cedars. They selected the best rabbits for food and skins and turn the rest loose to propagate for the next year. About two or three hundred were taken during each round-up. At least that's what I've been told.

Captain Charlie Beitzell was the last local person to own St. Catherine's Island. He sold it in 1926 to Benjamin R. Jacobs, apparently with his partner Daniel R. Forbes (although the deed does not mention Forbes). Next, we'll take a look at the commerce of the local area in the early 1900s before we continue our story.

Local Commerce

The natives of St. Mary's County are some of the most savvy and cunning business men and women around. Though rural and "laid back," most are sharp as tacks. There is something in the air that lets them know just how much they can get away with. This characteristic is not new. Robert Pogue relates two delightful seventeen century quotes regarding this native cunning:

"One Dutch captain named De-Cries said that although the Marylanders are extremely hospitable they are not proper persons to trade with. You must look out when you trade with them or you will be stuck in the tail. If they can deceive you they account themselves a Roman action and say they played him an English trick."

"The people of this place are a more acute people in general in the matters of trade and commerce than any other place in the world; and by their crafty and sure bargaining, do often over reach the raw and inexperienced merchant. To be sure, he that undertakes merchants employment for Maryland must have more of knave in him than fool."

The southern Marylanders believe that their land is God's country and that no man has any right to tell them what they can or can't do with it. Unfortunately, this type of attitude has led to the near depletion of most of the natural resources, seafood and otherwise, in the area. However, one cannot say this is a characteristic common only to St. Mary's County. In fact, the entire world can share in the blame.

The seafood industry is the backbone of the economy of the local area around St. Catherine's Island. The yield of oysters, crabs, and fish in the area ranks high with other areas of the River and Bay. There are thousands of individuals from Maryland who each year are licensed to crab or oyster in the Bay; even more Virginians are engaged in the occupation taking of seafood from the water. There has always been some animosity between the Maryland and Virginia fisherman, as explained by Fredrick Tilp, in his book "This Was Potomac River:"

"Fishing as a matter of states' rights resulted in pioneering the Potomac River compact of 1785, when representatives of Maryland and Virginia met under George Washington's sponsorship at Mount Vernon to deal with fishing and poles. Maryland owned the river to the Virginia shore line and agreed to allow Virginians to "fish it" in return for free entry of Maryland ships through the Virginia capes. The compact, in force to this day, was the first step taken in behalf of interstate commerce."

The heyday of the fishing industry lasted from after the Civil War until the 1920s. During this time, enormous quantities of fish, oysters, and crabs were taken from the Potomac River and Chesapeake Bay. The annual catch of sturgeon reached over a million pounds, from which 100,000 pounds of caviar were produced. Currently, the annual sturgeon catch averages is less than one fiftieth of what it was.

Sturgeon once ruled as the king fish of the River. In 1608, Captain John Smith said that "the river exceedeth with an abundance of fish... lying so thick with their heads above the water, as for the want of nets." He reported spearing fish to the bottom with his sword at low tide. With nets, "there was once taken 52 sturgeons at a draught, at another draught, 68 of two or three yards (each)." Frederick Tilp reports that female sturgeon might weigh up to 350 pounds. The roe was valued as some of the most delicious in the country. One can only imagine the sight to be seen from the banks of the Potomac as far north as Washington, D.C. of a sturgeon, "...occasionally throwing itself to a considerable distance above water, to the height of at least eight or ten feet, so that in the pause between the ascent and the descent, the whole fish seemed suspended in a horizontal position for a moment in the air."

Shad, herring, and rock fish were also plentiful in those days. At the peak of the shad and herring fishing season after the Civil War, as many as 22 million shad and 73 million herring were taken in a period of about eight weeks each year. A typical rock fish weighed between 25 and 120 pounds and one haul recorded three miles below Washington yielded 450 rock fish averaging 60 pounds each.

Another delicacy from the sea also practically trapped out of existence is the Diamondback Terrapin. There had always been thousands of terrapin in the Bay area and they were captured as far back as colonial times. Frederick Tilp says that:

"During the siege of Yorktown, Generals Washington and Lafayette lived almost exclusively on terrapin -- there being little else to eat. Tidewater terrapin abounded in colonial days, being sold by the wheel barrel full in Georgetown and Bladensburg for a pittance."

General Winfield Scott said in the early 1800s "This is the best food vouchsafed by Providence to man."

Potomac vessels going on a sea voyage generally included a supply of terrapins. There were so many during the 1800s that terrapin were fed to pigs.

The House Cove of St. Catherine's Island was well known for its prodigious number of terrapin. Walter Cheseldine and Harry Ellis were two of the local individuals who profited most from catching terrapin. The first Jefferson Island Club parties held on St. Catherine's Island oftentimes featured terrapin soup.

These delicious reptiles could be caught in many different ways. It was common for men to catch terrapin after a fresh freeze in January and December. They would break the ice and peer into the water, which was crystal clear to the bottom. The outline of hibernating terrapins was easy to spot and it became a simple matter of picking them up with a dip net. At one time, hunters simulated the end of the hibernation season by building fires in the marshes. The terrapins, thinking that such heat could only be summer, would come out and easily be caught. Hounds also were frequently used to sniff out and disclose the location of terrapin.

The modern seafood industry emphasizes oysters and crabs. The oysters found in this area of the Potomac are some of the best tasting anywhere. It may come as some surprise to many that the oyster is one of the most healthy foods available. Oysters supply much of the phosphorus, calcium, iron, iodine, copper and manganese required by the body. They are also rich in protein and contain vitamins A, B, C, D and G.

The oyster spawns when warm weather arrives in early summer. Millions of eggs are released and drift around in the water for a few weeks until they finally settle down and attach themselves to a hard surface. At this stage, the oysters are called "spat" and begin to grow. Many of the spat do not survive because they are unable to find an appropriate surface. Within three years, they are ready to be harvested and have grown to a length between three to six inches. Oysters feed on microscopic plants and vegetable matter that are plentiful throughout the Potomac River. In a 24-hour period, a single oyster might strain up to 60 gallons of water for food. Scientists estimate that at peak abundance in the mid-1800s, the Bay oyster population could filter all the waters of the Chesapeake every 3.3 days. Today's oyster population, reduced by disease and pollution, requires more than one year to accomplish this. In other words, the purity of the Bay is directly related to the number oysters, and we ought to treat them as a protected and endangered species, for our own benefit.

The earliest method of oystering was raking, which was learned from the Native Americans. Soon, the white men learned to "tong" oysters. Oyster tongs are between 14 and 26 feet long, depending on the depth of the water, and are shaped like scissors, with metal baskets and teeth at the end for grabbing up oysters. Oyster tonging is most difficult work. The tonger stands on the side of the boat, normally in the freezing cold with northwest winds whipping up the waves and soaking him with icy water. The tongs are dropped to the bottom, the oysters shoveled up, and the tongs pulled up to the top, where they are culled and the undersized oysters thrown back into the water. This method of oystering leaves some oysters on the bottom for further propagation. All the watermen on the Bay used tongs until the early 1800s.

Around 1810, the fishermen of New England found that they had depleted their oyster beds. It amazes me to think that about two centuries ago the oysters could have been wiped out. It's no wonder why when you understand how they harvested them. The New Englanders employed a dredge, which is a metal device dragged along behind a boat, scraping the bottom clean of oysters. There were so many oysters to be had in the Bay, however, that these "foreigners" came down in massive numbers and dredged as many oysters as they could and pirated them back to New England. Soon, the Bay oysterman realized that these New Englanders were stealing all of "their" oysters and began to dredge too, with the result that within ten years the Chesapeake oyster supply nearly was exhausted. In 1820, both Virginia and Maryland passed laws prohibiting dredging and requiring that fishermen of the Bay be native and licensed in one of the two states.

The watermen returned to tonging for 45 years until after the Civil War, when the oysters had replenished themselves to such a degree that both states once again permitted dredging in certain locations. During these years, the average take climbed to nearly 15 million bushels of oysters per year.

During this era, the oystermen who dredged often stayed out on their boats all winter under sail, selling their oysters to "buy boats." The crew would be wet, cold, and kept away from home for six months. Understandably, ship captains encountered great difficulty enlisting crew members. Some captains resorted to "stealing" drunks out of bars or from other waterfront locations and simply forcing them to work the entire winter. The lonely sailor would be promised wages in the spring but more than once these unfortunate fellows were "paid off with the boom." A particularly greedy captain would send the sailor on deck and purposely jibe the boat, knocking the man into the water with the boom.

Soon however, the dredging grounds again became depleted and the dredgers moved in on the tongers' territory, which led to fierce disputes called the "Oyster Wars." The Oyster Wars involve anyone, -- Potomac rivermen, Eastern shoremen, or Virginian -- who did not want the other to take "his" oysters. The watermen became even more enraged when the state of Maryland Oyster Navy (can you imagine that), charged with enforcing the laws of the River, told them where they were allowed to oyster. Examples of these disputes include dredgers dredging on tongers' ground, dredgers dredging on illegal round, dredgers dredging at night, tongers shooting at dredgers, dredgers shooting or attempting to ram tongers, and Oyster Navy chasing all of the above. Many shots have been fired and some lives lost in these crazy oyster wars. The height of the oyster wars occurred in the winter of 1889, when more than a dozen people died fighting around Hog Island Flats in the southern Potomac River. And battles were fought for years afterward about whether Virginia or Maryland owned certain of the oyster grounds around Tangier Island.

Crabbing is an important livelihood for many of the watermen around St. Catherine's Island. If you've ever lost sleep wondering what the rows of white markers might be that float on top of the water in summer, you will be relieved to know that they're markers for crab "pots." These pots are box shaped chicken wire structures with several entrances made to be much more difficult for a crab to exit than to enter and an upper deck where escape for the crabs becomes a virtual impossibility. The crab potters, using salted fish as bait, check their traps in the early morning or evening in small skiffs. The individual grabs the marker and pulls the trap up, opens one side of the pot, and shakes the crabs into a bushel basket. He then freshens the bait and throws the pot back into the water. Simple? Not really. Many crabbers have hundreds of pots out and it's difficult to pull them out of the water. However, crabbing is not nearly as arduous as oystering because at least the weather is warm.

As stated by William Warner in his book, "Beautiful Swimmers," no body of water in the world has been as intensely fished for crabs as the Chesapeake, nor for a longer period with such successful results." ... The national catch of all species annually averages anywhere from 250 - 350 million round weight, or "whole crab" pounds, worth approximately 80 million dollars." Not all crabbing was done with pots. Many use "trot lines."

A crabber would run a line from one anchored position to another perhaps a half-mile away. The lines were baited with eel or fish about a foot apart and were lifted over a roller on the side of the boat where the crabber waited with a net. For some reason, crabs tend to hold on the bait until it is within easy reach of a practiced netter. Many old timers still prefer these "trot lines." In 1870, a crab scrape was invented by L. Cooper Dize of Crisfield, Maryland. This scrape was essentially a dredge, but never became as popular as the pots, which were invented and patented in 1938 by B. F. Lewis of Hauyhogen, Virginia. Today, there are millions of pots in use to help satiate the human appetite for smashing up hardened animals to eat their flaky white meat.

Another extremely popular seafood item is the "soft shell" crab. A crab molts or sheds about 30 times in its life; that's their way of growing. Each time, the crab initially comes out with a very soft "paper shell." After their shells have hardened just a bit and reached a certain size, they are highly valued as "soft shell" crabs. Experienced watermen can tell which crabs are about to shed (peelers) and they separate them from the rest of the hard crabs. The watermen deposit the peelers in "crab floats," wooden boxes that allow water to flow through, and wait for them to shed out of their hard shell. Actually, that's what they used to do; the water has become more polluted and now crabbers erect an elaborate above-ground holding area with piped in salt water where the crabs shed.

Soft shell crabs are much more valuable than hard crabs and, therefore, are worth the extra work. In the 1980's, four or five million soft shell crabs were taken each year from the Chesapeake Bay. There is a great deal more information concerning hard crabs and if you desire to further your education, it would behoove you to read "Beautiful Swimmers," by William Warner about this wondrous creature.

There is one more type of seafood which, though not important any longer in the area around St. Catherine's Island, continues as a large industry in the Bay. This is the soft or steamer clam industry. These also are called "maninose" or "mano" clams. Soft shell clams have a "foot" which extends an inch or two outside the clam. The clam digs into the ground with its "foot" and then sticks it above the bottom to "breathe." Since these clams lie in deep water, at least over ten feet, the problems has always been how to capture them on a large scale. In 1950, Fletcher Hanks of Easton, Maryland patented a machine called the "hydro-escalator." This machine hangs on one side of the clam boat. Its steel mechanism reaches down to the bottom, forcing between 1500 to 2000 gallons of water a minute at the river bed surface, bubbling up clams and other objects, putting them on a conveyor belt and bringing them to the surface. This is indeed a very efficient form of capturing clams, but unfortunately it destroys the bottom nearly two feet deep, covering oysters and ripping up natural sea grasses.

Around the Island, those who operate the mano boats are not well appreciated. It even has been said that an increase in the siltation and filling in of the River, creeks, and coves, such as the house cove at St. Catherine's Island, has been one unfortunate after effect of the mano boats. I used to see them frequently years ago, but haven't seen these boats in some time.

Captain Sam

The best example of a successful waterman in the area around St. Catherine's Island in the Twentieth Century was Captain Sam Bailey. For many years, the most popular spot in the area was Captain Sam's Crab House. The building was located on the west side of White's Neck Creek across from the Jefferson Islands Club dock. The Crab House was managed by Eddie Bailey and did a thriving business in the 1950s and 60s. It was the center of the local seafood industry and a community meeting place.

The Captain was born on St. Catherine's Island in 1896. His father, James Theodore Bailey, was a caretaker for Mr. Pendleton. James Bailey was a River Captain very successful in the pound net business and must have held Mr. Pendleton in high regard for he named one of his sons Robert Pendleton Bailey. Three years later, the Baileys bought nearby St. Margaret's Island and lived there for 27 years until it was purchased by Mr. Robert Forbes in 1926 for $4,000. Captain Sam had fond memories of his early days and how he used to walk three miles to school, rain or shine. Sometimes he was lucky enough to hitch a ride in an old ox cart going up the road. The first boy or girl who arrived at the school house would build a fire and the next would run out to the well and draw the water.

By 16 years of age, Sam Bailey already had accumulated enough cash from oystering and catching soft crabs to buy a $1,000 boat. With this boat he continued to work the water, but also began hauling railroad ties, lumber, and supplies to pick up extra money. As far as wood for his own family was concerned, he said they never had to buy any because of the combination

of driftwood and the lumber mill on the Virginia shore. Captain Sam said the mill had a large shoot from the top of the high bank on which the millers would send the wood down into a barge. Oftentimes, the wood split or fell and they would throw it to the side where local people could pick it up and take it home. It was commonplace to sail over to Virginia and back. But if you lost the wind it might take two or two and a half hours to row. "You got used to it," said the Captain. Once a schooner sank just off the shore of St. Catherine's Island. Its hold was filled with coal and Captain Sam laughed as he remembered his family and friends using "nipper" tongs to recover coal for almost a year afterward. At least that's what he told me.

Colonial Beach on the Virginia Shore was the hot spot for night life back then. There were many saloons and restaurants and about 40 or 50 people from the area frequently assembled and sailed over for a little fun. Sometimes not all of them would make it back to the boat at the agreed time, "cause they'd get all drunk up and forget about the time, but that weren't no problem. We knew they'd get back sometime," Captain Sam said.

In 1920, Captain Sam, like many of the youngsters in those days, went to Washington to work. He opened a seafood business and promptly went broke. He returned to St. Margaret's Island and in 1922 borrowed one hundred dollars and started an oyster shucking house in Bushwood, a few miles up the Wicomico. He employed ten shuckers and took the oysters himself to Washington. In two years, he opened another house at Marsh's Point with 25 shuckers. But, "I busted again because I just spread myself too thin." He still had the truck from his business so he began to haul oysters and tobacco and whatever else he could find up to Washington. There were only a few vehicles on the roads in the early 30s and it was known that many of the trucks hauled illegal booze. Not only were there bootleggers, but other ruffians looking for whiskey to steal from the bootleggers. Four big men with powerful looking guns stopped Captain Sam's truck one night and held their guns in his nose while they search the truck. After digging through the oysters and finding no booze, they finally let him go, but Captain Sam said it was a pretty scary experience.

Over the years, he expanded his trucking business so much that he had driven to each one of the continental United States. He soon re-entered the seafood buying business and at the peak had 20 boats working oysters. Each would gather 100 bushels which would total 2,000 bushels a day. In 1961, Captain Sam's Seafood sold more oysters and clams than any commercial venture in the

State of Maryland. His sons Bo and Eddie managed the business, while Captain Sam directed the operation.

Through his dogged determination and cunning, Captain Sam had built an extremely profitable seafood business from that single boat purchased back in 1912. This is quite an accomplishment and clearly illustrates the tough business nature of the St. Mary's Countians. Captain Sam had no regrets about taking so much seafood from the river, "We wasn't the ones eating them and buying them - that was the city folk. We just fished 'em." The Captain passed away in 1980 and was given the largest funeral the county ever saw. A legend truly had passed on.

Boats and Builders

The first boat built in Maryland, other than Indian canoes, was a "pre-fabricated" shallop brought by the colonists from England. This was probably the last pre-fabricated English boat built, because of Maryland's abundance of fine trees such as oak, pine, fir, cyprus, cedar, laurel, and others that could be used in building boats and ships. There was never a great demand for large oceangoing ships, because the European traders gladly sent their own ships to the colonies to carry valuable commodities such as tobacco back to the mother countries. There was, however, a great need for all types of working boats, from the large schooners to small canoes and rowboats. Boats not only provided transportation, but communications and a livelihood from the River. The first boat builders in the immediate area established themselves along the shores of the Wicomico River, St. Catherine's Sound, and St. Clement's Bay. There have been many different types of boats built for specific uses over the years, such as pinnaces, shallops, skiffs, long boats, sloops, and others. The study of the wooden sailing boats of the Chesapeake Bay would require an entire book. A close look at one man, Captain Garner Gibson, will give us an insight into the local trade.

Captain Garner lived in a house up White's Neck Creek, where he operated a gas stop and repair shop until 1978. An extremely friendly man, rather slight in his old age, he was born in the year 1900. Whenever I used to ask him, "How are you today, Captain Garner?" he would reply. "Still on two, sonny, still on two." He constantly chewed tobacco and a little juice usually dribbled down his furrowed chin. A pint bottle of bourbon might be found hidden just inside the door of his shop. In his day, he was a helluva man.

Garner recalls working on St. Catherine's Island when he was a teenager, picking corn for Charles Beitzell. The water was crystal clear. "You could see ten feet down to the bottom back then," exclaimed Garner. "Neck of the creek used to be right much wider too, 'deed she was." Garner began building boats for John Cheseldine in the early 1920s. John Cheseldine was an accomplished boat builder and the son of Captain Kelly Cheseldine, who is believed to have invented the dory, one of the most popular river boats of all time. Garner and his brother, Buddy Gibson, learned the trade well from John and began building their own boats soon thereafter. Buddy Gibson perfected the dory boat that Kelly Cheseldine had invented. They are not built anywhere else in the world and were constructed specifically for oystering and working the water. They worked building boats from Christmas until September each year and oystered in the fall. Some of the boats they built were over 40 feet long and were constructed mostly of yellow pine, cyprus, cedar and white pine, usually taken from Charles County.

In 1928, Garner was the first to build the "box stern" boat, which soon replaced the dory. Edwin Beitzell states that Garner: ". . . squared off the bottom (of the dory) about six feet back from the transom and made a square stern. This caused the boat to 'plane' and obtain high speed which could not be obtained in the dory, even though fins or wings were projected from the stern. . . In 43 years of boat building, Garner built some 285 boats, for both commercial and pleasure use. His boats may now be seen in Baltimore, Deale, Crisfield, Washington, Alexandria and at practically all points along the Maryland and Virginia sides of the Potomac. Garner's largest 'box stern' was a 47 footer, built for Captain Sam Bailey, and George Kennedy reported in the Sunday Star of Washington on June 24, 1956, that he clocked a 36 footer built by Garner at 42 miles per hour when it passed the camera."

Watermen from up and down the River went to White's Neck Creek to purchase the boats and skiffs from the Cheseldine's, the Hall's, and the Gibson's. Mr. Forbes, who owned St. Margaret's and St. Catherine's Islands at the time, contracted with Garner to build boats for him. Garner also kept and maintained boats for Mr. Forbes for a number of years. He never built a schooner though.

I have fond memories from when I lived on the Island in 1975-76 of going to see Captain Garner. He would repair the Club's 42 foot wooden boat, the "Seahawk," when it needed it. I remember him and his crew working on the "stuffing box," the place where the propeller shaft exited the boat, which had to have a tight seal to keep water out, but also allow the shaft to spin. Wooden boats also had to be regularly treated; their bottoms scraped to get the barnacles off, recaulked, and painted. Because the boats were made of wood planks that swelled with the water, there was some cotton wadding that was hammered into the small spaces purposefully left between the boards. When the wood expanded after having been in the water, it would squeeze the "caulk" together to make a tight seal. But you had to know just how to do it to get it right so the boat wouldn't sink. One of the major reasons our old beautiful Seahawk was finally given away (to the St. Michael's Island Maritime Museum, though I don't know where the old gal is anymore) was because of this maintenance and the fact the old timers who knew how to do the work were dying off or no longer working. It's a shame when an art form passes on.

There were quite a few large schooners in the beginning of the 20th century in the area of St. Catherine's Sound. The most famous was the 68 ft. "Mattie F. Dean," built in 1884 and owned by Captain Matt Bailey, which held 2,000 bushels of oysters and only drew six feet when light and nine when heavy. The "Mattie F. Dean" was in use until 1944 as a "buy boat." Other schooners in the area were the "George B. Faunce," the "Ruth 'n Ella" owned by Captain Lum Bailey, who lived on Bullock Island, the "Joseph T. Brenan," and the "Ella S. Cripps." These boats sailed to where the oystermen worked and bought their oysters on the River so that the oystermen could continue and not have to return to shore after each full load. There were many other schooners used for trade up and down the River between ports for mostly non-perishable items. The closest ports to St. Catherine's Sound were Bushwood and Leonardtown.

Ports

Leonardtown lies at the head of St. Clement's Bay and for many years was the busiest port on the River. Originally named Seymourtown, it was renamed Leonardtown in honor of Benedict Leonard Calvert, the fourth Lord Baltimore. Frederick Tilp stated that, "more tobacco has been shipped from Leonardtown over a longer period of time than from any other Potomac port." For years, Leonardtown was a headquarters for traders and sailors. About 1930, when the roads to southern Maryland were improved, trucking became the major form of transportation of goods and the importance of Leonardtown as a port declined. Leonardtown still affords a beautiful view from atop a high bluff. Tudor Hall in Leonardtown is a handsome building which was once owned by the Key family, related to Francis Scott Key, who wrote the National Anthem as he watched the British bombard Baltimore. Today, Tudor Hall is used as the County library.

Most of the commerce from the immediate vicinity of St. Catherine's Island was handled through Bushwood Wharf, originally called Port Wicomico. Bushwood was part of the St. Clement's Manor granted to Thomas Gerard and was part of the dowry to Robert Slye who married Gerard's daughter, Susannah in 1652. In about 1660, Slye built the mansion "Ocean Hall" in Bushwood. After Slye's death, Susannah married John Coode, the leader of the infamous rebellion in 1688. Much of the planning for this revolution took place at Ocean Hall and further indicates the importance of the Gerard Manor in the evolution of the Maryland Colony. Ocean Hall still stands and was owned by a former member of the Jefferson Islands Club, John Mitchell. I think it was John who told me Ocean Hall is the only known building in the country with a cruk roof, used in Europe in the medieval days between the thirteenth and fourteenth centuries. I don't know what a cruk roof is, but it sounds impressive. Ownership of Bushwood Plantation changed hands many times during the eighteenth and nineteenth century until Edmund Plowden inherited it from his uncle George Slye and his family held it until after the Civil War. John W. Renehan eventually purchased the plantation and operated the wharf until his death in 1924. In 1935, the Quade family purchased the store and have operated it since, I believe, but I haven't actually been by there in a while.

History indicates that Maryland's first mint was established at Bushwood in the seventeenth century in an attempt to change the medium of exchange from tobacco to currency, though this effort was unsuccessful at the time. Tobacco was used to buy land, pay wages and taxes, and settle debts. About eighty years ago, Eugene Morgan, who later helped build the cross on St. Clement's Island, was playing near the area and found several coins in an old brick vault hidden in the river bank. According to Robert Pogue, Eugene's father thought this vault was a dangerous place to play and would not let him return. Soon, the site eroded into the Wicomico River and the coins were never recovered. Thus, Maryland's first mint may lie at the bottom of a river about two or three miles from St. Catherine's Island.

River transportation has changed dramatically since the first settlements. Ferries were established up and down the River in the early days. In the late 1700s, a few "horse boats" operated as ferries between Washington and Alexandria. The horses were attached to a revolving turnstile to power the paddles. Horse boats were not utilized in the St. Catherine's area, though. In about 1835, steamboats came into prominence and realized their heyday in the years after the Civil War. Steamboats served Baltimore, Washington, and Alexandria and stopped along the way at 112 ports; Bushwood, Piney Point, Leonardtown, Abell's Wharf, St. Clement's Island, Colton's Point, and Chaptico being in the immediate vicinity. These steamboats were normally 100 to 200 feet long and could carry a couple hundred passengers each. In addition, cargo might consist of anything from home supplies, such as sugar, flour, and salt, to livestock, such as oxen and cattle. Barrels of crabs, hogsheads of tobacco, wheat, whiskey, and other goods were transported by steamboat. (A hogshead is a big barrel, not actually the head of a hog.) Most steamboats until 1895 were side paddle wheelers, but later the "screw" propeller predominated.

Some of the popular steamboats that frequented the Bushwood Wharf were the "Northumberland," the "Talbot," the "Dorchester," the "Three Rivers," and the "St. John's" that ran the Washington to Colonial Beach route. In the twenty-one years of service of the "St. John's," it's estimated that she carried about two million passengers. These high sided steamboats were constructed for the rough waters of the Bay and many further displayed their stability when pressed into service during the First World War as cargo ships to Europe. Bushwood was the center of commerce for all of the small stores in the vicinity. There was a tomato cannery and large warehouse at Bushwood. Iron railroad tracks ran out the wharf on which supplies were rolled to the steamboats. Two oyster shucking plants, three stores, a flour mill, an ice cream parlor, and the headquarters of the Maryland Oyster Police were located at Bushwood. One of the stores was owned by Johnny Goodwin and built on the wharf over the water. The Depression and new modern roads forced many of the steamship companies out of business in the 1930's. After this, Bushwood, like Leonardtown, was left with only memories of greatness.

For many years, a store on the site of the present Club parking lot was owned and run by E. T. Oliver. Captain Matt Bailey operated one on the other side of the creek, later run by his son Eddie Bailey. Other country stores were run by Larry and Miles Palmer, Jim Bailey, and, later on, Thomas Wise at the site of E. T. Oliver's old store. There is no store on the water off White's Neck Creek anymore. I wish there were, because I remember going

into Eddie Bailey's years ago when it was the local hotbed of activity. Not much demand for a store like that anymore, unfortunately.

Doctor Jacobs and Mr. Forbes

In October of 1926, Benjamin R. Jacobs of Washington purchased St. Catherine's Island from Charlie Beitzell. A few years earlier, Daniel R. Forbes purchased St. Margaret's Island from the Bailey family. Forbes and Jacobs were partners and formed the St. Catherine's Island Corporation, which purchased St. Catherine's Island from Jacobs less than three months later on January 22, 1927. Exact details of this agreement are unclear, but it is known that Dr. Jacobs and Mr. Forbes planned to develop the Island and sell individual lots as summer cottages. Valid reports claim water pipes were installed under the land to serve the proposed cottages on the northeast corner of the Island, between the rows of lombardy poplar trees planted by Forbes and Jacobs. I remember those trees growing up, but they have long since died.

John Long, local jack-of-all trades, worked for Forbes both on St. Catherine's and St. Margaret's Islands. Long was a carpenter, boat builder, electrician, and plumber. He hired local help to assist him in building the two room cottage that formed the basis of the present Clubhouse. My understanding is that the cottage was constructed approximately 125 yards from the Potomac River (but that could be feet). Just think that erosion took all that land so in 1976, just before the wooden bulkhead was built, the oval part of the room was held up on stilts over the water so it wouldn't fall in.

The television room, living room with fireplace, bar and entrance way of the present building were converted from the old house. The bar had been the kitchen and there were two bedrooms in the television room, the partitions between which are marked on the ceiling by two wood planks. However, just as the plan to subdivide and develop St. Clement's Island had failed in the 1880s, this venture also was destined not to succeed.

Mr. Forbes was a well-to-do patent attorney from Washington, who married Edna May, daughter of F. P. May, who owned a chain of stores in the city. Mr. Forbes was a very generous man who got along famously with the local watermen and their families. It is told that he often purchased boxes of food and supplies for some of the poorer families in the area struggling through the depression years. He also sponsored parties for his friends and county residents to raise money for the local church. As a lawyer, he represented companies such as the Philippine Mahogany Company, the Old Virginia Preserve Company, and Cross and Blackwell (I actually remember Cross and Blackwell jars being used for glasses in the old Clubhouse.). He is known to have sailed frequently on the schooner "Mattie F. Dean" with Captain Matt Bailey.

However, Forbes and Jacobs had a falling out somewhere along the line. Supposedly, Forbes eventually sold out to Dr. Jacobs, but it is not certain when this might have happened. They always had a caretaker living on the Island and there were several during the twenty years that they owned the property. I was told Dorothy and Charlie Bannigan moved onto the Island and lived there from 1928 to 1930. They accomplished several improvements on the Island. Raynor Blair and his wife Gladys lived there the next three years.

Forbes and Jacobs drilled several wells; one in the Clubhouse pumphouse and the other in the shed outside the Farmhouse. A 22-foot high redwood water tank with metal bands around the circumference was erected on the present site of the Farmhouse shed. Water was driven by a ram pump up to the tower, which supplied the Farmhouse with water pressure. This tank held 2,000 gallons of water that were pumped from the ice house, the ruins of which still can be seen on the shore (if you dig through some underbrush). Years later the water table in the County dropped so much that both of those wells no longer would draw water. That ultimately led to the demise of the Farmhouse, since the deeper well drilled to serve the Clubhouse is now the only water source on the Island. Plans to run a water line to the Farmhouse never materialized.

Forbes and Jacobs were not able to do much with the Island. They reportedly raised hay and alfalfa until the mid-1930s and lost interest. For several years local people brought cattle to the Island to fatten them and keep the grass down. The Island encompassed approximately seventy acres then, and was completely cleared except for the pine and cedar trees on the southeast corner. To keep the land clear, the caretakers would wait until a day with the wind coming from the right direction, usually spring or in the winter, and set fire to the land. This practice has been used by local people for decades to keep land cleared and prevent underbrush from growing. At least that's what I heard. It was also successful in reducing the number of insects, such as ticks, chiggers and mosquitoes. This burning was discontinued in the early '40s and resulted in the Island being heavily overgrown by the time the Club began its operation in 1946.

In the 1920s and 30s, the Island was not without its share of intrigue, for it was apparently used as a site for a large 50-gallon copper still, run by Raynor Blair. Many local watermen, including Garner Gibson, Fuzzy and his brother Howard Wise and a few others, were said to have helped Raynor in this endeavor. It is even claimed that Mr. Forbes had a friend in the government in Washington who had something to do with the "revenuers," and for the most part, kept them out of the area. There were four or five other stills located on the mainland that were assisted by this connection. Fuzzy Wise laughingly recalled, "Yessir, we made some top-notch liquor on that Island. It was good, strong rye whiskey, the kind that would make your teeth chatter and your hair stand on end. We used to sell it to some lawyers up in Philadelphia who paid $4.00 a gallon for it. We could only get $2.00 locally. After we'd make it, we'd keep it in 55-gallon drums down in that spring house and surround them with saw dust to keep 'em warm. Howard and Garner used to put barrels of it in their boats and drive around so that the jostling of the waves and the heat would help it ferment quicker." *

Captain Garner agreed that the revenuers didn't come around too often, but recounted to me a tale of what happened one time when they did. "See, we usually always knew when the revenuers was coming, 'cause the boys up the road would find out and word would travel like wildfire. This one particular time, back about '31, we had a bunch of liquor stored over to Matt Bailey's store. We heard the government boys was coming, fast, so I got Fuzzy, Stump and some others and we quick carried a bunch of them 20-gallon kegs over to the Island in my police boat and hid it in one of the outhouses. We beat them revenue boys by about ten minutes." During the time, Garner Gibson had captained a police boat, inspecting oysters.

Mr. Forbes supposedly let Captain Matt Bailey store some of his whiskey on the Island, but one time the revenue agents caught the Captain with whiskey aboard the "Mattie F. Dean." The police took the schooner to Baltimore and held her there. But not for long. The way the locals tell it, "Old Matt and the boys just went right up there to Baltimore, took the boat, sailed it back, and never heard anymore about it."

During this era, one of the most destructive storms of the century hit the lower Potomac in 1933. Between August 22nd and 24th, hurricane force winds and tides ten to fifteen feet above normal racked the area. The River's seafood industry was severely hurt, hundreds of boats were destroyed and damaged, wharves wrecked and buildings flooded. One hears of how Raynor Blair was forced to climb to the top of the water tower near the Farmhouse to escape the rising tide. Captain Sam remembered rowing to the second floor window of Matt Bailey's store at the neck of the creek to rescue some vital supplies. He didn't say just what those vital supplies were, but they may have been liquid.

In 1943, the St. Catherine's Island Corporation (which as you recall purchased the Island from Dr. Jacobs in 1927) sold the northwest portion of the Island constituting about three and one-half acres back to Dr. Jacobs. There was a cottage on that section of the Island northwest of the House Cove that Jacobs and his wife apparently still wanted to use as a retreat. James A. White, a friend of Dr. Jacobs (who White's daughter Christine called "Uncle Ben"), was stated on the deed to be the President of the St. Catherine's Island Corporation.

In 1945, the St. Catherine's Island Corporation was liquidated. The property was turned over to Francis G. Boswell, an attorney from Alexandria as trustee for Jacobs, I believe. The arrangement between White on the one hand and Forbes and Jacobs on the other was rather complicated, but in an agreement dated January 3, 1944, it was clearly White's intention to acquire the Island so he could sell it to a group that wanted to establish a club on the Island. On June 28, 1946, the Jefferson Islands Club purchased the Island, because the main Clubhouse on the Club's Island in the Chesapeake Bay on Poplar Islands had burned to the ground. The parcel of land on the northwest corner was excepted from the deed and retained by Forbes. It is not certain at what point that portion of the Island was transferred to the Club. Nonetheless, it was clear that another chapter in the saga of St. Catherine's Island was about to begin.

Aerial view of the Island in
the 1950's.

Don Glassie greets President Harry
Truman at the dock for Party in 1960.

"Mattie F. Dean," last schooner from
St. Catherine's Sound.

The original cottage built by carpenter John Long on St. Catherine's Island.

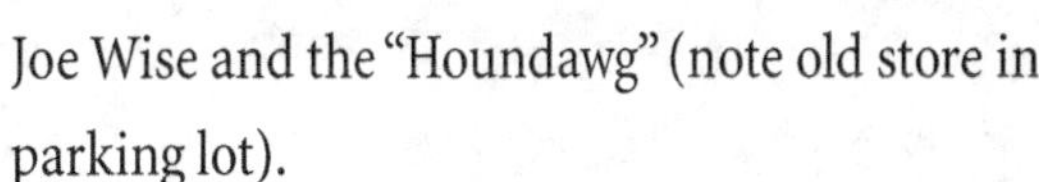

Joe Wise and the "Houndawg" (note old store in parking lot).

Joe and Rose Wise.

Joe Wise setting out decoys.

Concrete Cross at
St. Clement's Island
(note osprey nest on
top of cross).

Joe and Bernie Wise
barbeque chicken
on the outside grill
formerly in front of
the Clubhouse, now
under water.

Joe Wise shucking oysters in kitchen of Clubhouse.

Bernie Wise in the Clubhouse.

Mr. Forbes and Captain Matt Bailey.

Clubhouse on St. Catherine's Island. (Note land and trees in front, horseshoe pit in foreground - now all under water.)

Jetties constructed by Joe and Bernie Wise in front of Clubhouse.

Farmhouse in the winter.

"Uncle Don" Glassie.

Party scene in front of Clubhouse. (Now underwater.)

"The Island Girls"

U.S. and JIC flags in
front of Clubhouse.
(Also underwater.)

The new pool in 1960.

Dining room in the Club
House circa 1960.

"Dinner on the Mainland" in 1955 with President and Mrs. Harry Truman.

Riding the Seahawk to the Island for party with President Truman.

President Truman – "Retired Farmer."

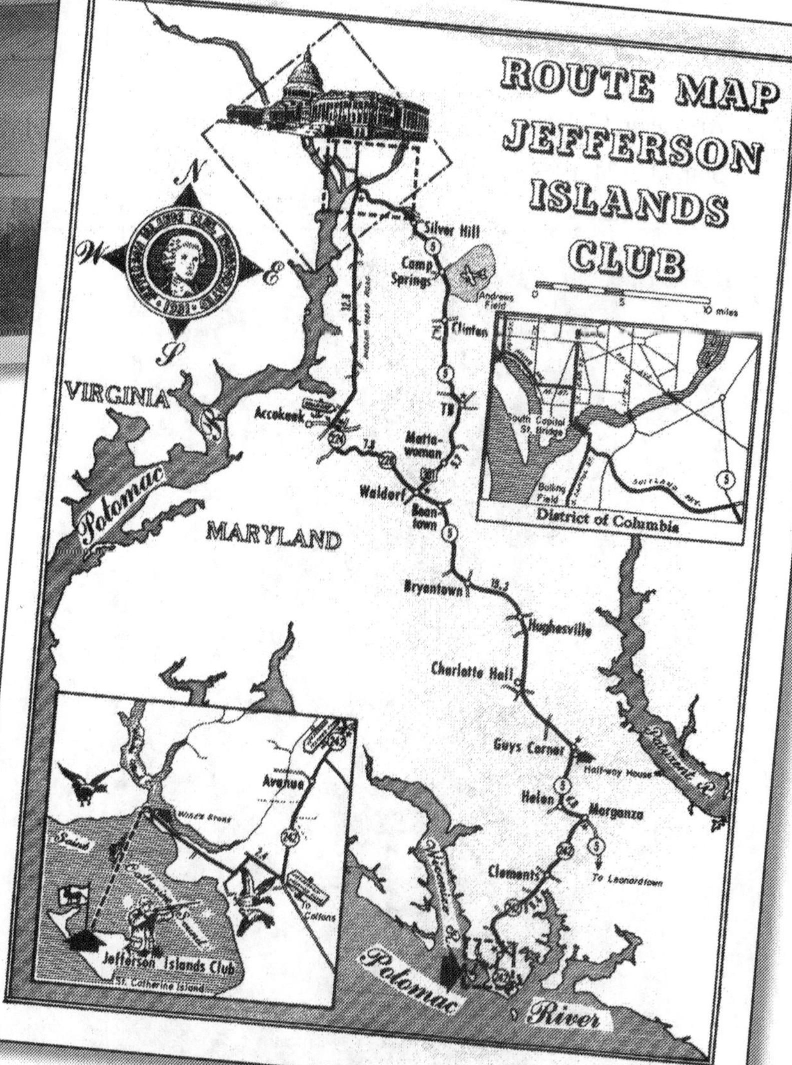

Old map to Jefferson Islands Club.

Club Officers and Governors 1960-61.

Officers for 1960-61

President Emeritus
HARRY S. TRUMAN

President
LESLIE L. BIFFLE

Vice Presidents
BERNARD M. BARUCH
CLAIR ENGLE
JOSEPH ALLEN FREAR, JR.
SAM RAYBURN
LANSDALE G. SASSCER
J. MILLARD TAWES

Executive Vice President
DON CAFFERY GLASSIE

Secretary
JOHN B. GORDON

Treasurer
THOMAS W. SANDOZ

BOARD OF GOVERNORS

F. GLOYD AWALT
BERNARD M. BARUCH
LESLIE L. BIFFLE
JAMES F. BYRNES
DON CAFFERY GLASSIE
JOHN B. GORDON
VANCE HARTKE
A. L. HUTTON
FRANK IKARD
ZEAKE W. JOHNSON, JR.
FELTON M. JOHNSTON, JR.
ROBERT C. JONES
JULIUS A. KRUG
S. KEITH LINDEN
WALTER S. MACK, JR.
WM. McC. MARTIN
JOHN L. McCLELLAN
LUCIEN H. MERCIER
FRANK E. MOSS
CLAUDE PEPPER
SAM RAYBURN
L. W. (CHIP) ROBERT, JR.
THOMAS W. SANDOZ
LANSDALE G. SASSCER
CARL D. SHOEMAKER
JULIAN C. SMITH
CHARLES M. THOMAS
HOMER THORNBERRY
JOSEPH P. TUMULTY, JR.
JAMES A. WHITE
SAMUEL J. ZEIGLER, JR.

Standing Committees

•

HOUSE COMMITTEE

JAMES A. WHITE, Chairman

F. GLOYD AWALT
CHARLES E. JACKSON
LUCIEN H. MERCIER
GEORGE F. GALLAND
DONALD MACLEAY

BOATS AND EQUIPMENT

CHARLES M. THOMAS, Chairman

PAUL M. RHODES
WILLIAM A. ROBERTS
M. DOUGLAS GIBSON
A. L. HUTTON
O. ROY CHALK

GAME AND SPORTS COMMITTEE

JULIAN C. SMITH, Chairman

JAMES O'DONNELL, JR.
SAMUEL J. ZEIGLER, JR.
THOMAS E. WALLACE
BARRON K. GRIER
HENRY P. THOMAS

COMMITTEE ON MEMBERSHIPS

RICHARD M. BOLLING, Chairman

LANSDALE G. SASSCER
HENRY P. THOMAS
ROBERT J. BIRD
RAYMOND A. WALSH

Article on Club from the Washington Star, May 24, 1964.

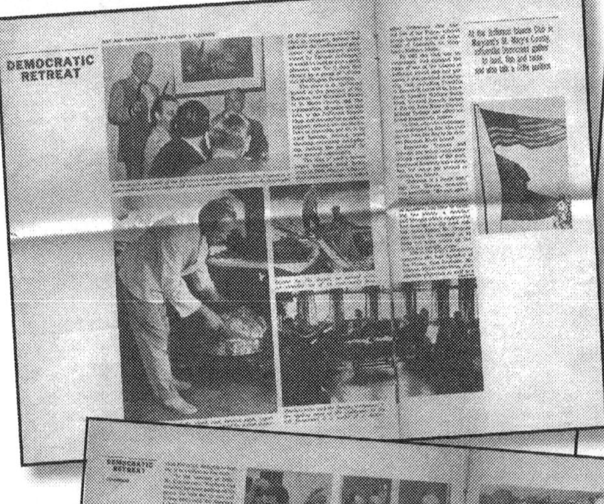

Letter from Senator Pepper to Don Glassie.

CLAUDE PEPPER
THIRD DISTRICT, FLORIDA

COMMITTEE ON RULES

MRS. MILDRED WALLER
EXECUTIVE ASSISTANT

Congress of the United States
House of Representatives
Washington, D. C.

JAMES F. SOUTHERLAND
ADMINISTRATIVE ASSISTANT

MISS SUE LEONARD
OFFICE MANAGER

WILLIAM A. ROBERTS
LEGISLATIVE ASSISTANT

June 28, 1965

Dear Don:

You gave us a grand party at the Jefferson Island Club yesterday. Senator and Mrs. Gruening and the Senator's sister, Miss Gruening, Mildred and I enjoyed it immensely.

You will find herewith my check for $37.50 for our party.

Warm regards, and

Believe me,

Always sincerely,

Claude Pepper
Member of Congress

Mr. Don Caffery Glassie
President
Jefferson Islands Club
1824 R St. N.W.
Washington, D.C. 20009

JEFFERSON ISLANDS CLUB

1130 - 17th St. NW, #320, Washington, D.C.   20036

<u>MID-SUMMER PARTY</u>

<u>August 18, 1968</u>

Our ISLAND PARTY in August will be a <u>Feesh Fry</u> -- with crabs.

DATE: 18 August 1968 (Sunday)

TIME: 1:00 P.M.

COST: Adults - $7.50 each
             The Young Set (15 and under) - $2.00 each

Our dietitians are planning some specialty items for the young set that might not like fish or crabs. There will be plenty of drinks for all, and a few contests, such as baseball throw, football throw, and other games for the young. The swimming pool is open and waiting for everyone to enjoy.

So -- y'all come! Make reservations early, and plan to spend the weekend if possible.

For those with children, it's cheaper to bring them than to hire a sitter.

Fill in the form below and return it with your check as soon as possible.

E. A. Terres
Program Chairman

- -

E. A. Terres
States Marine Lines
1130 - 17th St. N.W., #320
Washington, D. C.

Enclosed is check for $___________ to cover _________ adult reservations @ $7.50 each and _________ childrens' reservations @ $2.00 each.

____
(Signature)

Invitation to a "Feesh Fry" in 1968.

JEFFERSON ISLANDS CLUB

1820 MASSACHUSETTS AVENUE, N.W.
WASHINGTON, D. C. 20036

March 26, 1970

OFFICERS

HARRY S. TRUMAN
President Emeritus

LAWRENCE WOOD (Chip) ROBERT, JR.
President

EARLE CLEMENTS
DANTE B. FASCELL
VANCE HARTKE
CLAUDE PEPPER
JULIAN C. SMITH
JOHN SPARKMAN
J. MILLARD TAWES
Vice Presidents

DON CAFFERY GLASSIE
Executive Vice President

WILLIAM W. INGRAHAM
Secretary

THOMAS D. WALSH
Treasurer

EDWIN H. PEWETT
Chairman, Membership Committee

Dear Members:

Plans are progressing apace for the Game Dinner to be held at the Island on Sunday, April 12. Chip Robert and I have appointed a blue ribbon committee to make sure of every detail, under the chairmanship of Doug Gibson, who in real life is an expert on naval propulsion machinery.

The committee member in charge of the bear roast will be Tom Wallace, who in real life is a consulting engineer.

The committee member in charge of the roast goose is Chester Hogentogler, who in real life is the world authority on compacted soils.

The committee member in charge of the duck gumbo is Don Macleay, who in real life is a lawyer. Enough said!

The committee member in charge of venison is Bud Cromwell, who in real life is a TFX investigator.

The committee member in charge of oysters and crabs is Zeake Johnson, who in real life is Sergeant-at-Arms of the House of Representatives.

In charge of all other supplies and activities is Tommy Rose, who in real life is the Government's chief procurement officer.

Just in case you have already sent in your reservation and need to amend it to include more guests, below is another reservation blank for your use.

Sincerely,

JEFFERSON ISLANDS CLUB

Don Caffery Glassie
Executive Vice President

DCG:R

- -

William W. Ingraham, Secretary
Jefferson Islands Club
1820 Massachusetts Avenue, N. W.

ANNUAL WILD GAME DINNER
April 12, 1970
Cost: $7.50 per adult; $3.50 each,
children 8-18; $2.00 each,
children under 8

Enclosed is my check for $__________ to cover reservations for __________ adults and/or __________ children.

Signature __________________________

Invitation to Game Dinner on the Island in 1970.

The Club on Poplar Islands

The Jefferson Islands Club was founded on January 5, 1931. It had been the inspiration of several Democratic Party leaders, led by Senators Harry B. Hawes of Missouri and Key Pittman from Nevada. Senator Joseph T. Robinson of Arkansas was the Club's first president. These senators were great lovers of the outdoors, who appreciated and valued the pleasures to be found in quiet, peaceful settings--in community with nature. They, and the others who joined the Club, understood the importance of relaxation. Harry Hawes coined the Club motto, "Relax." Because of their hectic political lives in the nation's capital, they, as we, felt the need to "get away from it all." What better place than an island! And what better body of water for that island than the Chesapeake Bay!

It took approximately two years to acquire the islands, to garner an appropriate membership and to incorporate the Club officially. An important factor in the initial success of the Club was the support of the then Governor of New York, Franklin D. Roosevelt. The founders decided that the Club should be a retreat specifically for members of the Democratic Party; "Congenial Democrats." The objects of the Club, as contained in the By-Laws are to:

"…support, defend and advance the fundamental principles of the government enunciated by Thomas Jefferson," and "to provide a clubhouse with suitable surroundings and comforts, where members may assemble, discuss and promote Jeffersonian philosophies to the end they may become controlling in Federal and State governments."

There were 35 charter members, who included many of the most important and influential men of the twentieth century United States: Franklin Roosevelt, of course; John Nance Garner, Vice President; William D. Bankhead, Speaker of the House of Representatives; August A. Busch, Jr., of the perennially popular Anheiser Busch Company; Royal Copland, Senator from New York; Parker Corning, Congressman from New York; James A. Farley, Postmaster General; Joseph T. Robinson, Senator from Arkansas and Senate Majority leader; Millard B. Tydings, Senator of the great state of Maryland, and David I. Walsh, Senator from Massachusetts.

Bernard Baruch, a famous Democrat, was a charter member and one of the strongest supporters of the Club. During the First World War, Baruch served as Chairman of the War Industries Board, which was responsible for the entire industrial war effort. A well regarded advisor to four presidents, he served ably on numerous committees, including the Atomic Energy Commission. His fortune was made on the stock market and he contributed substantially to the success of the Club. Several life memberships were purchased by Baruch and given to influential government leaders. His penchant for contemplation and relaxation was well known. One can still sit on the "Bernard Baruch Bench of Inspiration" in Lafayette Square in front of the White House, where he used to ponder the problems of the country. Baruch died in 1948 at the age of 78.

E. Brooke Lee was the last original Charter member of the Jefferson Islands Club that I knew of and resided at the "Sweepstakes" farm in Damascus, Maryland, where I went to visit him years ago. Lee was a descendant of Richard Henry Lee, a leader of the American Revolution and owner of the Lee Stratford mansion in Westmoreland County, Virginia, immediately across the River from St. Catherine's Island. The Lee's controlled several ocean going trading ships in the colonial days. "Lighthorse Harry" Lee was another famous ancestor.

Brooke Lee was elected comptroller of the state of Maryland in 1919 on the ticket with Governor Albert Ritchie. He was Ritchie's most active political lieutenant and served as his right-hand man for many years. Governor Ritchie had been considered for nearly 12 years as a candidate for the Presidency of the United States and, as Lee said, "he almost made it." Lee also had served as Speaker of the House of Delegates. Mr. Lee was most proud of the fact that he led the second Maryland Battalion of the 115th Infantry Division during the First World War. It is interesting to note that William Preston Lane, destined to become Governor of Maryland, was adjutant of the Division and that Millard Tydings, also later a Governor of Maryland, served as a machine gun officer.

Brooke Lee knew many of the influential leaders of the government quite well and these induced many other charter members of the Club. He was good friends with Bernard Baruch, for whom Governor Ritchie had been counsel. Breckenridge Long married a cousin of Lee's, one of the Blair family. Brooke Lee is from the same family that was responsible for the famous Blair-Lee House in Washington, D.C. Lee was a close acquaintance of Joe Tumulty; Howard Bruce, an outstanding Marylander; Millard Tydings; Joe Davis, Millard Tydings' father-in-law and former Ambassador to Moscow; and Jim Farley. Brooke Lee also served as a regent of the University of Maryland and chairman of the Maryland Roads Commission. His son Blair Lee served as acting governor of Maryland while Marvin Mandel was out of office in the 1970s.

Governor Ritchie often took congressional delegations, sometimes with their wives, to the Jefferson Islands Club and Brooke Lee joined many of these trips. They usually did not stay the night, but went for a delicious afternoon meal and then rode in the Club "Commuter" boat back to Annapolis. A friend of Sam Rayburn, Alben Barkley, and Les Biffle, Brooke Lee retired from public life in the 1940s. After his retirement, he acquired and managed 22 farms in Montgomery County and was a breeder of the famous Polled Hereford cattle.

The Club continues to boast the historical membership of many prominent and influential men. A brief list of some of the past members is shown below:

President John F. Kennedy	Gov. Albert Ritchie
President Lyndon B. Johnson	Speaker Thomas (Tip) O'Neill
President Harry S. Truman	Asst. Secy. L.W. (Chip) Robert, Jr.
Bernard Baruch	Rep. Richard Bolling
Speaker Sam Rayburn	Gov. J. Lindsay Almond
Sen. Clair Engle	Rep. Jack Brooks
Gov. J. Millard Tawes	Sen. Harry F. Byrd
Sen. Vance Hartke	Sen. James O. Eastland
Felton M. Johnston, Jr	Rep. Dante B. Fascell
Walter S. Macke, Jr.	Rep. William Chappell
Sen. John McClelland, Jr.	E. Brooke Lee
Sen. Frank E. Moss	Rep. John J. Rhodes
O. Roy Chalk	Rep. Jim Wright
Rep. Albert Thomas	Sec. Arthur Goldberg
James A. White	Rep. Wilbur B. Mills
Gen. Julian Smith	Sen. Claude Pepper
Sen. Harrison A. Williams, Jr.	Rep. William S. Moorehead
Speaker Joseph W. Burns	Arde Bulova
Harry L. Hopkins	Sen. Virgil Chapman
Speaker Henry Rainy	Sec. Cordell Hull
Sen. A. Owsley Stanley	Ellsworth Bunker

These individuals all found different uses for the facilities of the Club. The Island often served as a site for meetings and conferences called by President Roosevelt; was used by Harry Hawes as a retreat to write some of his books, including "Conservation of Wildlife," "Big Outdoors," and "My Friend the Black Bass," and by Harry Truman, who loved to pass the buck and escape the rigors of Washington, to play some cards, and to fish a little down on the Bay.

The Club owned two of the islands of a small chain known as Poplar Islands. The Clubhouse, or "cottage," and its various support buildings were located on the island initially known as Cobbler's Neck, which also was referred to as Valliant's Island, named for the family that lived there just prior to the formation of the Club. Cobbler's Neck and the main Poplar Island were renamed "Jefferson Islands" by legislation enacted during the term of Governor Albert Ritchie of Maryland. In an early Club brochure, these islands were identified as "Wilson" and "Jackson." These names never stuck and the island on which the main clubhouse was situated is now known as Jefferson Island, with the larger Poplar Island retaining its original name. During the 1930s, the islands consisted of Cobbler's Neck of 34 acres, Poplar Island of 134 acres, and a third island, Coaches Neck of 100 acres. The Club never owned Coaches Neck.

In the 1630s, these islands had been known as Popley's Islands" and were owned by a gentleman named Richard Thompson. Richard Thompson was one of William Claiborne's henchmen and had joined the infamous Virginia Puritan in his battles against Lord Baltimore. Other early owners of Poplar Island included the former Dutch governor of Delaware O'Hyniossa, who had been forced to seek refuge in Maryland after the fall of the Delaware colony's Dutch government. The most famous holder of the island was Charles Carroll of Carrollton, the signer of the Declaration of Independence. Carroll owned it during the late 1700 and early 1800s having inherited the island from his grandfather, another Charles Carroll.

The islands were inhabited from the mid-1800s until the 1920s by many local families, some of which were Howeth, Valliant, Ridgeway, St. Claire, and Haddaway.

Poplar Island was the site of a town that at one time contained six or eight farms, a schoolhouse having nearly 20 students, a church, and one or two small shops. Horses, mules, sheep, and cattle were raised and several different crops were grown, including wheat, corn, tomatoes, watermelon, and tobacco. Of course, there were many watermen.

The last people reportedly to live on Jefferson Island were the Valliant sisters, Hattie and Mary. Their family had lived on the islands for many decades and Cobbler's Neck, later Valliant's, was owned by their father. It had become impractical for the sisters to remain on the island since they were growing old in years. Captain George Haddaway went to fetch them one day in the 1920s and transport them to a home on the mainland prepared by friends. The sisters refused to leave and Captain Haddaway was forced to return several times before they allowed themselves to be taken from the island. Deserted for several years, the islands was said to provide a perfect location for several illegal whiskey stills until raided by government revenue agents in 1929. For the next two years, the island was completely vacant, except for natural wildlife, until the Club purchased it in 1931.

After the clubhouse was destroyed by fire on March 5, 1946, and the location of the Club moved, the island has had many owners. A man named George Bailey built another clubhouse, which was later used by several corporations as hunting lodges. We will talk a little more about Bailey later on. Finally, the Smithsonian Institute received most of the islands in the late 1960s when William Elkins, a physician from Philadelphia, donated them. They were then pretty much left to erode into the Bay, and at one point were even called the "vanishing islands."

Today, however, it's exciting to note that the main island has been restored by a multi-million dollar exercise in replenishment. The harbor in Baltimore needed dredging, and there were not many good sources to place the "spoil," i.e., the mud, sludge, and gunk that resides at the bottom of the harbor. Through a massive project, the spoil was transported to Poplar Island, which was surrounded by huge holding fences. It is likely that vegetation will return to this resurrected island and it will be given a new lease on life. Here is what the Army Corps of Engineers says about the project:

"Poplar Island, recently on the verge of disappearing, is today a national model for habitat restoration and the beneficial use of dredged material. The U.S. Army Corps of Engineers, Baltimore District has teamed with the Maryland Port Administration and other Federal and State agencies to restore Poplar Island using dredged material from the Baltimore Harbor and Channels Federal navigation projects (only approach channels). Just off the Chesapeake Bay coastline, about 34 miles south of Baltimore in Talbot County, MD, Poplar Island is being returned to its former size and important ecological function while helping to ensure the economic vitality of the region. Approximately 40 million cubic yards of dredged material will be placed to develop 570 acres of wetlands and 570 acres of uplands."

"During the second half of the nineteenth century, Poplar Island experienced a significant amount of change. In 1847, the island was more than 1,000 acres in size. The forces of nature continued to alter the island. By the early 1900s, the continually eroding shoreline had split the island into three separate landmasses. Development on the island had evolved to include numerous farms, a post office, school, and sawmill, but the residents were becoming increasingly concerned about their shrinking real estate."

"It was probably Poplar Island's abundant wildlife and isolated beauty that attracted President Franklin D. Roosevelt and President Harry S. Truman to the location. In 1931 the Jefferson Islands Club was established to provide a weekend retreat for prominent Democratic politicians and businessmen of the era. By 1931, Poplar Island, the northernmost of the three islands, had been reduced to only 134 acres."

"By the 1960s, the main island was barely 80 acres. Over the next 30 years the islands continued to diminish in size and by 1990 the total area was less than 10 acres. In 1994, an interagency group, including the U.S. Army Corps of Engineers, the Maryland Port Administration, and Federal and State environmental agencies studied the feasibility of using Poplar Island as a beneficial use project for dredged material from the Chesapeake Bay navigation channels leading to the Port of Baltimore. Following the necessary environmental studies, it was determined that rebuilding Poplar Island and restoring over 1,000 acres of diverse habitat was a viable beneficial use of dredged material."

"In September of 1996, the project was approved for construction. A Project Cooperation Agreement was executed with the State of Maryland in April 1997. Construction began in 1998 and the project is expected to be completed by 2016."

How's that for a great story?

Shang ri-La

The setting for the Jefferson Islands Club on Poplar Islands was worthy of the names to which it was frequently referred, "Shang ri-La" and the "Playground of Presidents." The Club purchased Poplar Island and Cobbler's Neck, but not Coaches Island, as noted above. They were renamed Jefferson Islands by the State of Maryland (either by legislative action or proclamation of the Governor). The facilities of the original Clubhouse were magnificent. The house was a large two-story wood frame mansion painted white with green shutters. The interior was completely paneled with wood, mostly cedar. A large living room, with plenty of soft and comfortable leather chairs and a stone fireplace, sported hardwood floors. The house was protected by large oaks and poplars, and a finely cut green lawn spread out in the front and eased down to the white sandy beaches. Colorful flowers and small vegetable gardens trimmed the perimeter of the house. A large kitchen and dining room were capable of feeding an enormous lot of people. On the front side of the Clubhouse was a long screened porch, which had comfortable wicker chairs for the members to relax, sit, sip and leisurely watch the comings and goings on the wharf that ran several hundred feet out over the water. There were also many shady spots and comfortable tables and chairs that afforded private conversations.

The house had eleven sleeping rooms, ten with twin beds, "fine mattresses," and individual reading lights. A special Presidential Suite with a double bed for the personal use of President Roosevelt was designed. This room was simply furnished with cedar walls, a large dressing room, and bathroom. A headboard with a two-foot tall eagle and the "E Pluribus Unum" logo etched in it spread over the oak bed. Three large windows gave the President a view of the lawn and the surrounding harbor formed by the islands. There was also a sitting room in the Presidential Suite with a fireplace, and an extra room for the Secret Service. Except for special communication systems installed when the President visited the island, there were no telephones.

The insidious ring of the telephone was frowned upon in the early days of the Club, but today we have cell phones and can hardly avoid them even on the Island. The Clubhouse had one room with five beds called the "bull pen," according to Mary Jane Haddaway, daughter of the caretaker Capt. Bunzy Haddaway, where the Congressmen would stay who left their wives up town. Several other buildings stood behind the Clubhouse. One was the "sun room," where lockers enabled members and guests to store their guns, fishing gear, and various bottles of liquid refurbishment. The caretaker and his wife lived in one small cottage and other personnel and guides lived in another.

A modern skeet range was constructed for the use and enjoyment of the members, many of whom were avid duck hunters. The area around Poplar Island was a good spot for hunting many of the same types of ducks found at St. Catherine's Island. Certainly, there also was no dearth of geese. Ten duck blinds hid in and around the two Club islands provided good hunting. Pheasant and rabbits abounded on Poplar Island and there was a flock of "wild" turkeys. An article in the New York Times on July 25, 1939, described the exclusive Democratic composition of the Club and noted that, "the only rank outsider permitted to roam unchallenged in the region … is a 25 pound wild turkey that flew over to Jefferson Island from the mainland two years ago, joined up with the tame flock and now regards himself as a Democrat." A fresh water pond was dug on Poplar Island in order to provide a more natural habitat for these types of animals. It just might have been thickly planted with many types of grasses and vegetation deemed particularly tasteful to waterfowl.

If leaders of the Democratic Party were accused on occasion of going on "fishing expeditions" by their Republican adversaries, they would have been found culpable if those same Democrats had belonged to the Jefferson Islands Club. Fishing was a main source of entertainment and, indeed, the waters of the Bay provided an almost endless variety of fish to be caught by politicians so inclined. Rockfish, blue fish, trout, hardhead, and all other types normally found in the Chesapeake Bay were sought and caught by the members. The Club employed a fleet of three boats, each with captains. The "Commuter," also referred to as the "Jefferson Island," a well equipped boat built in 1926 with a length of 62 feet and a 14-foot beam, served as the main vessel used to transport the members from Annapolis. In addition, a 36-foot and a 30-foot boat were chartered primarily for fishing. Since many of the members preferred to cook their own fish or steam their own crabs or oysters, a barbecue pit was constructed. The Club owned several oyster beds in the nearby vicinity that were regularly harvested.

Members would call the secretary and make arrangements to reserve rooms at the island, much as they do today. They then would drive to Annapolis and meet the boat, which picked up those visiting the island every Friday at 5 p.m. and returned them on Sunday evening or Monday morning. The Bay Bridge had not yet been constructed, and it was a long ride across the Bay that was frequently subject to heavy winds, rough surf, and lots of cold water spray on the boat.

A picture hangs in the present Clubhouse on St. Catherine's Island of President Roosevelt and his entire cabinet under an expansive mulberry tree. According to the 1939 New York Times article, "Mr. Roosevelt's favorite spot for holding court on the island is under an old mulberry tree, planted long years ago and unfailing in its annual leafage. It is here that men speak their minds and free their souls." The seclusion of the island permitted frank discussion. The primary reason for the popularity of the Club among its members was privacy. Newsmen were rarely, if ever, invited to attend. Intimate conversations took place, many under that old mulberry tree. For this reason, there is a scarcity of information available concerning exact conversations and events that took place on the island. However, this was as intended. This makes recording the history very difficult, since many of the records also have been lost and most of the original members have matriculated to that sylvan Democratic Island paradise in the sky.

A few news accounts have been discovered that confirm President Roosevelt sponsored large conferences with Democratic leaders and assembled his entire cabinet at Poplar Island many times. It has been verified that in June of 1937, and again in 1939, Members of Congress were invited en masse to the island for conversation regarding several of the "hot" issues of the day. Senator Claude Pepper recalled attending the conference held in 1937. Pepper was one of the Club's strongest supporters.

Claude Denson Pepper was born in Dudleyville, Alabama in 1900, practiced law in Florida after graduating from Harvard Law School, was elected to the Florida State Legislature, and represented the Sunshine State as U.S. Senator from 1936-50. Pepper served ably on the Senate Small Business and Foreign Relations Committees and chaired the Middle East Subcommittee of the latter. Though he represented Florida in the U.S. House after 1962, everyone always called him "Senator." He was a staunch advocate for the rights of the aged as Chairman of the House Select Committee on Aging. When I spoke with him in about 1980, the Senator said, "I have a tentative plan to retire in the year 2000, but I may change my mind."

An unusual anecdote that I always loved, as reported in a Washington Post article, stated that Pepper was the victim of "one of the most famous speeches in one of the most bitter senatorial campaigns in modern history, when Pepper, branded as a leading liberal and sometimes as 'Red Pepper,' was defeated by George Smathers in 1950. In a speech which relied on his audience's unfamiliarity with big words, Smathers said that Pepper is known all over Washington as a shameless extrovert. Not only that, but this man is reliably reported to practice nepotism with his sister-in-law, and he has a sister who was once a thespian in wicked New York. Worst of all, it is an established fact that Mr. Pepper, before his marriage, practiced celibacy."

Nevertheless, the Senator has fond memories of the Club. "I first remember learning about the Jefferson Islands Club from Leslie Biffle, you remember him, he was Secretary of the Senate. He was a good friend of mine and his wife, Glade, was very good friends with my dear wife, Mildred. We always supported the Democratic Party and whatever events and functions might be scheduled. Mildred and I visited the island frequently," continues Senator Pepper. "We used to travel over to Annapolis with the Biffles, or the Blacks, Hugo and Mrs. Black, that is, both before and after he became a Justice of the Supreme Court. This particular conference in June of 1937 began with a luncheon for the wives of the Democratic Senators and many other high government officials. Did I show you the picture of Mildred fishing from the Club pier before the luncheon with Mrs. Black? The President wanted to speak with the members of the Senate, whom he was having some difficulty with at the time. I believe at that particular meeting the discussion may have centered around what had been going on regarding the Supreme Court. I would say the Club could accommodate about 60 or 70 people for an overnight event if necessary, but with so many of us attending at the President's meeting, we only stayed at the island for the day. There was a big luncheon with tables and chairs spread out on the lawn in front of the Clubhouse."

"I clearly remember to this day, many of those who were at the island for that conference," says the Senator. "Cordell Hull was there, and Jimmy Burns, Pat Harrison, I'm sure, Speaker Bankhead, Senator Andrews, also from Florida, and I believe Sam Rayburn was there, too. I'll never forget sitting in the living room listening to Key Pittman from Nevada regale us with stories of the Old West. He was quite a raconteur. Of course, the whole Cabinet was there. Joseph Robinson, the Senate Majority Leader, was there. He was my patron. He had assigned me to the Senate Foreign Relations Committee as soon as there had been a vacancy. Unfortunately, Senator Robinson died a month later in July 1937. He was President of the Jefferson Islands Club just before he died too."

As to what they normally did on the island, the Senator says, "Oh, we would fish a little, fix up a little barbecue of some fish or chicken, walk around the island a little bit, or take a ride in one of the Club boats. Or we would just sit around the Clubhouse and tell stories, talk, and have a libation or two, you know, just like we do down at the Club now. There was also good eating. Yes, always good eats." On May 30, 1989, the Senator departed for that Island Crab Feast in the hereafter.

Apparently, Roosevelt used these informal occasions to discuss legislative affairs more than just a few times. A 1939 article in the "Easton Star Democrat" reports that "at the retreat this week, President Roosevelt plans to visit for three days with Democratic members of the House and Senate. In relays of about 130 a day, they are expected to come out from Annapolis in the Club's boat. Party problems will be discussed; presumably the legislative program before Congress will also be mentioned in the course of the outing."

A New York Times article of July 25, 1939 reported that the "Secretary of the Navy sees to it that Jefferson Island Narrows has its share of lean, long rakish crafts moving nervously about the harbor when the President is on shore, and that each ship is equipped with a battery of search lights, if there should be a sudden demand for illumination at night." Thus, Mr. Roosevelt used the Presidential Suite and slept comfortably with Navy craft patrolling the island.

From the "Secret Dairy of Harold Ickes," the Republican in Roosevelt's cabinet, we learn the following: "I went down to the Jefferson Island in Chesapeake Bay on Sunday [in July 1935] as a guest of the Jefferson [Islands] Club, which is almost exclusively a Democratic Club. The officers and directors, almost without exception, are Democratic members of the Senate. I left the house at seven-thirty, picked up Secretary Dern, and arrived at the pier in Annapolis about nine o'clock. Senator Tydings was there to received the guests.... Boarding the "DuPont," a sizable and substantial yacht, we went down the bay to the island. The trip took almost two hours. We arrived at the island about eleven o'clock...."

"The President, with a party of which the Vice President [John Nance Garner] was a member, had gone down on Saturday. His party was just getting up when we arrived, as the result of a poker game the night before which lasted until four o'clock in the morning. The Vice President is supposed to be the best poker player in Washington, but the President took him into camp. He told me with great delight later how on one hand,

when there was a big jackpot, he had out bluffed the Vice President, inducing him to lay down two pairs topped by kings, whereas the President had only 7's and 4's. According to reports, this just about broke the heart of the Vice President. During the game, Senator Pittman remarked of the Vice President that when he bet ten cents, it wasn't merely ten cents, but the interest on $2 for a year. The Vice President was chaffed a good deal during the day on his playing, particularly by Congressman Rayburn, of Texas, but it didn't ruffle his feathers any."

"There was a plentiful cold lunch and abundant liquid refreshments. There was a little card playing, some clay pigeon shooting, and some crabbing, but generally people just sat around and talked and had a good time. Senator Joe Robinson was there as well as Senators Guffey, of Pennsylvania, Ryan Duffy, of Wisconsin, Dieterich, of Illinois, Radcliffe, or Maryland, Speaker Byrns and others. Of the members of the Cabinet, in addition to Dern and myself, there were present Cummings, Farley, and Roper.... We boarded our yacht for the return trip about four o'clock and reached Annapolis shortly before seven. We got into the worst traffic jam I have ever seen in this part of the country on our way back to Washington so that I did not get back until nine o'clock. This was a long session for a little fun, but I really had to go because I am more or less suspect as a non-Democrat ...."

Another story from the era is recounted by Christine White, daughter of Jim White. She was at the Club on Poplar Island for an outing with President Truman in 1945. She says: "That evening, not only did the President play the piano, but my father accompanied on the mandolin. After that, there was a 'boys only' rousing poker game."

"They played with a deck of yellow cards with the Pepsi Cola insignia stamped in the center. Dealing the cards face-down, the President remarked that the country had become mesmerized by labels. ... The President went on: 'On the other hand, doesn't the Jefferson Island Club have some cards with their own insignia? If not, why not?'

"One of the players was fortunate enough to think of a good reason: 'Mr. President, we're intent on building another bathroom at the moment.' My father interjected that he would take this up with the House Committee. Then the President advised him that he intended to run a country on necessity, not luxury, and that they were damn lucky to find a donated deck anywhere in the wilds of Maryland."

"Instead of taking it up with the House Committee, my father took up the cards and wrapped them in a type-written note to the effect that President Truman had played poker with them at the Island."

Perhaps the most sensational stories about those times on Poplar Islands come from a man who, with his wife Alice lived on the island and managed the Jefferson Islands Club for 13 years, and even stayed on the Island more than 10 years after the Club had moved its location to St. Catherine's Island. This was Captain Varnon ("Bunzy") Haddaway. His family lived on the Poplar Islands for many years and "Cap'n Bunzy" was a natural caretaker and story teller. The following comments are taken from an article in the Washington Post on August 13, 1970, written by Hal Willard.

"At that time, he was 68 years old, and described as 'tall, with close-cropped white hair, brown leather skin, the permanent squint of the watermen, chain smoker, a bubbling-over talker who was born, raised and lived all his life on, near and around Tilghman Island and Jefferson Island."

It was noted in the article that the old Clubhouse could ordinarily sleep 27, but when President Roosevelt came down, cots were used and space made for 70people.

In the Post article, we get our image of Harry Truman as a real firecracker from Cap 'n Bunzy.

"When President Truman was out there on Jefferson, visiting the Club, he let loose. He said to me one night, 'Captain Bunzy, do you suppose you and me could go out early one morning and catch some big fish before the rest of these sons of bitches get up?' 'Of course,' I said I thought we could, and we did."

"We caught eight fish, twelve to fifteen pounders, and when we got back, Mr. Truman had me string them up along the pier and then he grabbed the rope on the big bell we had there, and he began to ring and ting and he hollered, "Wake up all ye sons of bitches and see what you missed this morning!"

"Well, all those senators and congressmen came piling out of that clubhouse in their pajamas and I don't know when I'll ever see another sight like that."

Another reference to President Truman attending the Jefferson Island Club is in the book entitled simply "Truman" by David McCulloch. "At a conference of several hundred Democratic congressmen and senators at a clubhouse on Jefferson Island in Chesapeake Bay, [Truman] encouraged everyone to call him Harry and joined a game of stud poker on the porch. An unnamed senator later reported that Harry Truman played a 'damn good game,' while another eyewitness (also unnamed), describing what a good time everyone had, said, 'There was all we could eat and more than we could drink – only two people passed out.'"

Captain Bunzy also put on many large parties. On September 22 and 23, 1945, Russell M. Arundel was the host of a party at the Club in honor of former Congressman James Barnes of Illinois. The program of supplies for the weekend included, Bunzy swore, "500 cases of Budweiser beer donated; 300 cases of Mt. Vernon Straight rye whiskey, donated; 15 cases of bourbon, donated; 100 cases of Vat 69 scotch, donated, I forgot by who."

"There were 30 bartenders and President Truman played the piano. That was the weekend that a congressman from Kentucky, I'd rather not say who he was, apparently inspired by the quantity available consumed one entire bottle of bourbon before dinner. And when he came to the table he just sat there and somebody passed the mashed potatoes -- you know, the real creamy kind, and put them in front of him. He paid no attention and pretty soon began to sink slowly forward and first thing anybody know'd, his face was buried in those mashed potatoes! Somebody retrieved the Congressman and Bunzy said he hauled him out to the back porch, cleaned off the mashed potatoes and left him face down on the porch all night, figuring that was the best thing to do."

The article continues with a tale Bunzy told on Senator Key Pittman. "He owned a pair of pearl-handled revolvers and was famed for his marksmanship. After a few drinks," Bunzy said, "Pittman sat down on the sofa in the lounge, and unerringly shot out the lanterns all over the mantle." A picture of Pittman, the first president of the Jefferson Islands Club, hangs in the Clubhouse on St. Catherine's Island, though without his guns. Another picture shows President Truman twirling Pittman's revolvers at a card game. No one is remembered to have argued with the President during that game.

There is also a story about the time that Speaker Bankhead brought his daughter Tallulah to the island. "There used to be a lot of game birds on these islands," Bunzy said, "and somehow five red foxes got out there and was hunting them. So we decided to go after the foxes. I took Tallulah with me and I set her up near what looked like a good fox run and told her I'd go ahead and see if I couldn't flush them out. If I did, I'd yell 'Tally-ho!'"

"Well, I flushed them out all right, and I yelled 'Tally-ho!' for all I was worth. In a couple seconds, I heard two shots -- Bam! Bam! -- and I ran back there as fast as I could and there was Tallulah. She got two foxes on the run."

Another story was told by Mary Jane Haddaway. During the September party in 1945, she was 15 at the time and helping to serve the meal on Saturday night to President Truman and a group of about 45 before another batch of Congressmen were supposed to arrive the next day. "I was helping serve the table and I remember we had green peas … two bowls, one to go on each end of the table." Holding one bowl, she leaned down to place it on the table and inadvertently tipped the other bowl of peas down the President's back. The Secret Service agents jumped, and Mary Jane said, "I thought I was going to die!" The President turned around, saw the look on her face, put his arm around her and said, "Aw, hell, honey, don't worry about it. You'll have a story to tell your grandchildren."

Captain Bunzy Haddaway worked for the Jefferson Islands Club from 1933 till the Clubhouse caught fire in 1946. He stayed on to work for George Bailey who tried to start another club by building a replica clubhouse and selling memberships. This venture failed and in 1949 the Campbell's Soup Company bought the Island. They used it as a hunting lodge as did the North American Smelting Company, which purchased it in 1956. Captain Bunzy and his wife left in 1957, as a man who had been an institution at the Jefferson Islands Club for many years and who could proudly state that he worked for one of the most prestigious clubs of the day.

Dorothy White was the wife of James A. White, Administrative Assistant to Senator Key Pittman, and who played an important role in the transfer of the Club from Poplar to St. Catherine's Island. Mrs. White visited the Club on several occasions when President Truman was there. She said that the President was quite a gambler, who would stay up till late at night playing cards with the other men. He escaped to the island frequently, but Bess didn't like it and normally he went alone. Mrs. White said that the old Clubhouse was quite lovely. She remembers well a long time employee of the Club, Rufus Odom.

Mrs. White recalls that Rufus was "indispensable," a very short black man, about five feet tall, but very, very funny. He would meet them at the dock and help carry their luggage up to the house. He was the chime-ringer, butler, bartender, wood chopper, grass cutter, jack-of-all-trades, and practically a member of the Haddaway family. Rufus used to call those staying the night to come to breakfast with, "get up you-se people, I'se not gonna call you agin." One story, which Rufus loved to tell on himself was about what President Roosevelt had said to him. "Rufus, when I come down again, I'm agoin' to shoot an apple off of your head," and how Rufus replied, "No, sah. You ain't a gonna do dat, Mistah President, because when you come back to do dat, I'm a goin' to be away from heah."

Christine White recounts: "I remember a particular summer when my brother and I were 'lugged' down to a place called the Jefferson Islands Club, of which my father's boss, Senator Pittman, was President. Since we were small, we were not invited to go hunting, so the caretaker Rufus … was also our caretaker. He showed us how to play horseshoes, which we took to immediately. I could hardly lift and aim, but my brother was quite able. For the entire three days, we played horseshoes, whittled wood, and made paper planes out of magazine pages. … When the adults were around, whom I knew to be 'important,' Rufus was really the 'boss.'" When Rufus died on April 19, 1944 of a heart attack, the Club arranged for his interment.

It is not known what caused the fire on March 5, 1946 that totally destroyed the Clubhouse or exactly why the membership decided to relocate rather than to replace the house. John Gordon reported in a letter to the members that "building restrictions and materials shortages made it imperative that a new location be found immediately." In those days, membership in the Club was a much sought after privilege, with the long list of notables who belonged and a limit on the number of stockholder members. So, it was important that they have a suitable retreat.

The Transition

St. Catherine's Island was purchased by the Jefferson Islands Club in 1946 for $26,000. When the Clubhouse on the Poplar Islands burned, the members were advised that Senator Key Pittman had obtained an option in 1936 on another island in the Potomac River, St. Catherine's Island. The membership then voted to leave the old island and to move the Club to the new location.

The facts are that Jim White, an aide to Key Pittman, had been a good friend of Dr. Jacobs, the partner of Mr. Forbes in their ownership of the Island, under the name St. Catherine's Island Corporation. White hoped to establish a recreational club for administrative assistants similar to the Jefferson Islands Club. There was already a club for AA's in Washington, but White envisioned another more grand and effective club on St. Catherine's Island. When Dr. Jacobs and Mr. Forbes failed in their plan to develop the Island, White had become president of the St. Catherine's Island Corporation and attempted to form such a club.

The attempt by White was unsuccessful and the Corporation liquidated in 1945. He had stipulated that, unless one hundred members would be enrolled, he would not finalize his organization of the AA Club. When the Clubhouse on Poplar Island burned down less than a year later, Jim White worked through Key Pittman and John Gordon to bring the Jefferson Island Club to its current site.

The death of President Roosevelt, World War II, and the relocation of the Club brought about many changes. To a number of members, the days of the Jefferson Islands Club were gone. The new Island, as beautiful as it was, certainly did not possess anything as grand a structure as the two story lodge at the old site. The old Farmhouse was then the main building, for the Clubhouse had not yet been expanded. The new facility certainly was not in good enough condition to handle large conferences similar to those held by President Roosevelt.

Nonetheless, under the leadership of the new President, Congressman Pete Jarman, the Club forged ahead. Though some of the original members never even visited the new location, many others became avid supporters. With a new contingent of administrative assistants from the Hill, who had been contacted by Jim White, together with Washington area professionals, the membership gradually coalesced.

Two new caretakers, Joe and Bernie Wise, were hired. The Wise brothers, known locally as "Fuzzy" (Joe) and "Stump" (Bernie), or the "Wise Men," were dedicated individuals destined to continue with the Club for 26 and 29 years, respectively. Oftentimes, they worked day and night to guide hunting parties and to keep everything ship-shape for the members. Joe and Bernie nurtured the Club from an unoccupied island to a bustling social resort. Throughout, they became respected friends of the members who regularly visited the Club.

New leadership of the Club continued to emerge in the 1950s. Over the next 15 or more years, Jim White controlled the day to day operations, by virtue of being Chairman of the Club's House Committee. John Gordon was Secretary of the Club prior to the move and remained in that position for many years, staying active until his death. Gordon distinguished himself as executive secretary of the American Vegetable Oils and Fats Industries Association and on several international commissions. Charlie Thomas, a patent lawyer from Rockville, Maryland, vacationed at the Club frequently and owned several luxury cruisers (Katy Did I, II, and III, named after his wife), captained by Joe Wise. Most importantly, Leslie Biffle had been appointed Secretary of the Senate by Senator Robinson and soon was elected President of the Club, a title which he retained until 1962.

Another dedicated Club member who gave his wholehearted support was Lawrence Wood ("Chip") Robert. Chip Robert served as Assistant Secretary to the Treasury during the Roosevelt administration and as Treasurer and then Secretary of the Democratic National Committee in the late 1930s. Everyone who knew his wife, Evelyn ("Evie") Walker Robert, has said that she was one of the most amazing women they had every met. The Roberts lived for many years in the Mayflower Hotel and were high in the Washington social scene. It was Evie Robert who brought two donkeys down to the Island for one Sunday party. That didn't work out, because they kicked people. A picture of her and her pet lion hung on the walls of the Clubhouse until vandals destroyed it several years ago.

Senator Claude Pepper told me about the last time he went to the Club with Chip Robert. "It was the summer of 1976 when Mrs. Leslie Biffle, Chip Robert, my wife Mildred and I drove down to the island in Mrs. Biffle's chauffeured limousine. It was one of the most delightful experiences I shall ever have. The entire way down, and back, too, Chip regaled us of his many experiences throughout the world. We would say today that Chip Robert knew everyone. He had been in on presidential politics for several decades and told us many secret stories. Mildred and I would never forget that afternoon at the Island, eating crabs and sitting on the porch with Chip Robert." Others who always supported the Club were Senators Clair Engel of California and Virgil Chapman of Kentucky, Secretary of the Senate "Skeeter" Johnston, and House Sergeant of Arms Zeake Johnson, to name a few. The political influence these gentlemen retained continued to bring in new members, as well as to maintain the interest of many of the older members.

I recall one personal story about Zeake Johnson. I very distinctly remember walking with him along the beach facing the River south of the Clubhouse one summer afternoon, perhaps in the late '50s or early '60s. I don't know why it was just me and Zeake Johnson, but

I am sure there was no one else with us. I was young, obviously, and was holding a wooden duck decoy and would set it in the water and watch it float. The waves would push the decoy back to the sand. Zeake said if we threw it out further in the water, the waves would bring it back to us. So, he chucked the decoy out into the water, and we watched as it gently floated down the River and out of sight. I must have been sad, and perhaps shed a tear. Well, old Zeake felt terrible. A while later, he and his wife visited us at home and she brought me a paper mache, gray duck decoy that she had decorated with various baubles and glitter. It was very nice, but in my mind it wasn't a duck decoy, so I think I just let my mother have it for decoration around the house. Funny how some things stick with you years later, and then you can't remember what you did five minutes ago.

A Return to Poplar Island?

A little known event occurred that clearly indicated the desire of many of the members to return to the former days. In a letter dated November 5, 1951 and addressed to all members of the Jefferson Island Club, Secretary John Gordon announced that George K. Bailey, who had purchased Jefferson and Poplar Islands and built Poplar Island Lodge, a version of the old clubhouse, had passed away and the Island was being sold.

According to Peter Bailey in his book, "Poplar Island, My Memories as a Boy," his father had high blood pressure and, after several severe operations, died at the age of forty-four. Marian Bailey, George's widow, wanted to sell their Island after her husband's death. Mr. Bailey's lodge, on the site of the burned house, had 17 rooms, including five public rooms, 12 bedrooms and 5 baths. A new 600-foot wharf was installed as well as 12 duck blinds and other improvements. Peter Bailey's book is a very nice recollection of growing up on an island in the late 1940s, so you should read it if you want more information on that era.

The letter from Gordon delineated the pros and cons of both locations and requested the membership vote whether the old site should be repurchased and St. Catherine's Island sold. Gordon discussed the travel distance, noting the Jefferson and Poplar Islands were about 3 miles offshore from Lowes Landing in Sherwood, about 20 miles from Easton, Maryland, and 95 miles by automobile from Washington via the Sandy Point-Matapeake ferry. He noted that the new Bay Bridge, to be completed in 1952, would shorten the travel time significantly. He estimated travel time for the 65 mile drive to St. Catherine's Island to be a little less than two hours. He stated that the accommodations at the Poplar Lodge, which could hold about 24 persons, were better than the Clubhouse and Farmhouse at St. Catherine's Island, which could accommodate 18. He noted that St. Catherine's had about 60 acres, while Jefferson Island was about 37 acres and Poplar Island about 200.

The two properties had offsetting qualities and members responded both positively and negatively to the idea in strong terms. Jim White argued strongly in favor of remaining at St. Catherine's Island primarily because of the distance but, in addition, he pointed out that 25 new members had joined the Club with the understanding that their initiation fees would be used to build a new addition to the Clubhouse. White felt that the members in favor of returning to Poplar Islands would have been primarily doing so based on sentiment, rather than looking at the obvious advantages of St. Catherine's Island. He noted that the distance from the White House to Poplar Islands (including traversing the new Bay Bridge and the three miles by boat) was 99.3 miles, while the distance from the White House to St. Catherine's Island was actually 60.25 miles (including the three-quarters of a mile boat ride). So, he argued, a person could go to the Island for a trip of fishing or shooting and return the same day, which would not be possible with Poplar Island. White also mentioned the additional cost of $1.75 per car on the Bridge. He pointed out that there was space on St. Catherine's Island for a nine-hole golf course, too. I've thought of that possibility often, but there were always bigger fish to fry, and the upkeep would be significant.

Seth Richardson also wrote in favor of the new Island, partly because of the difficulties in calling to the old Island and making plans, because the only phone was located three miles up the road from Sherwood at Harrison's Store. In contrast, members could contact Joe or Bernie Wise at any time and they would immediately take you to the Island. Richardson said the hunting was much better at St. Catherine's Island, with more hunting blinds, and it was easier to get duck hunting guides at the new Island, too. He was obviously a hunter.

In January of 1952, Secretary Gordon announced that "the poll was overwhelmingly in favor of the return to our old stamping grounds." How about that? The vote in favor of moving back was 38 -21 with the other 44 members abstaining. A committee was formed by the Executive Committee at a meeting on January 11, 1952 held at the Army-Navy Club in Washington to determine whether the present St. Catherine's Island could be expeditiously sold.

Of course, the Club did not make the move back to the Chesapeake Bay, and the reason seems to be that a buyer for St. Catherine's Island could not be found at a suitable price. In fact, the letter from Gordon indicates selling St. Catherine's Island would be a key factor. Obviously, the Club would not have been in a position to maintain both properties. According to Peter Bailey, his mother was not able to sell the Island for another two years although there was much correspondence between her and John Gordon in the file.

With this crisis out of the way, and with the Club strengthening and gaining the support of new members rapidly, much was happening on St. Catherine's Island during those first years it hosted the Jefferson Islands Club.

The New Club Improves

When Joe and Bernie Wise began working for the Club in April of 1947, there was quite a lot to accomplish. During the ownership of Forbes and Jacobs, several caretakers had lived on the Island at various times. Just before the Island was purchased by the Club, it had been unattended for several years. Not much had been brought from Poplar Islands, they told me, except one chair and the boats.

Two of the Club's smaller boats had been brought to the new location, in addition to another that had been purchased shortly before. The "Commuter" was no longer in commission. These three boats were the "Houndog," the "Elcie V," and the "Mary Jane." Three wooden rowboats also were towed across the Bay and up the Potomac, but nearly everything else the Club owned had been burned in the fire.

"It was really a shambles over there when we started," said Bernie. "The grass was all grown up about two or three feet high, with big bushes and only a sheep path to the Clubhouse. All we had was a little push mower to cut the grass. We had to manhandle everything. Gawd, that was some work. We used to cut two acres regularly with that little mower. Now, I don't see how we did all that work. But it was fun then. We were horses."

Though they nearly worked their fingers to the bone, the Wise brothers managed the largest Island in the area, which gave them unique stature among the local people. They hobnobbed with many senators and congressmen who continued to escape Capitol politics at the Club, and the brothers benefited from the use of the Club's boats and equipment.

Bernie, born in 1911, was the older of the two, with Joe four years younger. Bernie was quiet, steady, and hardworking. Joe generally managed the operation and was one of the best story tellers one could ever be entitled to hear. They complimented one another beautifully and gained the trust and respect of everyone who visited the Island.

Both were born on St. Margaret's Island back in the days when "we used to have winters." Joe told stories of the snow being so high on top of the ice that they had to shovel a path across the ice just to get off the island to go courtin'. "Geese and ducks had a difficult go of it with snow covering everything," Joe explained. "They'd fly around for hours looking' for open water. We used to shovel the snow off a section of the ice and clear it off. Those birds would spot that opening, set their wings and come in to land, grinning from ear to ear. When they hit the ice, their feet would whoosh out from under them, they'd go belly up and slide into the snow bank. Funniest damn sight I've ever seen."

Their father was Thomas N. Wise, who worked in Matt Bailey's store in White Neck's Creek for many years until he married, after which he followed the water until about 1908. For the next 20 years, Thomas Wise was employed by the Tide Water Marine Police as General Inspector for the state of Maryland and was involved in the Oyster Wars. He was a Democrat and saw his career as a policeman end when the Republicans came into power in the local government. In about 1940, he opened a store that was located on the lot now used by the Club for parking. Wise operated that store until his death in 1955.

The Wises lived on St. Margaret's Island until 1924. Stump and Fuzzy followed the water when they were young, playing and working on it. During the 1930s and the depression, both worked somewhat regularly in Washington, D.C. Bernie worked as a landscape gardener for several years in the summer and returned home for the winter oystering and ducking seasons. Joe gained experience as a bricklayer in Washington during that time and also returned to the area during the winters. Mr. Forbes purchased St. Margaret's Island in 1924 and in the latter part of the 1930s, Bernie moved back to the island with his new wife, Dorothy, and his parents as caretakers for Mr. Forbes. Bernie and Dot had two children on the island. His parents moved off in the early '40s, but Bernie and Dot stayed on for another year or so. The facilities on St. Margaret's Island were, and are, beautiful. A large well-kept house with a big stone fireplace provided all the comforts of home. In later years a swimming pool was built, and being so close to the main land, electric wires were strung up and run over to the island.

Forbes built a small house for the caretaker behind the main lodge in order to convince Bernie to stay, but he and his family left in 1945 and Dot doesn't mind telling you why. "I hated it up there on that island -- - that's all there was to it. Cold, miserable, and lonely. I haven't been back up there since." For the next couple years, before the Club hired him, Bernie crabbed, fished, oystered, and ducked. Even after retiring from the Club, he still rose at the crack of dawn no matter what season, and worked his crab pots or tonged a few oysters. "It just stays in your blood."

The 1940s had not been pleasant for Joe, for he was on the other side of the world, fighting for Uncle Sam. He joined the army in 1942 and not too much later was part of the D-Day invasion as one of the shock troops on Omaha Beach. On August 8, 1944, he was captured and remained in prison camp until the end of the war. He looks back on his capture with a laugh and sparkle in his eye. It seems he and some of his buddies had found a specimen of some very fine French cognac and, accompanied by such a powerful force, he volunteered to go search out a German machine gun nest that had his unit pinned down. He found it alright, but along with it were enough German rifles pointing at him to encourage a restrained response. He spent the rest of the war in a German prison camp. "Hell," is how he described it to me. At the end of the war, Joe said he only weighed about 98 pounds and was more than just glad to get back home.

When Joe began working for the Club, his wife, Rose, went with him as a cook. For the next 12 years, Rose became the most popular figure on the Island, due to her excellent skills in setting delicious meals before hungry hunters.

Within the first year, the Farmhouse was renovated. Joe and Bernie put many long hours into cleaning, clearing, and fixing. Joe Oliver had grown up with "Fuzzy" and "Stump" and helped them quite a bit those first few years. It was Joe Oliver and Earl Sinclair who installed the plumbing in the Farmhouse. Prior to that there had been only one sink and an out-house. Jim White employed some carpenters from Washington and in the summer of 1948, sent them down to live and work in the Farmhouse to put the old structure in good shape for the new members. These carpenters, the Stonemans from West Virginia, were noted musicians. In fact, Pop Stoneman started a Bluegrass band called "The

Stonemans" that became famous. Donna Stoneman later became a regular on "Hee Haw" on television. The Stonemans rebuilt the storage shed and did much of the interior work in the Farmhouse. At least that's what Joe Oliver told me.

In the early years, Joe and Rose lived full time at the Farmhouse during duck season. They lived in the farm house in the North Pole Room upstairs. The Island was busy all day every day, and many years the Wises worked three months without a day off. Joe's son Terry also lived on the Island and got up every morning in the icy cold weather and drove his small skiff to the mainland to go to school. The house was heated with kerosene stoves and Rose remembers that they had to keep the water running, at least a dribble all night long to keep the pipes from freezing. The Farm house wasn't insulated either. It was cold. At that time, there was a well in the storage shed, as well as one in the pump house near the cottage, each nearly 300 ft. deep. The pumps were run by Kohler DC generators and the lights in both buildings were run by the same direct current.

The duck hunting was excellent, and that was one of the primary uses of the Club at that time. The 1952 letter from John Gordon confirmed as much, noting that there were some 27 duck blinds in operation in St. Catherine's Sound (making his point essentially that Poplar Islands was more secluded). The Club hunting rules for the 1952-53 season had a duck limit of eight, with a maximum per day take of two geese, and a possession limit of four. The season lasted from November 12 to January 10, a long season. The charge was $7.50 per day for a blind for each member and the same for a guest (max of one). The prices of the meals were listed as $1.50 for breakfast, $1.75 for lunch, $2.50 for dinner, and a room charge of $2.25. It cost less to stay for the night at Jefferson Island in those days than to have dinner.

Over the years, duck hunting was one of the Club's main "recreations," as Jim White put it. There are records of conversation in the minutes of Board of Governors meetings that went on in some detail about plans to plant the right kind of duck food around the Island.

There was initially no mechanized means of transportation on the Island. An old banana cart and wheelbarrow were all Joe and Bernie had to use for carrying luggage, tools, lumber, pumps, decoys, and anything else that might have to be carried back and forth from the cottage (as they called it for a while) to the Farmhouse. The dock was then down near the Farmhouse, almost a quarter of a mile away from the cottage. The old cart was better than nothing, and Joe says that he bets they put a thousand miles a year on it. "After a while, you got used to it. I pulled, and Bernard pushed." In the late '40's, a small Massey-Harris tractor, called a pony, was purchased. This simple four cylinder, 6-volt tractor was the workhorse that pulled stumps, hauled luggage in a small wagon, and was loaded with everything ever brought on the Island. It stood in the weather all year every year since then and ran until the 1980's. I loved that old tractor and, as a child, used to spend hours sitting on it driving all over god's creation. Funny how you can be in love with a machine, too.

In addition to cutting the lawn with the mower attached to the tractor, every year Joe and Bernie would select a day when the wind was blowing from just the right direction and set fire to a section of the Island. This aforementioned technique, appropriately called "burning," is a very efficient method of keeping the land cleared. They once planted about 20 acres with corn and rye on the cleared land, which was looked on very favorably by passing flocks of geese and ducks.

In those early years, all that was done by the members when they spent time at the Island was either hunting, fishing, story telling, eating, or drinking. Each of these was pursued with much vigor, and normally met with success. Joe and Bernie took fishing parties out all through the summer and they usually caught as many rock or perch as desired. What better way to relax for anyone from the city than to come spend a quiet day or two pleasantly fishing on the Potomac. The only force of nature that might cause one problem would be a summer afternoon thunderstorm, which can be treacherous and devastating.

Bernie remembers taking some "city folks" out fishing. "We were having a wonderful time," he recalls, "This man and his family had caught about 50 rockfish. I spotted a northwester brewing up on the horizon and told them it was about time to head in. Well, this fellow wasn't used to the water, and he didn't realize how rough those storms could get. So he said, "No, let's stay, we have time." A little bit later I said, "The storm is coming mighty fast, sir, I suggest we head in." He still wouldn't listen and they went right on fishing. Well, in about 10 more minutes, that northwester was on us -- she cut loose. Waves about three to four feet, lightning, thunder, rain -- peltin' down. The old "Houndog" was practically keeled over to the gunnels and that family huddled up in the bow of the boat a' cryin' and carryin' on. I knew we'd make it alright, so to teach them a lesson I told them they couldn't stay up in the bow or we'd sink. So they were all holdin' on to the side of the boat, rain pourin' down on them all the way back to shore. First lesson: always listen to the Captain of the boat."

During the hunting season was when it really paid to listen to the Wise brothers. "Now you take a north wind blowin' about 30 miles an hour, temperature about 5 below. So cold ice forms on your eyebrows and the hairs between your nose. You've got a dangerous situation," explains Joe. "Bernard and I had lived around the water all our lives, so we know what to do. But these city fellows -- sometimes -- Whew! By Gawd, I'd a thought we'd lost them." Bernie remembers the time that Seth Richardson and Burke Summers, who both visited the Island regularly during hunting season, were out in the blind on the river side. "It was really blowin' a blizzard that day. Snow comin' straight into your face, winds about 40 or 50, just snowin' to beat hell. Joe Oliver was guidin' for Mr. Richardson and Mr. Summers and he went out and told them that it was gonna get pretty bad and it was time to leave. It was only about a half-an-hour till sunset. Well, those two refused to leave the blind. Finally Joe left and came around to the cove and told me about it. We jumped in the "Houndog" and headed around the Island. The bow of the boat was bobbin' up about four or five feet and slammin' down into the waves, sprayin' freezin' water all over everywhere. I nosed the boat right up to the blind and held it as steady as I could. We yelled and told them they better jump in the boat now or we'd have to leave them out there for the night. Well, they finally jumped after a few minutes, but if they hadn't they would have been left there and frozen to death."

Joe recalls one old Senator, who used to love to hunt at the Club. "This senator was a helluva hunter. He'd take bourbon whiskey and a shotgun and go out in the blind. This one particular time, he must have fallen asleep and when everyone got back to the Clubhouse that evening, someone asked, 'Where's the Senator?' Well, we went back out to the blind, and there he was, hunched over with his gun between his legs and his head down almost to his knees. When he drank, his nose would run, and he must have been asleep for about an hour. There was a six-inch icicle hangin' down from his nose. We just broke it off and carried him back to the house. He was a good old soul."

Another famous activity was the card playing. Rose remembers waking up in the Farmhouse and coming down to cook breakfast at 4:30 a.m. Everyone would still be up playing cards. "Thousands of dollars on the table, sometimes," she said. "I just couldn't believe it. One time somebody won a car and gave it to Bernie.

That was his first car. Another time one man gambled away a summer home in Maine, I think it was Douglas Gibson. If the game was going good, they wouldn't even go out in the blinds -- just sit there and play cards."

In 1949, there was a bad storm and lightning struck the chimney of the Clubhouse, the generator house, and the old house on Captain William's Point, which burned to the ground. Joe rebuilt the chimney in the Clubhouse and about the same time built the outdoor fireplace and oven. The fireplace in the Clubhouse puts out some great heat, and I often cook oysters in a pan on the wood and melt butter in a mug on the hearth when we visit in winter. The outdoor fireplace was one of the largest and best built fireplaces in the history of the Island! It was big enough to hold a party in and could cook for several hundred people. It fell into the River when the bank underneath it eroded away in the early 1970s.

The original portion of the Clubhouse, first called the cottage, was built in 1940 by John Long. According to a survey of the Island dated February 1, 1952 and conducted by D. H. Steffens of Bryantown, Md., St. Catherine's Island consisted of 65.56 acres. The surveyor's chart includes a number of interesting tidbits. There was clearly a well on Capt. Williams point to the northwest of the Cove. The width of the land at its most narrow point was about 200 feet, and there was over 100 feet of land in front of the current Clubhouse, called the Cottage then. The Farmhouse was at its closest point about 50 feet from the water.

In 1953, the Club contracted with the Merando Company contractors from Washington, D.C. Merando built the cinderblock and woodframe four-bedroom south wing, the kitchen, and dining room for approximately $26,000. These additions were made as a result of the need for more space and the fact that many members had joined based on the assumption that the Clubhouse would be enlarged. The guest rooms each had twin beds, a dressing room, and private bath, including shower. It is interesting to note and somewhat coincidental to find out that this wing was designed by the architect Frederick Tilp, who also designed the plans for the county Courthouse in Leonardtown. Tilp was a friend of a prominent member, Gen. Julian Smith. Frederick Tilp lived in Alexandria, where I used to visit him, and was the author of the fascinating book, "This Was Potomac River," to which I refer often.

In 1954, the Executive Committee unanimously adopted a program to complete the construction of the Clubhouse by adding another four bedrooms, a Presidential suite, and a storage room on the north end of the cottage. These additions were made by Joe and Bernie Wise with local labor. The bedrooms are similar to those in the south wing. The Presidential suite was meant to provide accommodations like Roosevelt's room in the old Clubhouse on Poplar Island. A large paneled parlor and sitting room centered around a "heat-o-lator" fireplace. The sleeping room provided twin beds with a large dressing room. The bathroom has a tub shower.

The Executive Committee also voted to renovate the Farmhouse by installing two baths and new paneling throughout the interior of the building. The tongue and groove, beautiful red-wood, pine and cyprus paneling is still in the Farmhouse. At the same time, the Executive Committee decided to construct several jetties, also called groins, at a cost not to exceed $2,500, designed to arrest the erosion of the west bank of the Island (see below). These improvements were financed by loans from members. The Executive Committee's proposal was in reaction to the tremendous destruction wrought by Hurricane Hazel, which hit the area in 1954 and began a period of rapid erosion. Hazel itself took an estimated 15 feet of shore line from the Riverside of the Island in just a few days.

In a report prepared for Don Glassie, who was then Assistant Secretary of the Club, by the State of Maryland's Board of Natural Resources, Department of Geology, Mines and Water Resources, Joseph T. Singewald, Jr., Director wrote on October 21, 1954, that charts of the Coast and Geodetic Survey showed that "between 1868 and 1943, the southwest shore line [of the Island] receded a maximum of 240 feet at the north end, about 100 feet in the vicinity of the clubhouse, and a maximum of 180 feet south of the clubhouse. The eastern shore line underwent a maximum accretion of nearly 200 feet." The inspector, Mr. Turbit H. Slaughter inspected 3,200 feet of shore line on the southwest side of the Island and 1,800 feet on the east side. The Clubhouse was reported to be only 75 feet from the River. The Department recommended that the rate of erosion be lessened by construction of fifty foot long groins to catch the "littoral drift" of the River, which were predicted to result in sand being caught between the groins and building up the beach. Joe and Bernie built them, but they didn't really work, except perhaps as a temporary measure to slow the pace of erosion.

In 1955, a small dock was built at the site of the present pier in the Cove. This was built closer to the Clubhouse in order to enable guests to arrive and not have to walk quite so far to the Clubhouse, which by now was used more often than the Farmhouse.

Joe and Bernie still were working many long and hard hours. They did everything under the sun, literally, that had to be done. They cut the grass, kept the boats running, painted the boats, fixed the boats, kept the generators in operation, cleaned the rooms, and ran the fishing and hunting parties. While working in the Clubhouse on more domestic type operations such as mopping the floor, cleaning the bathrooms and making the beds, they referred to one another as "Josephine" and "Bernadine." To give you an idea of the hard work, look at a report of one week's record of Bernie Wise in the mid-50's. Week of November 4 to November 10:

Monday -- Changed oil, cleaned spark plugs in light plants. Put anti-freeze in motors, drained water lines from the dock.

Tuesday -- Repaired the roof on the Clubhouse, store porch chairs, and repair the yacht chairs.

Wednesday -- Put a last check on duck blinds. Putting decoys and rowboats and getting all the hunting equipment together.

Thursday -- Taking care of ducking and fishing parties.

Friday -- Taking care of ducking and fishing parties. Changing beds and cleaning rooms and taking care of laundry.

Saturday -- Taking care of ducking parties. Taking out the window in the television room, putting a door in its place.

Sunday -- Taking lockers to the Club and putting them up. Winterizing the Farmhouse. No ducking parties.

The Club was fortunate to have such a dedicated pair as Joe and Bernie Wise working through the growing years of the organization. Their contributions were deeply appreciated by the membership.

Uncle Don

In the past seventy five years since the Club was founded, many individuals have contributed their time, effort, and finances to the preservation of this organization and its goals. Nearly everyone who visits the Island is able to relax. Nearly everyone who relaxes is instilled with some love for the Club and the Island for there is a truly wonderful spirit of harmony. I have that love for the Island. But the man who may have given more than anyone else to the Club, in terms of his time, money, and soul, called this unique Island Club a "fraternity."

Donelson Caffery Glassie, referred to by old and young alike as "Uncle Don" when he was "still on two," became a member in the 1940s (with the first register entry being November 10, 1949), served on the Board of Governors for nearly forty years and held practically every office the Club had to offer. He began as Assistant Secretary to John Gordon in 1953, became Executive Vice President several years later, was elected President in 1962, and later was re-elected Executive Vice President for several years. He was at home just being at the Island with his friends and family. He was known to have a taste for a good drink and a beautiful woman (that would be my mother). He always treated old and young alike as mature people and loved to argue with any mature person. His stories could enrapture, whether or not you believed them. He often could be found "holding court" around the bar or in the Clubhouse.

Uncle Don was brought into the Club by Jim White. Don's father was a well known lawyer and served as Assistant Attorney General in Washington for many years. His mother was the daughter of Senator Donelson Caffery from Louisiana. Thus, Uncle Don was familiar with government officials. An engineer by profession, he found the Island a perfect place to utilize his knowledge. He supervised the construction of both wings of the Clubhouse, the docks, the installation of the heating, plumbing, and electrical systems, and the swimming pool. At one time or another, he probably knew all of the members, and remembered from where most of the objects in the Clubhouse came. Here is some of the historical background my father told me:

The famous dining room table, constructed of solid mahogany, was given to the Club by Senator Harry B. Hawes. The table was made in the Philippines and was presented to Hawes by the Philippine government in recognition of his assistance in helping that country obtain independence. Uncle Don tells of moving the table into the dining room. When the table had first arrived on the Island, Jim White directed that it be placed in the card room. It was actually a little too large, but White would hear nothing of moving it to the dining room where several members thought it should be. "One day several of us decided that we were going to move it, Jim White be damned. We measured the table and all the doors and discovered that it would not fit--it was impossible to move it into the dining room. Well, we talked about it and drank a bit, we moved it a little and pushed a little. About two hours and several drinks later, it was in place in the dining room. I'll never know quite how we did it."

Another great story revolves around that mahogany table. My mother told me recently that Uncle Don used to go down to the Island with a number of Members of Congress in the late 1950s, and that the Texas delegation went down several times. She said Dad rode down with Lyndon Johnson at least one time, so I know he was there, before he was Vice President, that is. Well, listen to this story that is excerpted from an article in the Enterprise newspaper in Lexington Park, Maryland, dated August 17, 1972:

"It was at the massive mahogany table in the dining room, where conferences of top level policy making matters were discussed, that Lyndon Johnson, a senator from Texas, was "told" he had to become Vice President. He wanted the Presidency, but former President Harry S Truman and Dean Acheson, Secretary of State, told him he had to accept Vice President. The two week conference continued to map out the political strategy. At times "there was some loud talking and some pretty strong words," [Joe] Wise recalled."

"At one point, when Johnson continued to hold out for the Presidency, one of the Democrats, (John Nance Garner, former Vice President) is reprted to have said, "Take it Lyndon, sombody's bound to take a pot shot at that young squirt, Kennedy, and you'll be in the White House in due time."

"You're the only man who can carry the South, Lyndon," former President Harry Truman is reported to have said." Hey, if it was in the newspaper, you know it's true, right?

The bar top was donated to the Club by Prue Savoy, a member who had fond memories of it and had obtained it when the Murray Hill Hotel in New York City had closed. It was installed by a carpenter named Husky, who worked at the Capitol. The original bar was not quite the same shape and was much longer. Mr. Savoy had bought the entire 80 foot bar and Husky brought a piece to the Island. He had to make it turn a corner to fit into the room. A brass toe rail was installed in front of it. The original toe rail eventually fell apart, and in the 1990's yours truly and Douglas Gibson replaced it. So, go belly up to the bar, rest your toes, and have a drink sometime. Douglas was one of my favorite friends, particularly after my father died in 1992. Douglas told me, "You know, Jeff, I've never not had fun at the Island."

The paneling in the living and card rooms was the original pine installed by John Long for Dr. Jacobs and Mr. Forbes when the cottage had been built. The dining room and foyer, which boast beautiful redwood paneling, were added later by a carpenter named Jenkins who worked for Archie Hutton, a long time member who owned the A.L. Hutton Company in Washington.

One of the sail fish that now hangs in the Clubhouse was presented to the Club by Leslie Biffle. The tarpon, which was repainted a bright silver by Joe O'Malley, had been caught by Jim O'Donnell, a member who held many world fishing records and recorded the first incident with the "swampwampus."

The swampwampus is a horrible looking creature who lives in the swamp at the eastern end of the Island. He has quite a friendly countenance, despite his ugly features. The swampwampus resembles an animal with the feet of a great blue heron, the body of a rhinoceros, and the head of an alligator. He survives on a modest diet of small children and feisty dogs. It is rare when one can catch a glimpse of this terrible creature, but his tracks may often be seen on the beach.

Uncle Don told me also about the old "Island Queen," a 1950 Kaiser Frazer automobile that was donated by Archie Hutton in 1955. It was brought over on an old barge, which rested so low that it appeared as if the big car was riding on water over to the Club. The Island Queen was used as transportation from the Farmhouse to the Clubhouse when most of the people used to stay in the Farmhouse and come up to the other house for meals. The words "Island Queen" were lettered in gold on each side of the car. A member named Bill Cunningham had great fun with the old auto as a means of rapid conveyance while rabbit hunting. Bill would sit on the front end of the "Queen" and hunt at night with the lights on while someone else drove. He had a great time shooting at the rabbits, which numbered in the hundreds. "You would have thought that Old Bill would have bagged a rabbit or two every once in a while," recalled Uncle Don, "but he never hit one."

The beginning of the end of the Island Queen occurred when its driver, who had parked it just outside the Farmhouse, woke up one morning to find it resting with only its blue top showing in five feet of water. Joe Wise insisted, "it was Jim Palmer, who had driven back to the Farmhouse the night before and had left the brake off. The next morning I came across to the Club and just saw that blue top sitting in the water, right in the middle of a bed of 150 bushels of oysters that I had just planted a little while before. We hauled it out with the tractor and got it going again, but she never was quite the same. Those oysters weren't hurt a bit, though."

Many of Don Glassie's friends became members of the Club. For a very long time, a fraternity truly existed at the Island. All the members were friends and used to go to parties at one another's houses and get together uptown in Washington when they were not at the Club. Tom Sandoz, Douglas Gibson, Ed Pewett, Henry Glassie, Don Macleay, Jim Palmer, Jim O'Donnell, Ed Terres, Tom and Joe Wallace, Ray Walsh, Alan Lloyd, Reed Fawell, Bill Beebe, George Galland, Bill Foote, Bill Blum, and many others and their families were all good friends in Washington.

A wife of one of these men said to me that, "after World War II, going down to the Island was one of the only truly fun things there was to do. It was one of the only places I can remember where the relaxation and peacefulness was the same as before the war. Since that war, things have never been quite the same, it's been so tense." Funny what effects war can have.

It would be impossible to recount all of the discussions that have taken place around the big dining room table, in the kitchen, in front of the fireplace, or around the bar. But one thing was certain, you would never know quite what to expect. Arguments were always popular. If someone made a relatively controversial statement when Uncle Don was around, another would immediately confront him and tell him he was an "old fool." It didn't really matter whether or not either argumentor had a valid point, or so it seemed, as long as there was a point to be made and a counterpoint to be debated. Many times the debaters switched sides in mid-argument.

Uncle Don recalled the night that a woman made the comment that she would need to buy an entire new wardrobe, because the high-heeled shoes had essentially changed the length of the hemlines of her dresses. "Well, that started it all," laughs Uncle Don, "for the next three or four hours we batted that one back and forth. It seemed ridiculous to me that a woman's hemline length would change because of the type of shoes she wore, so we argued, debated, kidded, measured, computed, re-measured, re-computed, called in witnesses, re-called witnesses, and re-worked the whole thing a few times over. We had ourselves a ball that night and never did reach a conclusion."

Another night, a group of gentlemen debated for 3-1/2 hours about whether all the water froze and dropped out of the air at 32 degrees or not. Engineering books were consulted, thermometers used, ice scraped out of the refrigerator, measured, heated and thrown in the air, with the result and conclusion that all of the moisture in the air does not freeze at 32 degrees. "Oh, yes it does," says Uncle Don.

A favorite ritual of Uncle Don was the sprinkling of "sugar" on the delicious desserts that the cook had concocted after a wonderful meal. A sample of the menu for dinner back when I was a kid growing up on the Island, prepared either by Mrs. Lillian Yates or later by Mary Dyson, might look like this: local green beans, corn, and beets, Southern Maryland fried chicken, freshly caught fried fish, crab cakes, soft shell crabs, ham and beaten biscuits, fresh sliced tomatoes, and baked potatoes. I think for $4 each person. Then, the cook would bring out some homemade applesauce cake, spice cake, or jello. All of the guests would "ooh" and "aah," and then moan when Uncle Don would say, "I think this needs a little sugar." "Sugar?" they would cry. And with that, Uncle Don would run out to the bar and bring back a bottle of rum or bourbon. He'd go around to each person at the table, put his thumb over the end of the bottle, shake it and shake it and shake it profusely, and let a bit squirt out onto the individual's dessert. "Ah, that'll make it a lot better, you wait and see." It usually did.

No matter who he was talking to, Uncle Don always had a story to tell. Either about the time he stood on top of the Washington Monument (which is true, although no one has ever seen a picture) or the one about trapping squirrels in Chevy Chase and letting them off on the White House lawn, or the one about the fact that "the only woman ever created by God was Eve. The Bible never mentions the fact that any other woman were created, so they must have fallen out of the trees or something."

My brother John has a story about hunting. "I remember going duck hunting for the first when I was seven. It was raining and Dad put me in some rubber waders — pants, not just the legs, what do you call them? But they were for a teenager and the waist reached to my chin, so he got a big fat rope and tied them up around my armpits with a giant knot. We went out and sat on whiskey crates in the blind in the rain for a few hours. And no ducks showed up to be fooled by our fake ducks out in the water, but when it was time to turn in, Dad let me shoot my shotgun for the first time: a 20-guage he'd modified by sawing a few inches off the stock. I stood on the crate and fired, and the kick knocked me off the crate; there was that spilt second before it was clear if this was a bad or good experience, but Dad just acted like I was a hero. I realized just how exhilarated I was, and then we started laughing, and hey, I'd just shot a gun! Hunting-wise, I did sort of become a conscientious objector by the time I was 15, but I'll never forget that moment."

Uncle Don always loved sailboats, but never got around to doing much sailing. One time he took one of the Club's wooden skiffs, used a long pole, made a sail out of a blanket, and took off around the Island. Joe Wise and he had the same birthday, November 22, and Joe would always toast with Uncle Don on their birthday, but since Joe didn't drink, he would get an eye dropper of bourbon and put it in a glass of water. That was the only drink he'd have each year (for the most part; I do remember him having a hangover one morning during the week when I stayed with he and Rose at their house like I used to some summers).

Joe and Uncle Don used to have some great fun, too. Out on the porch, a compass rose had been painted on the ceiling and a weathervane was to be installed with an arrow so one could see from inside the porch which way the wind was blowing. For many years, Uncle Don would say that Joe, an excellent shot, was going to lie on his back and shoot a hole in the roof with a rifle so that they could install that weathervane. It never did get done and no one ever knew if they were fooling or not.

Uncle Don was a sharp dresser and a man of leisure. He always dressed in the style of the day, and once, when he wore a yellow shirt, yellow belt, yellow pants, yellow socks, and yellow shoes to a party, he referred to himself as a "yellow-bellied girl watcher." As a man of leisure, he took great pains to construct wooden floats on which one could place a drink while sitting in the swimming pool. It would not be unusual to see six or seven people sitting in the pool with their drinks conveniently floating in front of them, a perfect way to begin the cocktail hour.

Uncle Don also knew most of the older members. This story comes from the Sunday Magazine of The Washington Star article on the Club dated May 4, 1964.

"One of the Club' s memories concerns the late Speaker of the House, Mr. Sam Rayburn. Mr. Glassie, who was something of an amateur physician, as well as the Club historian, delights in telling it to visitors to the Club. "In the summer of 1962," Mr. Glassie says, "Rayburn had strained his back putting on his pants. He told me he was suffering, and I said, Mr. Speaker, I have some horse lineament that's good for tough people."

"By God, I'll try some," said Rayburn. " So, sure enough, we rubbed it on his back, and later he said it was the only thing that gave him any relief."

Another story concerns the fact that no telephones were ever installed on the Island. And none ever will be. This story describes a meeting of the Board of Governors in the late 1950s. Again, from The Washington Star article: "Senator A. Owsley Stanley -- rest his soul -- was dozing at the meeting," recalls Mr. Glassie. "Someone mentioned having a phone put in to the mainland. The Senator woke up abruptly, banged his fist on the table, shouted "By God, no telephone," and promptly went back to sleep. That was the end of that."

There certainly has been no limit to the amount of genuine fun on the Island. Many people have spent countless hours enjoying the peace, quiet, and the spirit of relaxation found there. The Island means something different to everyone and the Club itself yields different responses in each of us. Over the years, Don Glassie embodied this spirit and strived to make it special for everyone fortunate enough to visit. I inherited his love of the Island; it's just in my blood now, perhaps more so now that Dad is gone. But I'm sure he is with Claude Pepper, Joe and Bernie Wise, and the rest of our departed members at that great big Crab Feast up there.

Social Events

Many people like to go to the Island and cuddle up in a big chair with a favorite book and read for days on end. Others enjoy the sport of fishing, either from a boat or right off the pier. But, throughout its history, the Jefferson Islands Club has sponsored social events and parties to allow members to mix and mingle, bring friends and neighbors to participate together in the joys of its delightful seclusion. As we have seen, President Roosevelt had his own type of social events and meetings for the political leaders of the day. Also, company picnics are held regularly at the Club. There are even parties held on the mainland, in Washington, D.C., to recreate the spirit of the Island.

The largest and most famous of these was the "Dinner on the Mainland" held on April 15, 1955 in the ballroom of the Shoreham Hotel. This was a fine affair held in honor of President Truman, Speaker Sam Rayburn, and Senator Alben Barkley. The guest list reads like a Democratic "Who's Who." There were approximately 200 people present including:

Bernard M. Baruch, Sen. Warren Magnuson, Renah Camalier, Sen. & Mrs. John L. McClellan, Justice & Mrs. Tom C. Clark, Sen. & Mrs. Mike Monroney, Mr. & Mrs. Clark M. Clifford, Gov. Edmund Muskie, Sen. & Mrs. Earle C. Clements, Mr. and Mrs. Christian Huerich, Sen. Claude Pepper, Sen. James Eastland, Burke Summers, Rep. & Mrs. Clair Engel, Sen. & Mrs. Stuart Symington, Sen. & Mrs. Sam J. Ervin, Jr., Sen. & Mrs. Millard Tydings, James A. Farley Sen. Fred Harris, Mr. & Mrs. Gilbert Gude, Congressman Wilbur Mills, Gov. W. Averill Harriman, Senator "Skeeter" Johnston, Secretary Cordell Hull, Senator Breckenridge Long, and Sen. & Mrs. Lyndon B. Johnson. Pretty impressive list, huh?

Speakers included Leslie Biffle, President of the Club, Rep. James M. Barnes, Chairman of the Dinner Committee, and the three honored guests. Music was provided by the orchestra Brusiloff and guests were treated to the singing voice of the noted tenor, Raymond Michael McGuire.

The dinner menu consisted of seven courses. Featured, of course, were Chesapeake Bay seafood dishes. Imagine the delight and surprise of the guests as they completed their meal and were treated to a dessert of "Spumoni Bombe Jeffersonian."

Christine White attended, too. She said, "I remember, as a sub-teen, my father asked me to put on my first evening gown and attend a Jefferson Day dinner with him. I was informed that the President was going to host the evening and that Mr. Biffle, one of my 'admirers,' would also be there. … When I arrived, it seemed like I was the only 'kid' there. … [An] enormous Epicurean dinner was placed before me, but the only things on the plate that spoke English were the Carolina yams. I ate those, drank ginger ale, and bolted two deserts. Everybody else was turning their chairs around to face the podium. As I turned around, I saw the President of the United States: Harry S Truman. We were in the front row. I did not anticipate being 'entertained,' so I told myself to 'look interested whether you are or not, don't tap your feet under your dress, and don't keep looking at the door.'

"But the President executed some beauties in terms of strident political remarks, aimed at Speaker Rayburn who countered that only 'inside remarks were permitted here.' The whole room laughed and applauded. These two were just warming up. The swift dialogue that ensued from Speaker to President was a marvelous example of 'fast-on-your-feet' innuendos. The laughter from the audience arrowed back at them and they were persuaded to go on. They were like two stand-up comics. So I whispered to my father: 'I didn't know that the Speaker and the President were stand-up comics." This event will certainly go down in the annals of the Club as the most prestigious dinner ever presented.

In the 1950s, a party was held at the Island in honor of Congressman James Barnes. A caterer provided a magnificent spread. There were 300 Maine lobsters at a pound and a half each, shrimp, pink salmon, bushels of Dungeness crabs, in addition to the usual fair of Chesapeake Bay seafood. For many years, Joe Wise was the head cook. Joe would erect his own special barbeque pit and cook whatever your heart (or stomach) might fancy. His barbequed chicken was causing finger lickin' before Colonel Sanders. Rose Wise helped with the early parties and could be counted on to brew up some tasty stew or chowder and some good St. Mary's County vegetables.

On May 1, 1960, another party was held in honor of President Truman and Speaker Rayburn. The President flew from Independence, Missouri, specifically for the party, just as he had in 1955 for the "Dinner on the Mainland." The President was brought to the Island on Charlie Thomas' yacht, the "Katy Did." Leslie Biffle accompanied the President to the Island where their entourage was greeted by Don Glassie and others. Pictures of this occasion still decorate the walls of the Clubhouse. The President wore a dark blue suit with a bow tie and his famous hat. He beamed as he signed the register that day "Harry Truman -- from Independence, Missouri -- retired farmer." He wore a special name badge imprinted "Guess Who?" It is not believed he brought any pistols to the Island that day, because of the great crowd.

My uncle, Ed Pewett, rode back to the mainland with the President and recalls Truman telling him, "You know, even in this modern age of Sputnik and space flight, I wish I could run for President one more time. I would teach some of those fellows a thing or two."

However, there certainly have been many parties to rival these in terms of the food presented. The Annual Wild Game Party and Dinner was a standard Club event for a couple decades since it was begun in 1960. Originally, the party was held at the home of a member and up to 200 persons might be found to enjoy such delicacies presented over the years as: wild goose and oyster gumbo, Chesapeake smoked chipped venison a la Presidente, campfire smoked haunch of wild boar Monticello, quail with juniper berries, chopped sirloin of gazelle, sauce "Elizabeth" Klingeman, caribou de Canada, North American anteloupe du jour, pickled deerhearts a la Miller, Canadian goose de Potomac, Paysanne Saint Catherine Island, Canard Savage, and Duck Gumbo Gibsonian.

These dishes were donated by Club members. They were often times cooked by Club members and almost never was a bad dish observed. For many years in the 1970's, the Wild Game Party was held at the Women's National Democratic Club near Dupont Circle in Washington and in 1981 at the National Guard Building on Capitol Hill. The Congressional Reception in January of 1981 was also held at the National Guard Building and was attended by over 300 persons, including 55 Members of Congress

The two most popular annual Island events have been the Crab Feast and Oyster Roast. In July, when the crabs are most plentiful and largest in size, the Annual Crab Feast takes place on a Sunday afternoon on the Island. Hundreds of people brave the summer sun to stand for hours before tables of spicy steamed Chesapeake Bay blue crabs. Crab cakes, crab gumbo and even non-crab dishes are offered. From 90 years old to nine months, people love to crack crab claws, pick at the back fin lump, lick their seasoned fingers, and relax with each other. My brother John said: "From the early days, I just think of platters of fried perch and softshell crabs and tomatoes and kale and corn on the cob. You'd take a couple of pieces of white bread and make a fat softshell crab sandwich with the claws and legs sticking out. And in my adult life I like to order softshell crabs, but they're usually small and sissified and I feel like I've never really had a totally, completely satisfying softshell experience since then." In 1980, over 350 persons attended the Crab Feast, in honor of then Democratic Majority Leader Jim Wright from Texas. Rep. Wright was flown in by helicopter on the warm, clear Sunday afternoon. Wright had visited the Island several times in past years and remembered listening to Sam Rayburn tell stories on the porch overlooking the River.

The 1981 Crab Feast celebrated the 50th Anniversary of the Club. The first Annual Harry S. Truman Award was presented to five members: Dante Fascell, Claude Pepper, Don Glassie, Douglas Gibson, and George Galland. Since then, other members who have received the award for services to the Club include Fred Peirdon, Charlie Cromwell, Pat Presely, Jon Swindle, John Kern (twice), Earl Comstock, and yours truly.

The Oyster Roast features the 'king of the shell fish" prepared in many ways. Man, woman, and child gobble down luscious raw oysters dipped in special sauce, lemon butter, or just plain. Oyster fritters, fried oysters, scalded oysters, and roasted oysters decorate the tables and test the palates of those so afflicted. The highlight of the meal occurs when the oyster stew is announced as ready. For many years, the Club Chef was Mary Dyson, a wonderful local black woman whose Southern Maryland style cooking couldn't be beat. Mary's cooking caused many a person to hold his or her stomach and moan with joy. Her oyster stew, plain and simply, was "the best." She always refused to divulge the secret recipe and if you could ever prod it out of her, you will have uncovered a treasure.

Many private parties also have been held over the years. In the early days, John Gordon sponsored many social group meetings, variously referred to as the "Breakfast Club," the "Mint Julep Patch," and the famous "Dirty Old Men's Foursome." For many years there were costume parties held on George Washington's Birthday. One year, my father went dressed up as a woman, and was using two grapefruit as "bazzoms." My mother reported it was so cold that he warmed them over a kerosene heater before putting them in his bodice.

During the years when Ed Terres was President, 1967 and 1968, he came up with several unique ideas, including an old fashioned "Feesh Fry" at the Island. An evening at Rosecroft attracted about 100 persons to the featured event of the night, "The Jefferson Islands Club Pace." Immediately after the race, Mr. Terres, George Galland, and Don Glassie presented the winning horse with its blanket. Many members also gathered at the Burn Brae Dinner Theater for a performance of "Oklahoma" that year.

Senator Sparkman once wore a green Irish hat to a St. Patrick's Day party, along with several other Congressional members. Mr. Terres was President when a Virginia and Maryland Congressional Day was held. Several members of the Congressional Delegations from Virginia and Maryland attended and the Lieutenant Governor of Virginia reportedly stopped by in a helicopter.

For many years in the 1960s, luncheons were held every Friday in the private Pershing Room of the old Army-Navy Club in Washington. Jim White organized these events at first and later Bill Ingraham, Secretary for several years, sponsored them. A rump business meeting on any important subject was held. The Club members would debate the issue and resolve the question unanimously, even if it meant tabling the discussion. The essence of the meeting came when members related the latest stories and jokes and kept abreast of political gossip. Chip Robert flew in from Atlanta nearly every Friday on the "Oily Boid" just for the luncheon. Sometimes he stayed for the weekend at the Island, but usually he returned to Atlanta that afternoon.

During that period, a ladies luncheon also was sponsored once a month with entertainment provided by the champion joke tellers of the previous weekly luncheons. Occasionally, Congressman Albert Johnson brought his mandolin and would conduct a sing-along accompanied by Jim White or Chester Hogentogler on the piano. Those were the good old days.

The 1960s

The 1960s were heralded in by the opening of the swimming pool, financed by loans from members. Joe and Bernie Wise hired local help and it was dug out by hand with shovels and picks. The pool was constructed in the shape of a three-leaf clover (a "club" in a deck of cards) with steel sides and a concrete deck, to make sure that no additional reinforcement would be necessary. The sides were originally sections of circular granary bins, made out of corrugated galvanized steel. The concrete was mixed on the Island from sand from the beach. Water was filtered and pumped into the pool from the River. Initially, the water was pulled from the Cove through long hoses, because it was felt the water would be cleaner without as much sand from the front. Nowadays, a small trash pump sucks water from right over the seawall. It's pretty nice anyway; the silky brackish water feels great on a hot day. The construction of the pool proved to be a boon and was used continuously during the summer all during the 1960s and into the 1970s. This also illustrates the fact that the Club was becoming more and more a vacation spot for the entire family. The pool was filled with children for hours.

Another reason for the construction of the pool was the fact that sea nettles, or jellyfish, were an extreme annoyance in the hot summer months. It might often be very painful to endeavor a quick swim in the River. Not only that, but several youngsters had the misfortune of stepping on old pieces of glass that had washed down the River to the sandy beach in front of the Clubhouse. When I was about five, I distinctly remember Ray Walsh, about a year older than me at the time though since passed on, lying on the kitchen counter with a huge bloody gash in his foot. Uncle Don and several men treated him, but it underscored the issues with wading around the shore with bare feet.

The pool was dedicated in a flashy ceremony by Father Scherer of Holy Angels, the local Catholic Church. Father Scherer dedicated the pool on that day saying, "It is presumed that the members of the Jefferson Islands Club who use this pool will be as wet on the inside as they are on the outside." The Club maintained a very close relationship with the Holy Angel's faculty and staff in those days and borrowed chairs from Holy Angels for the parties. On hot summer weekdays, a few nuns were rumored to have doffed their habits and dived into the pool when no one else was around.

Several trees and plots of bamboo had been planted along the shore in front of the Clubhouse in the mid-1950s and these trees provided perfect shade for evening settees during the summer. There was a set of wooden steps that led down to a 75-foot dock with an "L" shaped end. This dock was a perfect place for little children to fish (some big children were seen fishing out there, too) and for late night galaxy gazing.

The old tractor and wagon were integral parts of the operations. The tractor cut the grass and pulled the wagon that carried all sorts of things, including people. It was painted green and in those days had steps in the back and rails on both sides to lean against. When you arrived at the Island, Joe and Bernie would put the luggage on the wagon and drive it around the front of the Clubhouse. Your bags would be waiting in front of your room. People took rides on the wagon all the time around the Island. Darrell Wise, husband of current Club Manager Colleen Wise, remembers in those days driving the wagon around and people always hopping on and sometime falling off while it was going. I remember my father was thrown off at a party one year and broke his arm.

Another great pastime was dueling with two "one armed bandits" that were hidden behind the wall map in the bar. Young children played these slot machines for hours upon end using nickels kept in large mugs under the bar and in Uncle Don's locker. Of course, if the change dried up, the machine would be unlocked, the money removed, and the fun would continue. When slots were declared illegal in St. Mary's County, I've heard these two machines were thrown into the River by some law abiding member, or perhaps vandals stole them. Another one was surreptitiously brought down to the Island later on, but I think vandals did steal that one. If anyone knows where to get some old fashioned slot machines, I know a place to put them.

In 1960, a full length movie entitled "Dead to the World" was produced by a long time member, Ed Alfriend, with the Island and White's Neck Creek as the major location. The film starred Reidy Talton and Jana Pearce and was based on a novel entitled "State Department Murders" by Edward Ronns. The story, with music by Charley Byrd and Billy Taylor, is a spy thriller about the murder of a powerful Federal Agency Director Jason Stone (meaning, J. Edgar Hoover) and the hunt for the murderer, led by the accused Barney Cornell. Much of the footage was taken in the local area and Joe and Bernie Wise had cameo roles. I've seen the movie and have a copy of the film someplace.

Recently discovered documents indicated that the Club had taken significant steps in the 1960's to try and get electric power to the Island. Detailed plans were prepared in 1962 to bring electricity from Crew Point on the mainland just over one-half mile northeast of the Farmhouse. Armored cable was to have been run under the water and buried in a trench, according to the plans drafted by Kueffel and Esser Co. of New York. Under the channel off the northeast point of the Island, the cable would have been about 20 feet beneath the mean low water mark (as I read the diagram).

Another effort was made in about 1970, and the Club files show a different plan prepared by the Southern Maryland Electric Cooperative (SMECO). Drawings dated June 2, 1971 envisioned an electric cable being run from Joe Wise's house on the mainland west of White's Neck Creek 1945 feet to Bullock Island to supply Frank Fuqua's house, and then another 2650 feet to the Island at a point near the old Farmhouse. Submarine cable would have been buried at least three feet under the River bed (or about 9 feet below mean low water). The plan was to bring electricity to Frank's residence, and then provide the Club with the power. In a letter to my father dated June 19, 1972, Walter Smith, Assistant Manager for SMECO wrote and said: "Mr. and Mrs. Fuqua have indicated their desire to provide electric service to their house on Bullock Island. This reduces the amount of our investment assignable to St. Catherine's Island …, excluding transformers and meters, to be $12,258.00 …, with the net charge to provide the service of $11,343." In an earlier letter to my father dated December 24, 1971, Smith had said, "Improved material and equipment technology and installation techniques indicate an estimated installed cost approximately 30 percent lower than our 1962 study."

I know my father wanted badly to bring electricity to the Island, but the Club just couldn't afford it, par-

ticularly in light of the serious erosion threat. When we checked in 1994, the estimated price tag for electricity was $100,000 plus. It's unfortunate that the Club wasn't able to afford any of these electrical projects, because the amount of blood, sweat, tears, and money running the generators over the years probably would far exceed the costs of the installation of the electric line.

The Club has never had much money, and this story was only one indication of that. The idea of selling the Island has come up several times. In about 1970, a formal appraisal was conducted by William Lawrence and Frank Barley, based on comparable sales. Actually, I can't imagine any comparable piece of property in the area, other than perhaps St. Margaret's, St. Clement's, or perhaps Bullock Island. St. Catherine's Island is larger, but has no electricity, which would have to affect the price significantly, I would think. Anyway, this appraisal indicated the Island was about 50 acres at the time, based on a 1963 tax bill. Knowing that a formal survey was done in 1962 showing the Island was 65 acres must have been the cause for at least some relief.

The 1970 appraisal indicated that comparable sales were in the range of $8,000 to $17,000 per acre. The estimated usable land was considered to be about 35 acres. The appraisers valued the Island at about $4,000 per acre of such useable land, and about $300 per acre of 10 acres of marsh land, or about $3,000. The parking area was estimated at .08 acres with a value of $6,000. The report also noted that in 1970 storms caused a loss of about eight feet in front of the Clubhouse, and that Hurricane Hazel had taken about 12 to 15 feet. The appraisers recommended a seawall be constructed, and estimated the cost at about $30,000. With the value of the improvements on the Island, including the Clubhouse at about $51,000, Farmhouse at $4,000, pool at $10,000, the Island pier at $1300, the mainland pier at $300, barbeque at $600, and the sheds at $500, the total appraised value of the Island in 1970 was $218,000.00. How about that!

A memo to the members of the Club in 1970 from Chip Robert as President told something about the condition of the facility at the time. In the year from September 1969 to September 1970, the Club had five parties at the Island, with the Annual Game Dinner being very well attended. The fishing and ducking seasons were good, Robert reported, but there were the usual minor catastrophes. Both "light plants … conked out on the same day." That sounds familiar. The engine in the Seahawk lost an exhaust manifold. The swimming pool pump finally gave out after a "seven-year beating from the salt water." A storm blew off a section of the roof at the north end of the building, which also sounds familiar; there must be something up with the way the wind hits that part of the Island during a storm. Robert continued: "All of these mishaps have been taken care of and, happily, with a minimum of expenditure, and we are in full operation."

Robert noted that 17 members had died in the past few years, although he announced three new members, including Charles Hawkins, III, destined to become Executive Vice President of the Club. The memo also included a report on finances. In 1969, the Club had $21,262.30 in income, and $22, 814.65 in expenses. In three years, expenditures exceeded cash flow by about $1800. So, the Club was not prospering financially at the time.

Of crucial importance, Robert warned that the continuing erosion on the western shore of the Island was growing worse. He indicated that the Board had discussed the possibility of "granting a permanent easement to the Nature Conservancy and the Audubon Society in return for help in the matter. The easement would be for the benefit of the egrets, ibises, and the ospreys which now inhabit the southwest tip of the Island in great numbers." In fact, an undated brochure confirms that the Nature Conservancy was trying to raise funds to actually buy the Island and preserve it. The brochure focuses on saving the Island and its birds and said the Club was willing to sell the Island for $140,000 (a below market price) to accomplish the rescue.

Here's what Edward N. Schell, president of the Southern Maryland Audubon Society, and George Wilmot, Chairman of the Society's Conservation Committee, had to say in 1972 in a letter to the Nature Conservancy in support of the effort:

"The Southern Maryland Audubon Society recommends the acquisition of St. Catherine's Island (Jefferson Island) for a wild life refuge by the Nature Conservancy. St. Catherine's Island is the largest heron rookery in the western shore area of the Chesapeake Bay. It is the only western shore nesting sight of the snowy egret, the cattle egret, and the glossy ibis. In addition, it is the second largest in the state for the common egret and the black-crowned night heron. The Island is also a nesting place for the osprey and the waters in its immediate vicinity are important feeding areas for both the ospreys and the endangered bald eagle. The fact that St. Catherine's is an Island will render the preservation of the rookery less difficult and more assured than a main land site. … [D]ata show that the preservation of the rookery at St. Catherine's is essential to the future or Western Shore herons and is and important nesting site for the Middle Atlantic region."

The data referred to was in a letter from James Banagan to Schell in 1972, in which the number of nests observed at the Island per year was 8 osprey, 40 cattle egret, 125 common egret, 5 snowy egret, 3 Louisiana heron, 100 black crowned night heron, 2 glossy ibis, and 75 little blue heron. That's a large number of nests, not to mention birds. I remember watching the bird watchers come over to the Island when I was little as they headed down to the cedars to watch the birds. I guess they were counting nests, too. It's really too bad that, for some reason, perhaps destruction of their own habitat, most of those birds no longer nest at the Island. Of course, there are lots of osprey and heron around, and some eagles, still to this day.

So, we see that the Club entertained a number of efforts to save itself financially over the years. The idea to grant an easement for wildlife to the Audubon Society and/or the Nature Conservancy and/or sell the Island did not succeed. The Board of Governors also approved trying to secure a loan from the Conservancy, which didn't work out either.

In 1974, another idea was considered. Charles D'Arco, on behalf of himself and several undisclosed principals, made a proposal by which the Club would liquidate and transfer all assets and liabilities to D'Arco (debts estimated to be about $60,000). D'Arco would organize a new club with the same name, and turn over to the Club five acres for its use, and another ten acres to a charitable organization as a wild life refuge. This new club would be a proprietary endeavor like a country club, and D'Arco was to make many improvements on the Island. A $2,000 deposit was tendered to the Club as earnest money. The Board of Governors meeting on May 22, 1974 at the Chevy Chase Village Hall voted to approve the proposal. It is not clear what happened with this proposal, either, but a good guess would be that D'Arco didn't think it would be profitable. Later, in 1975, a loan was arranged that bought the Club a little more time, but things were not looking up.

Charlie Cromwell presents award to Maryland Comptroller Louis Goldstein, while Rep. Dante Fascell and Don Glassie look on.

Clubhouse teetering on edge of bank; porch at left was lost.

Lake Pierdon at south end of Pennsylvania Avenue, circa 1980.

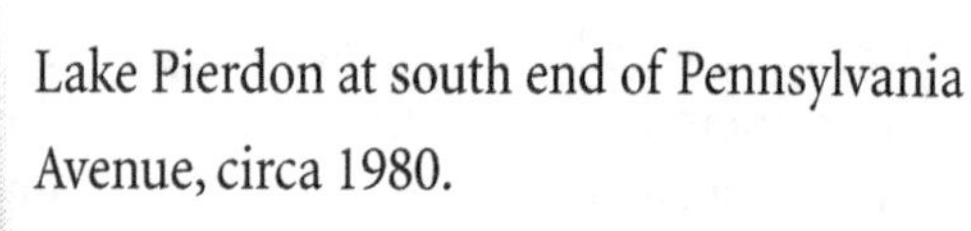

Seahawk and little boat stuck in ice; Muffin walking on ice. Winter 1975-76.

Invitation to visit the Island 1976.

JEFFERSON ISLANDS CLUB

900 SPRING STREET
SILVER SPRING, MARYLAND 20910

OFFICERS

LAWRENCE WOOD (Chip) ROBERT, JR.
President

EARLE CLEMENTS
DANTE B. FASCELL
DON CAFFERY GLASSIE
VANCE HARTKE
CLAUDE PEPPER
JOHN SPARKMAN
J. MILLARD TAWES
Vice Presidents

FRED A. PIERDON
Executive Vice President

CHARLES E. HAWKINS, III
Secretary

RICHARD T. DAVIS
Treasurer

Board of Governors
(in addition to the above)

Vincent P. Ahearn, Jr.
Charles H. Cromwell, III
George E. Galland
M. Douglas Gibson, Jr.
Henry H. Glassie
James D. Isbister
Donald Macleay
John W. Mitchell
Lansdale G. Sasscer, Jr.
Clyde H. Smith
Samuel Stanley
Thomas E. Wallace
Thomas M. Walsh
Harry W. Wells, Jr.

OBJECTS

"For the purpose of supporting, defending and advancing the fundamental principles of government enunciated by Thomas Jefferson.

"To provide a Club House with suitable surroundings and comforts where members may assemble, discuss and promote Jeffersonian philosophies, to the end they may become controlling in Federal and State Governments."

June 5, 1976

Hello Islanders:

This letter comes to you from the garden spot of the universe - Jefferson Island. After a few fallow years the drought has ended and our Island may once again blossom and become the haven from urbanity that we all desire. It is up to you.

We have made great progress recently, but all members must come down and use and enjoy the Club to continue these improvements.

We are not asking you to work, we are asking you to enjoy yourself. Bring your family and friends and have a great time. The purpose of our Club is to relax and enjoy. Summer is here and I remind you of the fishing, swimming crabbing, clamming, water ski-ing, and all the other outdoor activities including that ever popular sport sitting and sipping. It is all here waiting for you, but you have to take the first step.

I sincerely hope to see you before or at least for our June 27th party. But remember .. ... the best times to be had at the Island are the quiet weekends when one can enjoy the peace and beauty of what truly is one of the garden spots of the universe - our Island -

Pax Vobiscum

Jeff Glassie
Manager

Sea Biscuit Bob Boy and Jeff.

Committee on Oyster Stew 1979.

The Jefferson Islands Club Newsletter

Autumn 1982 · Special Issue

VICE PRESIDENT BUSH RECEIVES JIC CITIZEN OF THE YEAR AWARD

Vice President George Bush received the First Annual Citizen of the Year Award.

The First Annual Jefferson Island Club Citizen of the Year Award was presented to Vice President George Bush at a black tie reception and dinner held at the City Tavern Club in Georgetown on Tuesday, July 27, 1982. Club President Bill Chappell awarded a handsome plaque...

...accepted the award with ...and made some very in-...out the role of the United ...stated that he hoped he ...he Island soon.

Ninety four people attended the dinner, including twenty-eight members. Several congressmen were present, including former Club President Dante Fascell and Bill Emerson. A brief description and history of the Club preced-ed the remarks by Chappell and the Vice President.

Special thanks for organizing the event go to Executive Vice President, Charlie Cromwell and Dave Smith.

A few pictures of the reception and dinner follow on the next pages.

Club President Bill Chappell presented the award to the Vice President after a few introductory words.

First Citizen of the Year Award
presented to Vice President
George Bush, 1982.

Congress of the United States
House of Representatives
Washington, DC 20515-3603

July 22, 1993

President William J. Clinton
The White House
1600 Pennsylvania Avenue, N.W.
Washington, D.C. 20500

Dear Mr. President:

We are Members of Congress and members of the Jefferson Islands Club writing in support of Beryl Anthony's previous letter inviting you to accept the Club's annual Citizen of the Year award at a formal dinner in Washington this fall. We believe it would be fitting, appropriate, and consistent with the Club's history for you to receive this award.

The Club was founded in 1931 by Senators Harry B. Hawes of Missouri and Key Pittman of Nevada; charter members included President Franklin D. Roosevelt and Senator Joseph T. Robinson of Arkansas, who was the first Chairman of the Board of the Club. Presidents Truman, Johnson, and Kennedy also were members. You received this historical information on the Club in Mr. Anthony's letter.

Recipients of the Citizen of the Year award, begun in 1981, include then Vice President George Bush, Senator Claude Pepper, Speaker Jim Wright, Rep. Dan Rostenkowski, Rep. Dante Fascell, Rep. Jamie Whitten, Secretary Caspar Weinberger and Secretary Dick Cheney. The Citizen of the Year Dinner would provide you with the opportunity to address a broad spectrum of Congress and others in a neutral forum.

We urge you to accept this award and help us maintain a great tradition.

Letter signed by 27 Members
of Congress inviting President
William Jefferson Clinton to accept
the Citizen of the Year Award.

Program autographed by Richard Petty.

Rep Dan Rostenkowski accepts Citizen of the Year Award, 1989.

Rep. Jimmy Hayes, Leslie Hayes and Rep. Gene Taylor.

Secretary Dick Cheney and Rep. Jack Brooks.

Rep. Bill Emerson, a long-time Club member.

Rep. Beryl Anthony, Club President and Steny Hoyer,
whose district includes St. Catherine's Island.

Jefferson Glassie with Thomas Jefferson,
aka Bill Barker.

Rep. Billy Tauzin presents Citizen of the
Year Award to Rep. Don Young, with wife Lu and daughter Dawn.

Senator Blanche Lambert Lincoln.

Nancy Cole and Senator Trent Lott.

Rep Howard Coble, Honorary Chair
of the Club, presenting award to Rep.
John Dingell, with Pat Presely to right.

Jim Desmond speaks at a Citizen
of the Year Dinner.

A fitting tribute.

Molly on the half-shell?

A crackin' good time!

Several generations of Islanders.

Colleen and Darrell Wise
(note toothpick); Colleen is
current Club Manager.

Jeff and Natalie raise flags on the
Charles Hawkins flagpole.

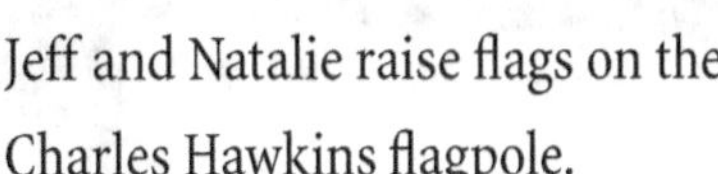

Warm your ass by the
Clubhouse fireplace.

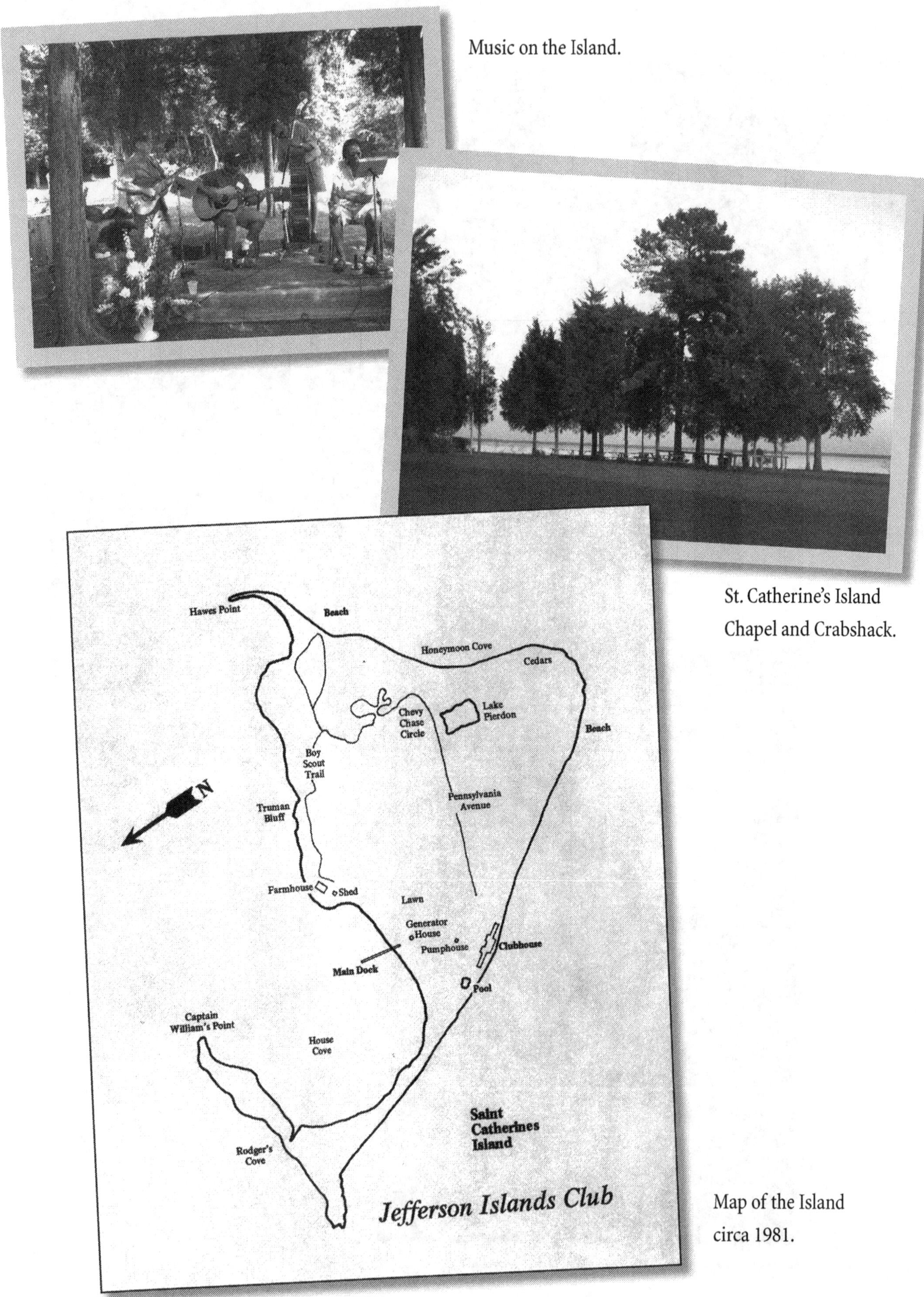

Music on the Island.

St. Catherine's Island
Chapel and Crabshack.

Map of the Island
circa 1981.

PART IV:
MODERN HISTORY

Rejuvenation

In the spring of 1975, Bernie Wise tendered his resignation. He served the Club well for almost 30 years, but now at age 65, he decided to retreat from a full time job to be able to spend his time at home. Joe Wise had left several years earlier to work at the power plant at Chalk Point for a healthier salary.

Membership had dwindled to about 50 and less than half were active. Correspondingly, dues income had been reduced and it might be said that the Club was now in "dire financial straights." The lack of income had prevented appropriate expenditures being made to maintain the facilities. Both the Clubhouse and Farmhouse needed extensive repair. The roofs leaked, the floors sagged, the plumbing and electrical systems were growing old, and the generator was about to give up the ghost. The "Seahawk" puttered along with a twelve-year old engine and was in need of bottom repair. The docks were rickety and the grounds were becoming overgrown. Worse still, erosion had accelerated to the point that the Clubhouse was about to fall in the River. In addition, the pool was being undermined by the constant washing of the water of the Potomac.

This decline had come about over the last several years due to a number of factors. Most of the leading Democratic figures who had belonged to the Club had passed away. Many of the other members had grown too old to enjoy the Island facilities. In two years during the late '60s, nearly twenty members died. Unfortunately, it had never been a policy to bring in younger members and there was no one to come to the rescue. With the facilities in rather poor shape, it was now nearly impossible to convince most people that the Club was a proposition worth investing their time and money. Most simply wondered how long it would be before the Clubhouse fell into the River. Joe and Bernie were gone, there weren't enough members, there was no money, and the Island was eroding away. Yes, things looked bleak for the Jefferson Islands Club.

The spirit that had characterized the Club and its members throughout its history was still alive, however. A small group of members still wanted to see the Club survive and regain its former popularity. Senator Earle Clements, Don Glassie, Douglas Gibson, Vince Ahearn, Charlie Hawkins, John Mitchell, Harry Wells, Sam Stanley, and a new member named Fred Pierdon refused to let the Club die. They sought out the assistance of two of the most important and influential men in Maryland, former Governor J. Millard Tawes and Al Smith, owner of the Citizens Bank of Maryland.

On a cold, dreary day in the winter of 1975, just before Bernie retired, Governor Tawes assembled a group from the Shore Erosion Control Division of the Department of Natural Resources along with several members. The Clubhouse was cleaned up as best she could. At the time, the furnace rarely worked, and it was lucky to get the lights and water going. Bernie Wise managed to get everything working with a kick or two, a prayer, and some good luck. Mary Dyson put together one of her masterpieces of oyster stew and roast duck with all the trimmings. After dinner, the Governor sat back in his chair with a cigar, told stories of the prominent history of Jefferson Island, and said, "Well, now boys, we just can't let this operation fall in the River, can we?"

So, here's what was done. The St. Catherine's Island Public Watershed Authority is a political entity entrusted with preserving the area of St. Catherine's Island. It is a nonprofit organization composed of the owner/members of the Club. After the meeting, plans were drawn up for a seawall to be constructed in front of the Clubhouse under the jurisdiction of the Watershed Authority. An interest free loan was arranged to provide financing through the Authority. At about the same time, the members also secured a loan through Al Smith's bank, Citizens Bank and Trust Company, to pay back debts and to finance the Club's rejuvenation. The key to the project was a larger membership. But someone also had to be found who would work for low pay and manage the operation; someone who would have enough pride in the Club to fix it up properly and enough naiveté to think that it could be done easily. Who might it be? Where could such a person be found?

I was attending the University of Virginia at the time, just about to graduate with a major in Government. I had no plans, no job, no wife, no girlfriend, and no idea of what to do about it. My parents, Don and Claire Glassie, had been bringing me to the Island since I was little over a year old. I visited the Island so frequently in the days when the Farmhouse was used as the main lodge for sleeping quarters that the room in which I stayed, the middle room upstairs, became known as "Jeff's Room" (at least to our family). When I was little, I used to sit on the tractor for hours and hours, though my feet wouldn't even reach the pedals. I also captained many an adventure to exotic lands far away, fought with pirates, and sank submarines at the helm of the "Seahawk" firmly tied to the dock. Each summer for several years I was invited down to the Island to live with Joe and Rose Wise for a week or two at a time. I rose before sunup with Joe and went out to fish his crab pots with him, sitting on the bow of a skiff for several hours while Joe did all the hard work of pulling up the pots, shaking out the crabs, scraping the seaweed off with wire brushes, and re-baiting. About all I did was use crab tongs to fetch a stray crab or two that might have crawled under the seat or up to the bow of the boat.

I helped "Josephine" and "Bernadine" mop the floors and make the beds in the Clubhouse. I remember cleaning out the pool and cutting grass every week. Joe and Rose used to take me to Leonardtown during the summer festival and I played the games and rode the merry-go-round with the other children. Joe used to call my sister Claire (who, bless her heart, really hated the crickets at the Island), our friends, and me the "mosquito fleet," presumably because we were small and good bait for mosquitoes. There was nothing more fun in the world than sitting and listening to Joe tell stories about the ducks, hunting stories, fishing stories, and the like. My brother John recalls: "I think Joe used to do this thing with his cigarette where he would flip the burning end with his tongue inside his mouth and then flip it back out again. He had lots of tricks that we all loved, and it was always a thrill to follow him around, or to go real fast in his skiff if you got to ride with him, for instance. Bernie was the straight man and a sweet man and funny in his own right, and a hard worker, and I always thought a slightly unsung hero."

One of our favorite adventures was to pile into the green wagon behind the tractor and have Joe drive us down to the cedars. We would all be still, trying to quietly slap the mosquitoes, when Joe would suddenly stand up clap his hands, and the egrets, the herons, the hawks, and eagles would jump up from the trees by the thousands and fly around in a white cloud over our heads, screaming, crying, soaring, and diving. As indicated earlier, there were hundreds of birds there; an impressive site.

It was too horrible for me to think of the fact that the Club might fall apart. What the hell, I was ready to go live on an Island. So, I applied for the job. A good friend of mine, Terry Cullen, with whom I had gone to grade school and high school, was also willing to go along and help out. We were hired and a week after I graduated from college we went down to the Island to live.

Jeff and Terry

The only thing that we didn't know about running and maintaining a club, an island, and its facilities was everything. Neither Terry nor I had any knowledge about engines, motors, or pumps. We were city boys turned loose in the country. What's a generator? You mean to tell me, that the wind comes from different directions? The tide rises and falls every six hours, huh? Oh, I see, this pump brings the water up from the well and pushes it through the pipes? You need a certain water pressure for the shower to work properly? And this pump is electric so we have to run the generator, now I see.

Terry and I brought down our harmonicas, which neither of us could play, some clothes, and our fishing poles. We planned on catching lots of fish. Unfortunately, we were successful and caught so many fish that within two or three weeks our freezer was jammed to the gills, so to speak. For two years, I couldn't look at another perch.

Terry thought this was all very strange. He is 105% Irish, with red hair and freckles. Very athletic, he is always willing to try something new. He comes from a family of nine boys (they all cheered when they finally had enough for a baseball team) and two girls. The only thing wrong with the Island, thought Terry, was that there weren't enough family around, so every few weeks, he would import about a dozen relatives and friends from Washington and Scranton, Pennsylvania. We had lots of fun the first several months we worked on the Island.

It was certainly not all fun, though. Just a week or two before Terry and I had moved in, some local vandals trespassed on the Island and wrecked the place. They broke every door, window, and light fixture they could get their hands on, as well as all of the members' lockers, which were still stored with liquor and supplies. They stole pictures and opened cans of food and threw them at the walls. They smashed toilets and other plumbing fixtures. They visited the Island again one or two days before we arrived and broke whatever else they could find.

Luckily, the new Executive Vice President Fred Pierdon was a boy scout troop leader and brought the scouts down to the Island to help. They earned merit badges for accomplishing such tasks as cleaning up destruction wrought by the vandals, cutting a new trail through the woods, now called "Boy Scout Trail," and putting a new roof on the Farmhouse. The scouts did a very good job in cleaning up the mess, but the possibility of vandals "visiting" the Island while we lived there was a constant fear. We were not sure that these local ruffians would have any hesitation about pulling a gun and shooting someone. For that reason, we brought a dog along.

Meet Muffin. She was a brown and white pure bred springer spaniel, with papers as long as your arm and leg. She was about four years old at the time and was as much a product of the city as Terry and me. She was to be my constant companion for the next fifteen months. The first night we landed on the Island, it was very dark and there was no moon ("It's so dark out here, I feel like a vampire," said Terry incredulously. "You mean the moon isn't out all the time?") Somehow we lost Muffin as we walked up to the Clubhouse to eat our first meal on the Island. Of course, first we had to turn on the generator, which Fred had taught me how to do about a week before. Amazingly, it turned right over and started. Although we were going to live in the Farmhouse, there were no kitchen facilities there and we had to eat our meals and store items that required refrigeration in the Clubhouse where there was a propane gas refrigerator and stove. ("Yea, Terry, I'm sure that these big silver bottles have pressurized gas in them. I think Fred said that we use gas for the stove and hot water heater, too," I said. "You mean we have to carry these big huge bottles back and forth on the boat all the time?")

I was worried that Muffin might have picked up the scent of a deer, followed it into the bush, been ambushed, and trampled to death by razor sharp deer hooves. We didn't see her for a few hours and I was ready to give her up for gone. After dinner that night, we strolled back down to the dock and guess what? The spirit of Harry Truman be praised! There was good old Muffin terrified out of her paws and shaking for all she was worth in the "Seahawk." She certainly was glad to see us. Apparently, she had run off after one or another of the thousands of new smells she would soon discover, had lost us, and gone back to the "Seahawk" to wait for our return. With that crisis solved, we turned in, ready for the next day and the beginning of our jobs.

Our first task was to fix everything we knew nothing about. To get started, we had to make the Farmhouse livable. It had not been inhabited for ten or fifteen years. We spent a substantial time fixing windows, putting up screens, cleaning, throwing away junk, and, as Terry said, "reclaiming the Farmhouse from the wasps." We each picked a room in the upstairs of the Farmhouse and fixed it to our refined tastes. The room formerly called "Jeff's room" was in such bad shape that we closed the door and locked it until we could get a chance to work on it. Later, we cleaned it up, set up our stereo and television, and it became our living room.

One of our first lessons was finding out that everything took three times as long on an island as it did on the mainland. Take for example, getting the mail. At home in town, you would run downstairs, open the door and the mail would be there. On the Island, you walked from the house down to the dock, out the dock, got in the boat, drove across to the mainland, tied up the boat, walked to the car, got in the car, drove up the road to the post office, and picked up the mail. As those who have lived on an island know, you have to carry everything several times, too. Down the dock, into the boat, down the dock again, put it on the wagon, drive up to the house, and carry to where it should be. Needless to say, this gets tiresome very quickly. At that time, the generators ran on gasoline and filling it up was a real task.

We bought gas from Captain Garner Gibson, who became a great friend. He always told us a story or two when we came by. We contracted with him to haul the "Seahawk" out of the water and repair it. The Captain still was working on boats even though he was nearly 80 years of age. His workshop was a ramshackle barn-like structure which allowed boats to be pulled up or pushed out directly into the water. I don't know how it lasted through some of the more fierce storms, much less stood up at all. It must have been older than Garner and accumulated many varieties of junk, old engines, boards, hammers, bottles, etc. as decoration. One of my favorites was a sign above the water faucet which said, "Cut Spicket Off." Anyway, Garner and his men repaired the hull as good as new, though he warned, "that old engine ain't worth coot's feet, sonny."

We regularly filled up the "Seahawk" and five gallon cans for the generator with gas. Those five gallon cans! When filled, they weighed about forty pounds each. We had about fifteen of them and would place them all on the back of the boat. When we got back to the Island, we carried them, two at a time, down the 200-foot pier to the generator. Terry and I hauled so many five-gallon cans of gas that Terry remarked, "Jeff, if I have to keep carrying these cans much longer, pretty soon I'll be able to tie my shoes without bending over." Soon thereafter, we obtained our first 55-gallon drum, hooray! Those metal drums were fairly easy to place empty on the back of the Seahawk, fill with gasoline, and then drive over to the Island dock. You had to have the right tide, but from there, we would dump them off the Seahawk, roll them down the dock, and use a small hand pump to get the contents into the larger generator gas tank. I wasn't too keen on looking like an orangutan, either.

Another problem that annoyed us a great deal was the lack of kitchen facilities in the Farmhouse. Imagine yourself relaxing after a hard days work, sitting on the porch of the farmhouse, watching the sunset. Then think of a cold beer or a bubbly soft drink. Then re-member that you had to walk almost a quarter of a mile to the Clubhouse to get it. Within a couple of weeks, Terry and I cried, "Enough." We appropriated some rough cut oak wood intended for the repair of the docks to build a kitchen in the Farmhouse and purchased a small gas stove for $30.00 from a local merchant. We moved the gas refrigerator from the Clubhouse and moved the electric one we then had at the Farmhouse back to the Clubhouse to replace it. The electric refrig-erator was of no practical use to us in the Farmhouse, because it would not keep our items cold since, to save gasoline, we only kept the generator on for four or five hours in the evening. The water pressure built up in the plumbing system during this time would keep for most of the next day if we used it sparingly.

The fact we had to turn off the generator every night led to great satisfaction for the one who had performed the task the night before. ("It's your turn to go down and turn off the generator tonight, isn't it Terry?") Actually, I also remember that we eventually found a small little generator with a one gallon tank that would run the Farmhouse, and then shut off when it ran out of gas a couple hours later. You just had to be ready when it went out.

That rough cut oak is some of the toughest wood God ever created. The small kitchen we constructed on the porch of the Farmhouse is extremely solid. We used sixteen penny nails and wore out our arms banging them in. I remember after a full day of hammering, my arm eventually became so weak that - while attempting to drive a nail up high - my hammer fell back and, un-able to garner the strength to stop it, hit me on the head. My own hammer! That ended my carpenter work for

that day, I can assure you. Nevertheless, our new kitchen proved to be very functional and is so strong that it will probably remain long after the rest of the Farmhouse has decayed away (which won't be long, unfortunately).

For almost two months, Fred Pierdon's son, Art, lived with us on the Island. Art was several years younger and an excellent mechanic. This was a skill that neither Terry nor I possessed and we learned quite a bit from Art, as well as becoming good friends. The old "Seahawk" en-gine was kept alive, the generator maintained, and the pumps running smoothly due to Art's efforts. He also overhauled the 30 year old tractor, which still was used to pull the wagon that hauled everything from boats to supplies to luggage to the members themselves. We used the tractor to mow the grass for a while, but the sickle arm mower gradually succumbed to the wear and tear of old age. From then on, we used hand mowers and borrowed riding mowers whenever we could. Terry was convinced that the real answer was a herd of sheep, but none could be found and that idea never reach fruition.

It seems to me that I began to detest painting in ear-nest during that first summer on the Island. We painted chairs, the tractor, the wagon, the pump house, the gen-erator house, the shed, and much of the Clubhouse. We wanted to improve the appearance of the Club as much as possible to attract new members. We tried to pretty things up, but there was really only so much we could do. A new roof was needed on the Clubhouse, and a con-tractor was hired. Within a short time, he had taken the first draft of money and "gone south." So, we patched the roof here and there. Let me tell you that working with rolled asphalt roofing and tar on a black roof dur-ing the middle of August was a hot project. Still, we patched many of the leaks and were able to seal most of the Clubhouse. We cleaned and repainted some of the sleeping rooms. It was a constant struggle, and to make matters worse, we had more trouble with the vandals.

One Sunday afternoon, when there weren't any guests on the Island and Terry was on the mainland running some errands, I was at the dock replacing a part on the "Seahawk." I had just eaten lunch at the Clubhouse and about an hour later, remembered that I had left some tools there. Upon opening the door to the kitchen, I dis-covered snow in the dining room! The large table and all the chairs were covered with a powdery white substance. I was absolutely amazed and dumbfounded until I no-ticed one of our fire extinguishers lying on the ground and some pictures and a few other objects missing. The vandals! I ran to the porch and looked down the River. Not a boat in sight! I ran to the back of the house. No one at all. In just a short hour or so, these hooligans had come into the Clubhouse, played their pranks, and gone. I don't know whether my returning had startled them while they had managed to escape, but they sure frightened me. For the record, they also stole a half case of Shawnee Springs canned peaches, which are still the best peaches in a can anywhere.

On account of this, I kept a shotgun in my room in the Farmhouse. I never wanted to use it, but it seemed to be practical, especially since we didn't know the nature of these local roustabouts. They were constantly tearing down the Jefferson Islands Club sign at the end of River Springs Road and shooting holes in it. One night, however, the gun was used. I will let Terry tell you about it:

"It was just about sunset one evening and Jeff was on the mainland making some phone calls. Muffin and I were sitting in the Farmhouse when I noticed the low sound of an outboard motor puttering around the Island. I looked out and there were three or four fellows sitting in a little white skiff, peering at the house, and motoring around the shore. They looked like trouble-makers, so I grabbed the gun from upstairs. By the time I had figured out how to load it, they were around the other side of the Island. Muffin and I walked down to the Clubhouse and I knew that they could see me plain as day. I thought that the sight of me with a gun and a dog would scare them off, but they kept right on coming."

"I figured the only thing that I could do was to fire a warning shot in the air over their boat. Well, I fired, but not being a very good shot, it came a little too close. I nearly hit those buggers! Anyway, they jumped about four feet in the air then hit the deck. I heard one of them yell, 'Those guys are crazy. Let's get the hell out of here!' They headed the boat in the opposite direction as fast as it would go. Well, we never had any trouble after that."

In spite of our difficulties, Terry and I thoroughly enjoyed the summer. We learned quite a bit about the wind and the water and the basics of life. We lost touch with many of our acquaintances, who thought we were nuts to live on an Island, but kept contact with our closer friends. Terry's cousin, Richard Dempsey, and my brother, John Haywood Glassie (who we called Haywood from time to time) lived with us for about a month. Just about everything had its humorous side, and we laughed our way from one problem to the next. We hung life jackets in the Clubhouse, which by then was hanging over the River, just in case she started to go down. The floors in the Farmhouse pitched and rolled and, since we were afraid some one might get going too fast and lose control as they walked a particularly steep section, we placed a mattress outside on the ground so they would have a soft landing after going through the window.

Terry and I both were amazed when we discovered peculiarities like "chinch" bugs, or stink bugs. Neither of us had ever imagined that a bug, a little funny look-ing grey bug, could expel a smell that would knock you off your feet. These were found at various times in pro-digious quantity in the shed or, for that matter, in any place where one would least expect it. At the cry of a "chinch bug," we would grab our noses, light matches, and head for fresh air.

We fished so much at first that we got tired of it, but then the fish found us. One night when we were driving across the Sound in our new 14-foot blue fiberglass boat with a 40-horse motor, a fish jumped out of the water and landed in the front seat next to Terry! He yelled and leaped so high in the air that I thought that he was going to trade places with the fish. It was the biggest fish we had ever caught! Evidently, the fish were attracted to the running lights of the boat for we "caught" several others this way.

The deer on the Island became used to us (Muffin really didn't care too much about deer) and would of-ten come up within 20 feet of the Farmhouse porch. A substantial herd has occupied the Island for years. The thick undergrowth of honeysuckle, bayberry, and other varieties of vegetation provides good cover and plenty of feed. It has been estimated that there have been as many as 40 or 50 deer living on the Island. They swim on and off easily, for they are powerful swimmers. When the number of deer gets too large, and they eat everything up to the "browse line," the hunters thin out the herd. When we walked the path around the Island in the late evening, we usually spotted a deer. We became great enemies of some other local inhabitants, however, some of the little ones.

In all my years of visiting the island, I had never seen a tick. Seemed like several millions of them moved on the Island that summer. It really wasn't too bad after we got used to them, but we would normally find one every once in a while on one of us or Muffin. Terry didn't con-sider pulling ticks off the dog to be his responsibility. He told me, "Since Muffin is your dog, you pull the ticks off her." We soon discovered that these little creatures would not pose much of problem if you avoided high grass.

We reserved the Island one weekend for our own party, called the "Third Annual Party." Since there had not been two earlier annual gatherings, we thought that would be an appropriate title. We invited everyone we knew and charged $1.00 admission. This entitled the guest to all the hard crabs, barbequed chicken, beans, corn, and potato salad he or she could eat and all he or she could drink. It was a beautiful crisp day, and in honor of the occasion, we flew the only flags that we had -- an American flag and a Japanese flag. Our friends swarmed all over the Island and truly enjoyed themselves. They fished, canoed, swam and lay around in the sun. This had been planned as sort of "test run" party so that we might be able to sponsor the Club's Annual Crab Feast shortly thereafter.

One of the only mishaps that occurred with the boats happened on this night. Just after the sun had set, people began to realize that they had to return home. We had advised them that the last boat would leave at 7:00 p.m., but it took a while to gather everyone together. One friend asked Terry for a ride, and they jumped in our little blue boat and began to take off. Terry tells the story better than I:

"Before we knew it, about ten more people had jumped in the boat. We cast off and began heading for shore. All of a sudden, the boat began nose-diving like a submarine into the water. We were sinking! 'Abandon ship!' I cried. Well, you should have seen all those frightened people jump. Guys and girls jumping off the boat right and left. Of course, the water was only about three feet deep, so we were in no danger. But as everyone jumped into the water, Rick Macsherry, who was sitting next to me, with legs crossed and cigarette held fashionably in the air, said aristocratically, 'Those fools!' We rescued all those flailing about in the water and I docked the boat."

"As one of the only two authorized captains of the "Seahawk," I then decided we needed a bigger boat and announced, "All ashore that's going ashore, get on the Seahawk." Within a few minutes, there must have been fifty people on board. I revved up the engine and we cast off. It just happened to be one of those nights with no moon. Everyone was singing and talking, and as we got to the dock on the mainland, I could hardly see where I was going. I yelled for the people to help guide me into the dock. That was the fatal mistake. Those on the left of the boat yelled, "to your right, to your right" and those on the right hand side of the boat hollered, "to your left, to your left." Well, I figured that this meant I was right on target so kept her straight as she goes. I was on

target, all right. We slid straight into the dock, smash! Actually, no damage was done, but I'm sure those people were glad to get off the boat."

The next morning, we made arrangements for everyone who had stayed the night, approximately 50 people, to eat breakfast over at Captain Sam's Seafood House, then run by "Butch" Morgan and his wife "Pinky." This Restaurant was across White's Neck Creek from the Island parking lot, and has since been razed. Butch and Pinky had become good friends of ours and cooked up a special breakfast at a cut rate. At about 10:00 a.m. in the morning, we all hopped on the boat and headed ashore. Muffin always had a habit of running around the gunwales (pronounced "gunnels"), running around and around, for what reason I do not know. Somehow, she was knocked off and with all 50 on board, we ran through a well disciplined "dog overboard" drill. Muffin was saved and the party ended with a fine breakfast.

The Crab Feast held a little later in the summer was the first for several years. It was very successful and about 60 people attended. Despite the hardships and our naiveté, people were enjoying the Island again and we were making great progress. Our major task for the summer has not been mentioned. This was saving the Clubhouse.

Erosion

As you may recall, the earliest historical accounts available place the size of St. Catherine's Island at about 180 acres in the 1630's. Today, it is less than 40 acres. We have previously seen with horror the story of the Poplar Islands, which were reduced in size over the same period of time from a total of perhaps 1,000 acres to barely 50. St. Clement's Island probably would not exist today were it not for the efforts of the St. Mary's County Historical Society and the complete bulkhead constructed around the Island by the state of Maryland. In the monumental book "Chesapeake," by James Michener, we learn that it is the nature of an estuarine system for the water to reclaim land deposited in the beginning of the process. Still, it is heart-breaking to observe the complete washing away of Devon Island at the conclusion of the novel. Unfortunately, this fate looms ahead for all islands in the Chesapeake Bay region that do not receive adequate protection from erosion. These islands were deposited by the process which formed the estuary now called the Chesapeake Bay millions and millions of years ago and are now being washed in continuation of the same process.

The causes of erosion are multifold and the pace has been accelerated by man and his habitation of the area. The "wetlands," like marshes, were nature's way of maintaining the foothold of the land in the tidewater region. These wetlands consisted of innumerable varieties of vegetation whose roots dug into the soil and held it tightly, preventing the water from reclaiming it. The grasses and weeds diffused wave action in addition to simultaneously cleansing and purifying the water. These wetland areas existed all over the Bay. These marshy areas not only held the land and cleaned the water, but provided a natural habitat and feeding grounds for all varieties of fish, crabs, and water fowl. Today, the wetlands are vanishing. Part of the reason Hurricane Katrina was so destructive in Louisiana was that the wetlands had been eradicated and there was little buffer for the immense storm surge.

The earliest destruction began with the original colonists as they cleared land to farm. Top soil from plowed land washed into the Bay and was deposited in river bottoms and in the wetlands where sedimentation smothers plant growth at the roots. The cultivation of farm land near to the water and the subsequent reduction of soil filtration and increased water run-off reduces underground water levels. This causes the drying up of creeks and streams, the raising of river flood levels, and the filling of navigational channels, not to mention smothering oysters. All aspects of life dependent on the Bay and its tributaries suffer because of sedimentation.

The use of detergents, pesticides and chemicals combine to form the most destructive force to our rivers and streams. Not only are fish, crabs, oysters, clams, all types of water fowl, and land animals affected, but the irreplaceable forms of vegetation that purify and hold the land are wiped out. Raw sewage, which in the 1980's was still being dumped into the River at the rate of over 400 million gallons per day, also kills plant and animal life. According to Frederick Tilp, at least twenty-one species of fish and wildlife in the Potomac River region have become or are endangered with extinction, and he wrote that several decades ago. It is a shame to think that the islands located in this region may be near extinction themselves. It is not only bad enough that the wetlands must suffer their elimination as a result of secondary effects of man's habitation, but man has also deliberately abolished the wetlands by using them as sanitary landfills for the disposal of trash.

When we went to work for the Club in May of 1975, the reasons for the erosion did not seem important. What was important was that the Clubhouse was begin-

ning to hang over the edge of the bank and was in real danger of falling into the River. It is hard to believe that so much land had been lost, so let me repeat some of the startling statistics. A study of the Island had been made in 1954, by the Maryland Department of Geology, Mines and Water Resources, which stated that "the charts of the coast and geodetic survey show that between 1868 and 1943, the southwest shoreline of St. Catherine's Island receded a maximum of 240 feet at the north end, about 100 feet in the vicinity of the Clubhouse, and a maximum of 180 feet south of the Clubhouse." The Clubhouse was originally built approximately 125 yards from the river. In 1954, the Clubhouse was situated only about 75 feet from the bank. The rate of erosion had been small between the 1930's and 1954, but hurricane Hazel began the most recent trouble when it destroyed nearly 12 to 15 feet in a matter of several days.

The 1954 report went on to say that "absolute protection against erosion can be obtained only with a bulkhead. However, the rate of erosion can be materially lessened at less expense by means of groins to catch the littoral drift (of the river) and by supplementing this with artificial fill." The construction of a seawall was not then within the means of the Club. You will remember that jetties were constructed in front of the Clubhouse by Joe and Bernie Wise. For about 10 to 15 years these wood jetties, approximately 75 feet long, helped decrease the rate of erosion somewhat. Several trees and a large patch of bamboo were planted directly in front of the Clubhouse to assist holding the soil. I remember when different types of seaweeds and grasses grew thickly in front of the Island to help hold the land.

Although the Clubhouse was nearly on the brink of going for a dip, we were heartened by the fact that the construction of the seawall had finally been contracted for and was to begin shortly. We were afraid, however, that a summer storm might come up before the wall could be erected. Erosion was taking its toll everyday. The porch in front of the Clubhouse had lost its support and had been shored up by concrete blocks and a wooden post so that it was nearly level but unstable to walk on. The round living room hung over the bank. The screened porch immediately in front of the Presidential suite also was beginning to fall in. We even developed a plan of action to save the furnishings of the Clubhouse in the event it started to tilt towards the water. It was so close that if you walked straight out of room number one, you would fall about eight feet down into the River.

A plan also was devised to provide a temporary hedge to the erosion. A makeshift wall was constructed of plastic bags filled with sand and cement forming a concrete mixture. Terry, Art, and I probably filled over 1000 sand bags, though it seemed like millions. This was our most important task, which we despised in an equal extreme. We literally spent weeks filling bags with sand at low tide, mixing in the cement, tying the bags up tight and placing them in a wall which resembled a typical combat sandbag barrier. The wall was about two or three feet high and protected the most vulnerable areas of the Clubhouse, especially directly in front of the dining room all the way to the Presidential suite. We sandbagged the ends of the Clubhouse, which were crucial spots also. Not to let any resource go unused, the old Island Queen and the 1941 Cadillac that had belonged to my father and brought to the Island at some point were dragged from their resting places in the weeds and pressed into service as bulkheads on the beach.

A normal exercise upon returning to the Island from the mainland would be to walk to the Clubhouse and check to make sure that none of it had fallen in the River while we were gone. We watched the River toss the sandbags around and we were constantly repairing our dykes. It was a tedious task and we waited for the contractors to arrive so that we could stop worrying about the Clubhouse and give up our most hated job. The contract had been let in July to the Charles Wroten Company from Hampton, Virginia. The wall was to be financed by a 25 year interest free loan from the State of Maryland; more on that later. Wroten was scheduled to begin work immediately, but they did not show up with their house boat, dredge, cranes, and barge until September. They dropped off all their equipment, went back to Virginia, and we didn't see them again until the end of October. The amount of time they wasted and the good weather lost was inexcusable. Fortunately, the Wroten Company had recently been purchased by the Quality Sanitary Engineering Company, which sent a man named Jim Bates to get the project going. If it hadn't been for him, the wall might not have been constructed in time. It was a winter I'll never forget.

Winter On The Island

As autumn began and the first flock of geese settled into the cove, life began to take on a new look for Terry and me. The relatively carefree, warm summer days were coming to an end. We were like the grasshopper in the fable of the ants and the grasshopper preparing for winter. The days began to shorten and to turn chilly. The northwest wind began to blow. Duck hunting season was coming on and, whereas it had been easy for me and

Terry to act as general caretakers and fishing guides, the prospect of being hunting guides was another story all together. We began by reconstructing duck blinds and re-conditioning the wooden decoys, fashionable today as living room decorations. I would point out that there were literally hundreds of wood decoys in the old shed outside the Farmhouse when I lived at the Island. There are none left now. I suppose even wooden ducks can become extinct through the acts of man.

Rising and shining at 4 a.m. proved rather disagreeable to Terry and me. Not just waking at 4, but getting out of bed -- Brrrrrr! Taking the "Seahawk" over in icy waters to pick up Mary to cook breakfast for the hunters, setting decoys out before dawn, and then taking the hunters to their blinds was hell in ice. We were no Joe and Bernie, I will tell you that!

At 7 a.m., our day seemed half over but had not yet really begun. From then on, we had to guide for the hunters, bring them in and out of their blinds, retrieve their felled ducks, pick up the decoys, and take Mary back after dinner.

Chasing the crippled ducks was the worst problem. Hunters normally find them, "put them out of their misery," and take them back for dinner along with the other killed ducks. It is hard to catch them though, because they're wounded and can dive even though they can't fly. It would be possible to shoot them, but at that close range you would end up with nothing but duck feathers and feet. So, the common practice was to bop them on the head with an oar, which would knock them out or finish them off. I would imagine that skillful boppers could hit the duck on the first try and easily scoop them up. This was not the case for me, because I had never bopped a duck in my life.

The worst experience I had was one rough day with the wind blowing northwest about 20 knots. I was using a 14-foot metal boat with a five horsepower Sears engine, which would pivot 360 degrees and did not have reverse. I was after a crippled mallard, but every time I stood up to bop him, the wind blew the boat around, the motor turned about 180 degrees, and as I bopped I was turned completely in a circle and thrown to the bottom of the boat. My long suit has always been persistence, so I attempted to bop this mallard for about 15 minutes. Each time, I stood to bop (there are no sitting boppers -- one can not get a good enough back swing to bop while sitting) the same results would occur; an errant bop, a dived duck (who would resurface eventually about 10 yards away), a turned and blown boat, revolving motor, and a crash to the floor of the boat. In doing this, the wind and the waves would spray freezing water all over my body, an uncomfortable yet positively invigorating feeling.

Though I guided that year, I decided that I would not hunt anymore for personal reasons. I think this poem, related in "Beautiful Swimmers," by William Warner, tells why:

> A hunter shot at a flock of geese
> That flew within his reach.
> Two were stopped in their rapid flight
> And fell on the sandy beach.
> The male bird lay at the water's edge
> And just before he died
> He faintly called to his wounded mate
> And she dragged herself to his side.
> She bent her head and crooned to him
> In a way distressed and wild
> Caressing her one and only mate
> As a Mother would a child.
> Then covering him with her broken wing
> And gasping with failing breath
> She laid her head against his breast,
> A feeble honk… then death.
> This story is true, though crudely told,
> I was the man in the case.
> I stood knee deep in the drizzle and cold
> And the hot tears burned my face.
> I buried the birds in the sand where they lay,
> Wrapped in my hunting coat,
> And I threw my gun and belt in the Bay
> When I crossed in the open boat.
> Hunters will call me a right poor sport
> And scoff at the thing I did;
> But that day something broke in my heart,
> And shoot again? God forbid!

Unfortunately, Terry didn't like plucking and cleaning ducks, or the freezing cold at all. One day he said to me, "This is crazy, I'm too cold. I'm leaving." That was the end of that.

Not too much later, Fred Pierdon said that I would freeze to death if I stayed in the uninsulated Farmhouse during the winter. The water pipes would certainly have frozen if I didn't. He had discussed this with Jimmy Oliver who had inspected the house with Fred. I then moved to room #3 in the Clubhouse.

Jimmy was a local gentleman who was providing invaluable assistance to us by taking phone messages and relaying them to me by CB radio regarding scheduled visits to the Club. He and his wife Helen were two of the nicest people I'd ever known and assisted me in more ways than I can count during my stay on the Island. Their son Jimmy was about my age and was one of the most skillful mechanics and handlers of equipment and tools that I ever knew. He helped me out on numerous occasions and eventually worked as manager for the Club for several years.

About this time, Jim Bates arrived on the scene and decided to keep his crew on the Island during the week and live in the Clubhouse. This arrangement worked out very well and I became good friends with Jim and his right hand man, Elmer Ray Potter. Jim was a great leader and could operate any piece of equipment used in construction. He had never built a sea wall, but he saw that the Clubhouse would fall in if he didn't build it right away. So he did.

For the next four months, Jim and his crew worked through the coldest weather of the year. Oftentimes, they'd wake up with their equipment frozen. A crane with an air-driven hammer drove 14-foot wood sheathing 6 or 7 feet into the ground. Piling were driven behind the wall and tied to it so that the wall would not fall into the River once it had been back filled with dirt. The wall itself had been constructed about 15 feet out from the bank. It was fortunate the tide was nearly always low during the winter due to the northwest winds. These winds pushed the water down the River and out the mouth of the Bay. It sure made it cold working, though.

Thus, our sand bags had served their purpose and saved the Clubhouse from falling in until the wall could be built. The 600-foot wall was completed in April of 1976. Unfortunately, we lost the porch in front of the Presidential suite. One night, during an extremely hard north blow, one of the men came into my room and said, "Jeff, I hate to tell you this, but your porch just fell into the River." I looked at him and, having become sufficiently immune to all types of problems and disasters, said, "Well, I suppose that's the way it goes. I certainly can't get back out there and pick it up." The sea wall had been constructed to about 20 feet from the porch at that point.

Jim Bates and Elmer Ray Potter and their crew helped me survive that winter. After ducking season, there wasn't too much I could do by myself. I engaged in some odd jobs around the Island, but basically took it easy. I was so cold. Elmer Ray was a great cook and every night we were treated to a new dish. I actually gained weight during the winter. Elmer Ray and Jim would sit in the kitchen with me and some of the others and tell some great stories.

We experienced more than a few adventures during that winter. The sound froze up and we had to break ice frequently to get to the mainland for supplies. One night, after making our evening run to the store, fog and ice closed in on us.

Well, we had to get back to the Island. However, in the middle of the sound with ice flows all around, we ran out of gas. We couldn't see the Island so we commenced yelling, "Help! Help!" to Frank Fuqua, who lived on Bullock Island, between St. Catherine's Island and the mainland. Captain Frank was to become Manager of the Club when I left in October of 1976.

Frank Fuqua went out to the end of the pier and guided us back to the Island with a signal light. That night, if there had been a band on board, I would have told them to strike up a tune because I was sure we were goners.

Frank and his family had left the hustle and bustle of the city ten years before and had gone to live on their island, which Frank's father had purchased in the late 1940's. Prior to that, it had been owned by a Mr. Smith, President of the American Automobile Association, who built several nice houses, a long pier with a fenced in gazebo at the end, and an underground generator and wellhouse. Mr. Smith had employed 30 to 40 local men during the depression years in completing the work. Before him, Captain Finney Bailey had lived on the island as local waterman and a sail maker. And way before that, it had been part of St. Catherine's Island, as you know, but is now about a half mile away.

When the sea wall was completed in the spring, Jim Bates was assigned to another job and Charlie Wroten was to complete the three groins. Never has a more dilatory man lived than this gentleman and it took him almost three months to complete the jetties. It was another two or three months later before we could convince him to remove his equipment away from the Island, which included a 60-foot barge piled with junk and a bright orange, ugly dredge-house boat.

I had another very scary experience that winter. One Friday evening with only Muffin as my companion, I sat down in the Clubhouse by the fire to write a little before going to bed. It was still cold out, about 30 degrees. We had been having a little trouble with the generator, so when the lights flashed and finally fell dark, it seemed no great matter for me to pull on my boots and walk down to the generator house to start it again. As I got close to the generator house, I noticed that, Oh my God!,

there were flames shooting out the windows of the generator house. Understandably, this excited me tremendously and I ran down to the generator only to remember that there was no fire extinguisher there. Flames were spewing out of the generator itself! I ran back to the Clubhouse, grabbed an extinguisher, hustled back to the generator house and extinguished the fire.

Oh no! The fire sprang back to life! Now I remembered another fire extinguisher in the Farmhouse. I sprinted down there, grabbed it off the wall, and flew back down to the generator house and extinguished the fire. You're kidding! The fire jumped back to life again, whereupon I remembered there was another fire extinguisher in the Farmhouse so I ran back up there again, grabbed it, and back down to the generator house. Muffin thought this was more fun than chasing ducks and she was racing in circles and around trees and all over. Thank goodness that the fire went out on my last try.

I was not sure exactly what other steps should be taken in the event of a fire such as this. I was a little shaken up. I called on the CB for, "Anyone, anyone, have you got your ears on?" Frank Fuqua answered, I told him the problem, and he came right over. Here was another of the many times Frank helped me out and we were becoming good friends. Together, we drenched the fire to make sure it was out, drained all the water out of the Clubhouse, and put anti-freeze in the traps and sinks. I decided that I didn't want to stay on the Island on Friday night with no water, heat, or electricity, so I drove back to Washington. This had been another in a long line of "disasters" that I was beginning to shed like water off a duck's back. I also began to look forward with great anticipation to the return of the warm weather. The next summer was to be a good one.

Pleasant Summer Days

In the late spring of the year, I said to myself, "Self, wouldn't it be nice to have a horse on the Island?" Yes, I thought, so I bought one. I had only ridden a horse a few times, but I figured that it would be no big deal. Actually, in my last semester at UVa, I'd taken a horse riding course for one hour of college credit, so I thought I could handle it. I bought an old brown, sway-back mare from Robert Anderson, a real horseman just up Route 234 in Clements, Maryland, who also raised Belgian pulling horses. These resemble the famous Clydesdales. In simple words, they are huge.

It was a bright sunny day when we led my new horse on to a small barge and took her over to the Island. I'm not sure whether she or I was more frightened, but she proved to be a rather good sailor, and hopped right on and walked right off the barge onto the Island. I was afraid that if I let her go, she'd run off and I'd never catch her, so I kept her tied for a few days. I had spent quite a bit of time building a horse shed out of old planks from the dock. I was careful to face the open side south so the north wind wouldn't chill her. I nailed roofing paper all over to keep the wind out and made a barbed wire pen for her to stay. Whenever anyone asks me what it was like to live alone on an island, I cite the example of this horse shed and how the simplest tasks can become difficult. Just having one other person to hold up the other end of a board certainly would have been a great help.

Soon I realized that she wasn't going to run off, so I let her loose. What a great lawn mower and fertilizer. I didn't know exactly what to name her. In addition to Muffin, I kept another dog for a while named Crackers. One friend suggested therefore that I should name the horse Biscuit and have Muffin, Crackers, and Biscuit. That sounded good to me, but I didn't want to use someone else's suggestion for a name. So I thought that "Sea Biscuit" might be a good idea for a name after the famous race horse. No, that wasn't right. Well, how about naming her "boy" since she is a girl. No, too stupid. Hey, I've got it! She was christened "Sea Biscuit Bob Boy."

It took me a little while to figure out how to ride her, but I did get a saddle, reins and all those horse accoutrements. I wasn't doing so bad until one day when we're racing (she had two speeds -- stop and race) and she stepped in a rut caused by some of the heavy equipment for the seawall and both of us tumbled onto the ground. I was lucky she didn't fall on me, but I did manage to break my arm in the process. Since I had broken my arm three times before, this was a piece of cake, except for the fact that I didn't know how I would get off the Island and up to the hospital by myself. Luckily, Ty Fuqua was on the Island. Ty was a lanky, bright boy with blond hair and a quick wit. He was Frank's son and lived on Bullock Island. He had been working part time after school to help me with some projects around the Island. He drove me over to Frank's Island, and he and Frank took me up to the hospital in Leonardtown. It seemed like Frank was rescuing me regularly now. The break didn't quite get set right, and if you put change in my right hand it will roll right out onto the floor if I'm not careful. But I managed; what else was I gonna do?

The Club now had a staff of one with a broken arm and a part-time helper. We still were able to accomplish a lot. Several of the members began redecorating rooms in the Clubhouse. Charlie and Marti Hawkins used the Presidential Suite whenever they came down and spent a lot of time and energy making it fit for a President. Marti is a tremendous popular and ebullient woman, who used to ride "Sea Biscuit Bob Boy" from time to time. This was no small deed, since most people who attempted to ride her were given an impromptu tour of some thick bushes or a quick seat on the ground. Douglas and Marie Gibson visited quite often and worked on various projects around the Clubhouse. Mr. and Mrs. Charles Hawkins, Sr. redecorated room #6 and always were at the parties. Mr. Hawkins served as a distinguished Congressional Committee staff director and took great enjoyment reading and relaxing in the Clubhouse. His charming wife, Collette, always made you feel like you were the greatest guy on earth.

Fred Pierdon, his wife Lou and daughter Julie, one of the most beautiful girls in the entire universe, spent more time than anyone on the Island and were tremendously important and helpful in the rejuvenation of the Club. Fred held the office of Executive Vice President for five years. Fred would tackle any problem be it mechanical, electrical, or nautical with untapped energy. The only problem was keeping track of him; more on Fred later.

Joe O'Malley visited the Island quite frequently and also had a penchant for tackling undesirable tasks. Joe could out-argue anyone except for maybe my father. My cousin Judy Glassie and her husband at the time Jim Somervell began weekending regularly that summer. Jim love to fish and consulted "solunar" tables to predict when they would be biting. Of course, he never got even a nibble. My parents spent quite a bit of time on the Island and again shipped Haywood, who was 16 at the time, to live with me for nine weeks during the summer. John was an invaluable help and gave us a total of three usable arms. Plus, we had a great time.

The Clubhouse was now in excellent shape. The "Seahawk" had been the recipient of a brand new engine and much tender loving care. A coat of and paint had made her look better than she had for years. We worked hard and the cumulative effect of the year's progress had made a noticeable difference. I had returned to the Farmhouse in the spring, after wintering in Room #3 at the Clubhouse. Haywood and I gave the Farmhouse a major face lift. We fixed the porch, which afforded a pleasant view of the beautiful Island sunsets. Haywood painted the tractor with a bright smiley face on the front, and it came to life. We re-carpeted and decorated to the point that old Captain Charlie Beitzell would have been proud. We listened to Bruce Springsteen cranked up on the stereo on the second floor of the Farmhouse. Haywood says, "There's no doubt in my mind that I played the best air guitar of my life in that upstairs room in the Farmhouse with the deer head in it. I think Muffin's Island years were the best years of her life. It was a heaven of dead fish to roll in." It was a good summer, and Club usage increased dramatically.

We were now busy with guests nearly every weekend and had proposed a regular Sunday afternoon social schedule. For the first party of the year, I decided to surprise everyone and fix the pool, which had nearly been lost to erosion. Even though the sea wall had been built and saved the pool, we still had some problems. We didn't have a proper pump with a large enough capacity and not enough hose. The pool needed patching for some of the steel had rusted out. It also needed a good coat of paint. These obstacles were quickly overcome with an old trash pump, some auto-body filler, and sky blue paint on the sides. We put some screen filter around the end of the pump's hose to keep the jelly fish out and ran it out in to the water. Guests for the first party of 1976 were surprised by a full swimming pool. It leaked a little, but so what. Yes, boys and girls, we were on our way back. Membership in the Club increased substantially that year, and we could hardly keep up with all the work.

We were in for one more catastrophe before the summer closed. A fierce squall built up from the southeast one Sunday afternoon and roared up the River. Afterwards, Haywood and I walked down to the Clubhouse and noticed something peculiar. We went inside, walked out to the porch in front of the dining room, looked up and saw the sky. Where was the roof? Either a tornado had touched down or the fierce wind had flipped it up and back over onto the Clubhouse. Haywood and I looked at each other and shrugged our shoulders. What else is new? A little boat had flipped over in a storm while tied to the dock just a few weeks earlier.

With the insurance money received from the roof, we were able to replace the roof and were once again back in shape. One of the major lessons that I learned from my time spent on the Island was that you can never underestimate the power of the wind and the water, nor fret over its results. You must simply be prepared for the worst to occur all the time.

It had now been almost 15 months since I had come to work on the Island. I loved every minute of it, but I thought that it was time to get back to civilization. I announced my resignation in the summer, to be effective after the September party in honor of Governor Tawes and Al Smith. Frank Fuqua was hired as the new Club Manager and worked with me closely the month before the party. We geared up and put on one of the best parties ever. Mary prepared her normally delicious fare and a crowd of almost 150 persons attended. Among them were Joe and Rose Wise and Bernie Wise. I'd been grateful for their help and was glad to see them there. I'm sure it brought back many memories for them.

Governor Tawes came and really enjoyed himself. The Governor was then over 80 years old but was able and quick of wit. He was presented with a plaque honoring him for his contributions to the Club, most importantly obtaining the sea wall. Al Smith was named to life membership in the Club, a distinguished list which includes: Bernard M. Baruch, Gordon Grayson, John Nance Garner, Cordell Hull, James A. Farley, Harry L. Hopkins, Pat Harrison, James F. Byrns, William B. Bankhead, Stephen Early, Edwin M. Watson, Harry S. Truman, John F. Kennedy, and James A. White.

I was given a share of stock in the Club that I was truly honored and gratified to receive. I will never forget my experience on St. Catherine's Island working for the Jefferson Islands Club. Part of my spirit will always remain on the Island and I'm sure that there are others who feel the same.

In October of 1976, the Club hired Frank T. Fuqua as Manager of the Club. Frank's family owned Bullock Island for over twenty-five years. As a young boy, Frank spent his summers on the island. He crabbed and fished and studied the water. You probably will not find a more knowledgeable individual concerning local lore and general "island" philosophy. Frank was an extremely competent manager and enjoys that distinct advantage of being able to observe the Island from his front yard. This was particularly important with regard to the security of the Club and facilities. Remember the difficulties encountered with local vandals in the spring of 1975.

When the Club was busy, and it was been extremely busy at that time, Frank worked weeks at a time without a day off. He was supported in this venture by his charming wife, Betty. She was an exceptional lady. Can you imagine having to break ice, brave wind and sea to get to work every morning? She was an employee at the naval station in Lexington Park and for years when they still lived on Bullock Island had to take a boat to her car to get to her job. Blessed with a fantastic, artistic talent, some of her canvases have graced the walls of the Clubhouse. She is a steady woman who always kept a tight island.

Mrs. Reta Boyce was Betty's sister. Reta for several years was the members' link to Frank. All reservations and messages were phoned into Reta, who relayed them by phone, radio, or in person to Frank. Remember, that was in the days before cell phones. We must not forget her husband Bud, a versatile handyman who worked at nearly all of the Club parties during that era and on other special projects.

Ty Fuqua, Frank and Betty's son should be recognized here also. Ty was an island boy, born and bred, and helped me a lot around the Island when I lived there. He took after his father in his tall frame and excelled in basketball at high school. Frank was a star in his own right in the early 1950's. He played for DeMatha High School and the University of Maryland. In fact, he was the second player, after Gene Shue, to receive a basketball scholarship to Maryland. A pro career was in store for Frank had it not been for serious knee problems.

Late 1970s

With the daily operations of the Club well in the large hands of Capt. Frank, the Club now turned to the serious rejuvenation of its membership. Lawrence Wood (Chip) Robert, Jr. had been President for several years, but passed away in late 1976. Don Glassie approached Congressman Dante Fascell from Florida and requested his assistance to lead the Club. Mr. Fascell readily accepted the challenge. Dante Fascell was to be the key to the rejuvenation of the Jefferson Islands Club. He was elected President in June of 1977, and I was elected Secretary. Vice Presidents were former Kentucky Senator and Governor Earle Clements (who used to write me nice letters about the Club), Senator Claude Pepper, Senator John Sparkman, Governor J. Millard Tawes, and my father. That was pretty cool, although they were all rather old at the time and none are with us now.

First elected to Congress in 1954, Fascell was reelected every term since. A staunch Democrat, he restored the political tradition of the Club. Elected President in May 1977, he took charge of the Club's reorganization. The Executive Committee and the Board of Governors began meeting in the Rayburn House Office Building in the evenings. The first meeting of the era was held on Wednesday, June 29 in Room 2255 Rayburn House Office Building. At that time, you could just tell the guard in the parking garage that you were going to a meeting in Mr. Fascell's office and you could park there. Not today, because you might have a bomb in your car. Dante would be turning over in his grave.

Fascell provided us with new leadership and we went to work. I remember spending lots of time in meetings at Dante's office. He would give us all a beer and cigarettes or cigars. We used to talk about all manner of things at the Board meetings, from pipes to plumbing, to generators and oil pumps, to boats and engines. Dante was right there doing his damnedest. We would go out for something to eat after the meetings and Dante often picked up the tab.

Usage continued to increase, party attendance grew, and every year we made more progress. The financial situation, by no means ever rosy, improved dramatically. Richard Davis and then Bob Davis (no relation) served as Treasurer and organized the Club books. Despite his hectic schedule, Dante Fascell took the time to oversee the policy decisions of the Board. More people began to attend the meetings. In 1975, the average attendance at Board of Governors meetings was probably about five people. After Dante Fascell took charge, nearly twenty dedicated members attended each meeting.

Douglas Gibson and Don Macleay, along with Don Glassie, represented the old guard on the Board. Invaluable services were provided by Vincent P. Ahearn, Jr. and Charles Hawkins, III. As top executives of the National Sand and Gravel Association, they had practically run the Club for several years (I was hired to work with them in 1976). Vince served as Secretary and Treasurer and Charlie assumed the secretarial duties for several years. Both were instrumental in obtaining the bank loan from Al Smith.

Harry Wells and Joe O'Malley were two younger members (at the time) who applied quite a bit of the legwork on projects undertaken by the Board. Harry worked on marine and estuarine developments concerning the Chesapeake Bay Region. O'Malley served as Club Attorney for several years and has spent countless hours on vital endeavors, from constructing the crucial second mortgage to fixing pipes and even working on the ad hoc Farmhouse Septic Tank Committee.

Fred Pierdon had became a member in 1974. Due to his boundless enthusiasm, thorough knowledge of all mechanical matters, and great love of the Island, he had been elected (i.e., drafted) Executive Vice President in

1975. Fred was another key to the success of the Club. Whatever needed to be done, Fred did it. He spent weeks on end at the Island. An avid hunter, he must be credited with accomplishing the greatest part of the physical renovation of the facilities of the Club at that time. Haywood later said: "There's one image that just seemed to repeat itself over and over and over during that time: a group of middle-age men bent over and around some broken engine or pump or generator or furnace, trying to fix it for the tenth time. It seemed so bleak, but people like Fred and Dad and Joe O'Malley were always so optimistic, and they had so much strange fun doing it. They loved it."

Strong supporters during those years also included Charlie Cromwell, Marion Bevard, Carl Miller, Joe Burnham, Liz Linkins, Jeff Rosen, Dale Andrews, Jon Swindle, Douglas Gibson, Terry Parsons, Ernie Kaulfuss, Jim Somervell, Al Dinsenbacher, Menard Doswell, Harry Wells, and the list goes on. It's crucial to have an organized membership, with regular meetings, to promote camaraderie and initiative.

In a newsletter from about that time, Fred Pierdon as Executive Vice President provided a comprehensive report to the members, which gives a feel for the types of things going on. Fred announced that there had over 200 people at the Oyster Roast (eighty more than were expected). Fred reported on a raffle being held to raise funds for a 19 piece stainless steel Queen Cookware set, with each ticket being a dollar. Not sure how much was made on that, but likely not much. A new diesel generator was in operation, and several of the rooms in the Clubhouse had been renovated by members. Other members interested in working on a room were asked to contact the House Committee Chairman, Doug Gibson. There was a new boat, a Chris Craft (maybe 20 feet), the Mary-Ark, which was named after Fred's mother and the Ark that brought the colonists over. A new radio system was being set up to connect the Manager Frank Fuqua with his sister in law, Reta Boyce, for taking reservations for Club use. Fred noted, " In keeping with past tradition, they will not provide a direct phone link to the Island." Twelve members joined that year. Mary Dyson was still available to cook meals for members, and that was always a treat. It's been hard to find a cook recently; no one wants to go over and cook all day at an Island anymore. Fred reminded members there were 9 rooms in the Clubhouse and six in the Farmhouse, which was in full operation. Both the Clubhouse and Farmhouse often were at full capacity on weekends. Boat launching ramps were used on both the Island and mainland. and

many members brought their boats down; we used to water ski around the Cover for hours in those days.

I remember Dante Fascell asking me one time to ride along with him to the Island to show the Club to Frank Moore, who was the Director of Congressional Relations in the Carter White House. This was back in 1977, the Democrats were newly (albeit briefly) back in charge, and Dante was champing at the bit to get the administration interested in the Club. We drove down in Dante's car. On the way down, Moore asked if someone could maybe take him out for a sail. We had a red daysailer for a while; Fred Pierdon, Joe O'Malley, my father and I had picked it up at an auction for $300. I learned to sail on that boat, but it wasn't in great condition. When we got the Island, we found that Dale Andrews and his family were down for the weekend. Dale had a 14 foot O'Day and we promptly dragooned both he and the vessel. Well, Dale's boat might have been in better shape than mine, but not by a long shot. Basically someone had to sail her (that would be Dale), someone had to tend the jib (me, thank you very much) and that left the third person – the aforementioned White House Director of Congressional Relations – to perform the very important role of bailer. This entailed constant scooping and dumping of River water using an empty Clorox bottle with a cut-out bottom. I will always remember tooling across the River, the boat at a rakish angle, and Frank Moore frantically bailing while asking Dale and me "Hey, you boys aren't gonna dunk me are you?"

In fact, one of the really great things about the Island is what a leveler it is. We all come from different walks of life back in D.C., but at the Island we're all equal as we sidle up to the bar or a pile of crab. I remember Claude Pepper in his latter years arriving in a black suit and tie and scurrying up to the crab table otherwise peopled with members in swim suits. Dale Andrews recalls once, when as a young attorney, he had researched an issue concerning the Privacy Act for a client and had been grappling with a particularly troubling remark in the legislative history by Dante Fascell. The next weekend Dale found himself next to Dante at the Crab Feast. Dale turned to Dante, recounted the point from the legislative history and said "Dante, did you really mean that?" Dante put down his crab knife, squinted back across the table and said "Damn right I meant it, Dale." Then he went back to slurping backfin.

Another story that Dale also likes to recount involves an early trip to the Island when he and his wife, Patricia Black, were first dating. They were enjoying one of Mary's great meals and there was only one other person at the table, a tall slender fellow dressed in a workout suit. Pat, always a great fan of the space program, mentioned that she really thought NASA needed a greater commitment by the government. The other fellow at the table asked her why and continued to ask her questions about space travel. Pat went on for about 30 minutes answering question after question. Dale was squirming throughout this because, unbeknownst to Pat, he knew who the other fellow at the table was. It was Bill Nelson, then a Florida Congressman, now one of its Senators. Senator Nelson, of course, was one of the only Congressmen ever to fly in the Space Shuttle; a fact he never even let on to Pat!

The generosity of the members became evident in 1978. The idea of a "Potomac River" second mortgage was initiated by John Mitchell. He had been introduced to the Club by Earle Clements, an avid Club supporter. The second mortgage was financed by eighteen members and provided the Club with needed money for pressing financial obligations. The Board of Governors approved the plan in 1978, after a thorough review of the financial situation. A committee of Bob Davis, Charlie Cromwell, Joe O'Malley, and John Mitchell put together the details. The plan involved placing a second deed of trust on the Island, which secured the promissory notes from the members. The $40,000 raised was used to pay off existing debts and taxes, the mortgage brought up to current, and the outstanding seawall payments made. This was one of many short-term solutions that helped the Club avoid bankruptcy and selling the Island. The notes to the members were all paid off by 1987.

So, in 1979, things actually were looking up again. The annual meeting was held on January 17 in good old Room 2225 Rayburn, and a comprehensive plan and budget was approved by the membership (26 members were actually present). Reports were submitted by the Membership, Boats, House, Hunting and Fishing, Social, Grounds, and ad hoc Legal Committees. Expenses were estimated at some $55,000, and income of about $47,000, with the balance made up by the second mortgage funds. There were fifty regular dues paying members at $450 per year. A meetings schedule was set forth for the year, with Board meetings once per month, mostly at the Rayburn building. We even sold Jefferson Islands Club tee-shirts and etched glasses that year.

The Early 1980s

After two years as President, Dante Fascell handed the leadership of the Club to Congressman William V. Chappell, also of Florida. Bill Chappell took further steps in increasing the efficiency and the membership rolls of the Club. Chappell maintained a desire to return the Club to its former prosperity and popularity. He spent numerous relaxing weekends at the Island and gained additional Congressional support. Chappell helped the Club host a number of parties on the Hill and at the Island. Chappell envisioned the Club just as the founding Senators Hawes and Pittman did fifty years ago. A perfect island gem, away from the hustle and bustle of official Washington. And no telephones! (At least that was the mantra back then; maybe now we could say: No fax machines!) Many other Congressmen joined the Club at Chappell's initiative (before the ethics rules started prohibiting memberships at different than regular dues rates for Senators and Members). The Club also began to enjoy the support of a number of corporate members.

In 1980, Tip O'Neill, Jim Wright and John Rhodes became members of the Club. Majority Leader Wright was flown in by helicopter to the annual Crab Feast in July. He recalled visiting the Club many years earlier with Sam Rayburn and other House leaders. The Representative from the largest Congressional district in Maryland, which included the Island, Roy Dyson attended the 1981 Jefferson Island Club Congressional Reception on the Hill, the Crab Feast, and subsequently became a member. Roy was always a great supporter of the Club.

Also in 1980, Charles Cromwell was elected Executive Vice President. Fred Pierdon had served ably for five years and had helped turn the Club around. Cromwell continued the progress without even breaking stride. Charlie is a tireless leader, working behind the scenes to help make the Club run smoothly, as well as become well-known on Capitol Hill. It is this type of person that makes the Club go. He also served as Club Treasurer, a thankless job, from 1990 until 2006.

A tornado hit the Clubhouse in 1980 on June 29. It demolished room number 8 and damaged room 7, too. Amazingly, my Uncle Henry Glassie's two stepdaughters were in one of the rooms and were literally picked up and carried out on to the lawn. The both escaped major injury, but it was a very traumatic experience. The Clubhouse seems to attract wind gusts coming up the water and zooming up the bank, presumably creating a vacuum on the top of the roof and lifting off the roof. As you recall, it happened before, and would happen again.

Another episode occurred in 1980 directly related to me. You remember that I had brought Sea Biscuit Bob Boy to the Island in 1976. While I lived on the Island, I think everyone enjoyed her around. She provided a picturesque sight, grazing in the grass from a distance. She was very friendly, although a little feisty to ride. When I left the Island, Frank and I decided she would be OK. He was to give her some corn or "sweet feed" on occasion. She had learned to eat all sorts of vegetation around the Island, drink the salt water from the River or fresh from Lake Pierdon, and back into the bushes to escape the cold northwest winds. In other words, she was happy.

For some reason, I also had brought over another horse that Robert Anderson sold to me. A younger male, white, with one blue eye and one brown. I don't even remember what we named him now. No one ever rode him. Also, he bit some people; I remember Charlie Cromwell had been bitten on his stomach. He was practically unapproachable (meaning the horse, not Charlie). Sure, they looked really wonderful romping around the Island, but there was an issue, and eventually people got fed up with it. Horse manure.

Admittedly, I had been lazy about this. The idea of taking the horses off the Island was somewhat difficult, and sentimental. Also, it isn't exactly easy to do. I had transported Sea Biscuit Bob Boy off once or twice, I recall, to get her hooves trimmed. And so, I knew she would step into the Seahawk (we'd lay boards down to make sure her feet didn't go through the "ceiling" of the boat). But handling the other horse would be a challenge. I can't remember how or when we took him over in the first place.

Anyway, Carl Miller finally wrote a letter to the Board. The horses also were eating a lot of natural flora, and some that he had planted to attract ducks and geese. I had to do something. I contacted Robert Anderson and asked him to help me persuade the horses onto the boat and also to buy the horses back. He came to the Island and, like a horse whisperer, easily convinced them to get on the boat and we took them to the mainland. I think he paid me $200 for Sea Biscuit Bob Boy, so I lost $100 on the transaction, having initially paid $300 for her. That was a very said day, and I lost a good friend. I just hope she didn't end up as glue.

In 1981, over 300 people attended the Crab Feast in honor of the Secretary of the Army, Jack Marsh, and the Secretary of the Air Force, Verne Orr. I have never quite understood the peaceful members of Jefferson Islands Club supporting the Defense establishment, but we have had a number of contractors as members, and if it helps pays the bills and keeps the Club going, I'm OK with that. Congressman Chappell attended and presented the Harry S Truman Award to five deserving members: Dante Fascell, Claude Pepper, Don Glassie, Douglas Gibson, and George Galland. Certificates of Appreciation were also presented to Joe and Bernie Wise, who attended and visited the Island, perhaps for the last time. There is a picture of the Clubhouse of us all on that day. Chappell was there, as well as Roy Dyson.

Bill Chappell also was responsible for creating the most important ongoing event the Club has had; the Citizen of the Year Award. This annual tradition has kept the Club afloat since 1982. Vice President George H.W. Bush accepted the First Annual Jefferson Islands Club Citizen of the Year Award at a black tie dinner on Tuesday July 27, 1982 at the City Tavern Club in Georgetown. Ninety-four people attended the dinner, including twenty-eight Club members, and Dante Fascell and Bill Emerson. Special thanks for organizing the event were due to Chappell, Charlie Cromwell, and Dave Smith.

I didn't have the money to attend, but was asked to give a brief history of the Club. I had mentioned in my talk that the former Vice President in the Roosevelt Administration, John Nance Garner, had been a member of the Club. During his remarks, Vice President Bush noted that Garner had remarked that being Vice President was like a "bucket of warm spit" (except I heard Garner had used a different word than 'spit'). I also was the photographer for the event, and we published a special edition of the Club Newsletter with thirteen pictures to celebrate the event. Subsequent Citizens of the Year have included Secretary of Defense Caspar Weinberger, Senator John Tower, Speaker Jim Wright, House Foreign Affairs Committee Chairman Dante Fascell, House Ways and Means Committee Chairman Dan Rostenkowski, Secretary of Defense Dick Cheney, Appropriations Committee Chairman Jamie Whitten, Judiciary Committee Chairman Jack Brooks, Senator Robert Byrd, House Transportation Committee Chairman Don Young, Rep. Bill Emerson, Senator Trent Lott, Commerce Committee Chairman John Dingell, Senators John Breaux and Thad Cochran (in the same year, as a tribute to civility in the Congress), Speaker Dennis Hastert, House Commerce Committee Chairman Billy Tauzin, Senator Ted Stevens, Senator Jim Inhofe, Commerce Committee Chairman Joe Barton, and Rep. Duncan Hunter. Quite an illustrious and bipartisan group, I must say. And the event has always netted us enough money just to get us into the next year. It is a wonderful and lucrative tradition.

In 1982, a Capitol Hill reception also was held at the National Guard Armory on March 22. This event was very well attended, and I remember having a slide show rolling during the reception with pictures of activities and events at the Island. In that era, party themes varied from Mother's Day to Father's Day, from the Octoberfest to the Septemberfest, and from fishing tournaments to Thomas Jefferson's birthday. A "bonfire dance" was also held one year, but no one really knew quite what that was. For several years in the late '70's and early '80's, there were parties at the Women's National Democratic Club near Dupont Circle in Washington. In 1979, the Wild Game Party had been held there, with musical entertainment, for $15 per person!

It was also reported in a Club newsletter that a robbery had occurred at the Clubhouse in the winter, in which thieves took ammunition and liquor from members' lockers, as well as an antique slot machine that had replaced the earlier ones that had also been stolen. What a drag. People should not steal other folks' stuff. Also in 1982, Frank Fuqua resigned after 5 years as manager of the Club. My old friend Jimmy Oliver was engaged as the new manager. A newsletter from that year also reported that House Committee Chairman Dan Pewett was still looking for volunteers to adopt the rooms in the Clubhouse and spruce them up.

The New Seawalls

You will recall that the first wooden bulkhead seawall was built in front of the Clubhouse in 1976. The cost was $100,000, financed by a 25 year interest free loan from the State of Maryland. Actually, under this statutory plan, St. Mary's County paid for the seawall and then was reimbursed by the State (as I was to learn later). But the first seawall only protected the Clubhouse, and the neck of the Cove was then beginning to break through. In the late 1980's, the water of the Cove and the River would actually meet at high tide. It wouldn't be long before a big storm breached the slim finger of land between the main part of the Island and Captain Williams Point to the northwest.

Aside from almost losing the Clubhouse in the mid-1970s, one of the easiest ways to measure erosion at the Island was by taking an annual walk across the spit of land that loops around the Island's harbor. When I was a kid, this was a broad expanse of land forested with persimmons and other trees. In fact, back in the late 1960s or early 1970s when George Galland was Executive Vice President of the Club, according to Dale Andrews, George came up with an ingenious way to bail the Club out of some of its constant financial woes. George was the senior partner at a Georgetown transportation law firm with offices at Canal Square off of 31st Place. The architect for Canal Square was Arthur Cotton Moore, still one of the great architects of Washington. George got into the habit of lunching with Moore and, after picking up the tab on a particularly good lunch at the City Tavern Club, George convinced Moore that he should become involved in trying to save the Island.

Several weeks later, Moore showed up at George's office with a set of plans for a community of weekend homes that, believe it or not, would have been built along that spit of land forming the House Cove. It was quite wide back then. Moore's idea was to fence that section off from the rest of the Island, provide a gate to the Clubhouse area, and then construct and sell vacation homes that would be conveyed with a membership to the Island. George presented this plan grandly to the Board of Directors, which promptly rejected it. George was disappointed, to say the least, but anyone looking at what happened to that land over the last few decades could see the impracticality of the plan. I remember walking the cove with Dale Andrews when he first joined the Club back in 1977. Even back then there was maybe only 50 feet of wooded land. Just before the Cove was finally saved with the rock wall, there was only a thin spit of sand.

In fact, we had to start sandbagging again. I wasn't exactly happy about that, because I had done so much sandbagging (so to speak) when I lived on the Island. However, we had very few options. Several weekends we gathered maybe twenty or more people and built sandbag mini-seawalls to protect the thinnest part of the land. Men, women, and children were pressed into service. The sandbags were either plastic or some sort of tough coarse material. When we had been sandbagging in 1975, we added some cement into each bag so that (theoretically) the wall would end up being a concrete wall and withstand more wave pressure. This time, we just put sand in the bags, tied them up, and stacked them into walls about two or three feet high. Whether the sandbags actually saved the Cove, I don't know, but the seawall to shore up the land arrived in time! Yay!

Jon Swindle was the member who was most directly responsible for getting the new seawalls built. He spent scads of time on this project; it may have cost him a wife or two. Seriously, he worked really hard on making these projects succeed, and certainly is one of the people who can be credited with saving the Island. Jon also is an avid hunter and has brought in many new hunter members, who always work hard to keep up the equipment and blinds. Jon has been deemed the "consummate host" in a photo on the Clubhouse wall.

The rip rap seawall that protects the Cove was built by Jim Gunn of the Coastal Design company in 1986. The cost was about $250,000, financed by another twenty five year interest free loan from the State, as was the first seawall. When the wooden bulkhead seawall was put in, Jimmy Oliver had told me, "You've got a 40 year wall there." It hadn't occurred to me at the time that the wall wouldn't last forever. So far, it's been about 30 years, and it needed shoring up recently (and more rock was added in 2005), so maybe he was right. I hope it lasts longer.

Anyway, after the first bulkhead seawall was built, the shore line also began eroding more rapidly at the southern end of the wall and, within 10 or 15 years, it had carved a great bay shaped swath out of the Island. So, we had to fix that too. Estimated additional cost: $260,000. Again, this would be a 25 year interest free loan from the State, but the annual payments were adding up. All three seawall payments would total about $25,000 per year in 1990, quite a chunk of our budget. Gunn also built the third seawall south of the Island, and it's a beauty. It was very well done and provided a picturesque long vista south of the Clubhouse. These rip rap walls should survive and protect the Island for a long time, I hope.

In addition, there were problems at the north end of the Island. The shore line toward St. Margaret's Island had been eroding, albeit more slowly, and a severe hurricane might have taken it away and breached the Cove from the north. If that happened, the punishing northwest winds would begin eating away at the area around the Farmhouse and toward the dock. It seemed as if we were being assaulted from all sides.

The State proposed a different program for this erosion control project. Sand would be pumped about a mile away from a project a mile up the Wicomico River, where they were dredging out the channel between St. Margaret's Island and the mainland, and then placed on the northwest shore of St. Catherine's Island. This would add about two acres to the Island. It was further proposed to shape the sand into several half-moon shaped bays, with rip-rap walls constructed parallel to the shore line. The idea was that these bays would form a sort of "living" or "non-structural" wall that would blend in more with the environment.

The problem was that this scheme was not a 25 year interest free loan, but only available under a 50-50 matching grant. The total price of the project was $200,000, which meant the Club had to come up with $100,000. A few years earlier, as you will recall, the Potomac River mortgage (as John Mitchell called it) raised about $44,000. But this was a much larger project. How would we ever raise that amount?

I remember one night after a lot of discussion at a meeting up on the Hill, Jon Swindle suggested that we issued bonds that could be convertible into stock. His idea was that members would buy bonds, which upon default of the bond terms would convert into stock. So, if someone bought $10,000 worth of bonds, that would be converted into 10 shares of stock at $1,000 if the Club could not repay the bonds. In that event, the bondholders would then own a majority of stock, which otherwise was limited to one share per member. Then, they could force a sale of the Island and theoretically recoup a profit if the Island sold at a high price.

Well, this plan took an awful lot of effort to implement, but we did it. The Club raised $111,000 that paid our share of the matching amount for the seawall, plus allowed us to put in a new deeper well and refurbish the swimming pool. The water level in the two old wells had dropped because of significant population increases in the surrounding areas. This ultimately led to the demise of the Farmhouse, but the new well constructed at the pumphouse by the Clubhouse still works well.

We had hoped to raise $165,000 and put in a tennis court, as well as upgrade the electrical facilities. We didn't raise enough for those projects, but what the heck. A number of members put up a significant amount of money to preserve the Island, again. The bonds were paid back, later than anticipated, but when issued we had warned that the Club might not be able to pay them back at all. As an associate attorney at the law firm Baker & McKenzie (having gone to night law school from 1981 to 1985), I arranged for the legal work to be done for the transaction.

The seawalls have been a major success. It's sort of difficult to walk up to the north end to see the results of the work, but it's worth the effort. Those half-moon bays are still intact and have not eroded at all. We gained back a couple acres of land, which rapidly was covered by tough Island vegetation. The efforts Club members had made were specifically recognized when a few years later, we were in financial trouble again.

The 1990s

The 1990s proclaimed a new era for the Club. Jimmy Oliver had done a great job as manager for several years. He kept the equipment and machinery in top condition, despite sometimes adverse circumstances (i.e., no money, and the River weather). Jimmy departed after a few good years. I always liked Jimmy. His oldest son and my two oldest were all born on March 18; what a coincidence! I think of Jimmy when I see the nice picnic table area under the cedars and pine trees just east of the Clubhouse, because Jimmy initially had cleared out all the underbrush so we'd have some shade trees.

The Islands trusty Seahawk ultimately had to move on while Jimmy was manager. She had dry rot and the engine problems were becoming just too much to cope with. The Island secured a new boat, aptly christened the Seahawk II (my son Jay won the contest for naming the new boat – pretty clever, huh?) The original Seahawk was donated to the Chesapeake Bay Maritime Museum and Jimmy Oliver had towed it over there across the Bay. Dale Andrews, his wife Pat Black, and their two sons Devon and Colin remembered sailing from Annapolis to St. Michaels for a weekend that summer. After tying up at the marina, they walked in toward town and there, tied up in a working slip, was the original Seahawk, looking glad to find an old friend. Devon and Colin clambered on board one last time, and came back to say a final good-bye before sailing back across the Bay the next day. I tried to locate the old gal years later at the Museum, but nobody could tell me where she'd gone.

Charlie Hawkins then hired Colleen Thompson as Manager. She was the spouse of Darrell Wise, the son of Flea Wise, brother of Joe and Bernie. Colleen is a very hard-working, savvy person. She knows how to get things done. Colleen served as manager until about 1995, then took a sabbatical, rejoined the Club in 1998, and has been the Manager ever since. I think Colleen has really turned out to be a great Manager; the Clubhouse and grounds have never looked better than they do at present. And everyone loves Darrell, always with a grin and toothpick in his teeth. He tells some great stories about the old days. He also knows how to get things done around the Island. Colleen and Darrell have been great additions to the Club family.

There were some very positive developments that started out 1990. As one example, a nice reception had been co-hosted by the Club and the Louisiana Congressional Delegation in honor of Congresswoman Lindy Boggs, a long time supporter of the Island. It was held in the posh Ways and Means Committee Hearing Room in the Longworth House Office Building. The Club was becoming well known on the Hill and I remember attending the reception. Unfortunately, Lindy Boggs daughter passed away that day, and the Congresswoman could not be there. Very sad. That perhaps was a portend of some other problems to follow.

The issue was that membership was still lagging. Charlie Hawkins was doing a great job as Executive Vice President, and there was an energized Club "base." But energy doesn't always translate into money. In 1992, things again looked bleak financially. Charlie sent out a letter on June 2, 1992 saying that the Club had reached a "financial crossroads" that threatened the Club's future. There were only 33 stockholder members, 10 junior, senior and non-resident members, and 48 Congressional members (but they only paid $50 in dues, if any, at the time). The 1991 seawall payment was overdue, and the Island could be placed for tax sale as early as November 1992, with the sale sometime in January or February of 1993. The Club then would have had six months to reclaim the Island from the person who bought it at the tax sale.

Charlie also pointed out that a recent appraisal of the Island by the tax assessor showed an estimated value of over $600,000. The Club's mortgage was about $195,000 and over $140,000 was owed to the bondholders (including interest). The Board considered the situation serious and presented several options. These included a special assessment of $6,000 per member and a permanent increase of dues to $2500 each; sell the Club to a group of 20 members for $20,000 each, which would end up owning the Island and deciding who could use the Island after that; move to sell the Island as quickly as possible and assessing the members an amount sufficient to avoid a tax sale, perhaps $1,000 per member; or a guarantee by each member recruited not later than July, which would result in 30 or more new members. There was a stockholders meeting on June 23, 1992 to resolve the issue.

I was an associate attorney now at the law firm of Jenner & Block. I was to come up for partnership soon. Needless to say, I was busy. Had three kids, ages 9, 7, and 5. Was supposed to bill 1900 hours a year. But I couldn't stand to see the Club to go down, so I stood up at the meeting and said I thought we should try to get 30 new members. The members said, "OK, then you be Executive Vice President." Drat.

But I had to do it. For the love of my father and mother, Sea Biscuit Bob Boy, and Joe and Bernie Wise, and many more, I had to do it. Truth be told, it really energized me. When I look back at the files today, I can hardly believe how much time I spent as Executive Vice President those few years.

The Board of Governors first adopted a plan to get back on track. One of the initial steps undertaken was to contact Louis Goldstein, Comptroller of the State of Maryland, and try to seek relief from the seawall payments. I met with Mr. Goldstein, who had been to the Island many times before, and who supported the tradition of the Club. Not only that, but he actually admired all the time, work, and resources Club members had made over the years to help protect the Island. At the Board of Public Works hearing I attended, he essentially criticized some other groups for coming to the Board to get undeserved tax relief, but praised the Club. He said the Island is "one of the few islands left" in the Potomac, and that the Club had "done a magnificent job to preserve the Island." He gave the go ahead to the Department of Natural Resources to work out a refinancing plan with the Club, essentially approving our request for a four year moratorium on the seawall payments. We eventually worked out the arrangements with the State and with St. Mary's County and finalized the deal in 1994. The Washington Post wrote an article in July 1994 saying that the Club had been granted a "bailout." Republicans on the St. Mary's County Council tried to make it sound like a Democratic insider deal. I was just trying to preserve the Island and that's what I told the reporters, but it was sort of a slanted article.

With breathing room now secured, we focused on membership and operations. One of the first steps was holding a reception in honor of Dante Fascell, our former President who was retiring from Congress and from his post as Chairman of the House Foreign Affairs Committee. That would bring in some much needed revenue. But membership still was the key. We launched an effort to bring in 30 new members. In the first couple months after I became Executive Vice President, we held a number of Family Picnics and similar events at the Island. The Family Picnics were day affairs, and we provided burgers and dogs and the pool was open. We only charged $25 per family, so it was affordable and increased use.

We also modified the membership dues and stock payments. We decided to hold any stock payments we received in escrow until we had achieved a certain number of members. Soon thereafter, as I recall, we also decided to let individuals be members without buying a share of stock in the Club, which had been a requirement since the Club's inception. However, it was felt the stock requirement was a disincentive to membership. The Club had the authority certainly to permit non-stockholder members to use the Club. Of course, only stockholder members can vote, although any member can be on the Board.

The committee structure was reinvigorated. Having worked with nonprofit organizations for years, I believed – and still do – that an active committee structure is the best way to get things done. In addition, we asked all members to bring at least three potential new members to the Island during the year, or at least give us three names of persons to contact. I don't remember if this was very successful, but we did get some names and some new members.

In 1993, there were several more family picnics held at the Island, with a focus on trying to get people down with kids. Based on my experience, the Island is a great place for children. It's sort of a grandpa's farm, where kids can roam and parents don't have to worry about traffic and strangers, just mosquitoes and jelly fish. It's a wonderful place for youngsters to traipse around the shore and poke at dead fish, certainly a rite of passage that everyone should enjoy. We worked hard at bringing in family members. And Jon Swindle did a great job enticing hunters to join.

During these years, Beryl Anthony, Democratic Congressman from Arkansas, was the Club President. Beryl was extremely active in the Club. He went down to the Island many times and used to love hunting there. He even donated his boat to the Club. It was a green metal fishing boat and lasted quite a long time. Beryl was the one who came up with the idea for a new party on the Hill, the State of the Union Reception. Beryl figured that the night of the State of the Union address given by the President was one night when Members of Congress would be "captive" and not able to go somewhere else before the speech. He was right. Back then, we had one of the only events on the Hill that night, and always had great turnouts for the Reception, with perhaps fifty or more Members of Congress. They loved to attend our event because we brought up a wonderful spread of fried oysters from the Island, with oyster stew and raw oysters as well. Chef Patsy Bailey, wife of Eddie Bailey who had run the store across from the Club's parking lot years ago, also prepared wonderful beaten biscuits with Southern Maryland stuffed ham.

Another thing I believe the Congressmen liked about the Jefferson Islands Club receptions was that we didn't really have any agenda, other than staying in existence.

Well, of course, providing a Clubhouse with suitable surroundings where members could discuss Jeffersonian philosophies was our agenda, but we definitely did not have a specific lobbying or issue goal.

When Bill Clinton was elected President, it was an exciting time for us, because Beryl swore he would get the President down to the Island (even though Beryl had unfortunately lost his re-election bid). That would have been really cool, but I wanted to be able to have a Citizen of the Year Dinner in honor of the President and make a ton of money. So, with the help of Jeff Rosen and others, we prepared booklets with information about the Club, including photos from the old brochures. Senator Joe Robinson from Arkansas was one of the founders of the Club and its first President, so that was a nice tie-in, too. With the help of Bill Brewster, a Blue Dog Democrat from Oklahoma who visited the Island frequently and is still a great supporter with his wife Suzi, we also sent to the President a request signed by about 30 Members of Congress asking Clinton to accept the Citizen of the Year Award. I was convinced that we'd get the President to one of our events.

Unfortunately, nada. No luck. Someone said the President's scheduler asked Vernon Jordan about the invitation, and he apparently said he didn't know anything about the Club, so they turned us down. I don't know what happened, but I still think Bill Clinton should attend one of our events, dammit. His middle name is Jefferson, for cripes sake.

Also in 1993, we had a wonderful 250th birthday dinner for Thomas Jefferson on May 25 (not his real birthday) in the Montpelier Room of the Madison Building of the Library of Congress. Doug Metz, head of the Wine and Spirits association, was the dinner chair and arranged for gourmet chef Brian Patterson to provide a wonderful menu for a meal reminiscent of the Jeffersonian era, including oyster soup, smoked goose with cranberry relish and Monticello greens, loin of venison stuffed with exotic mushrooms with gratin of roots and tubers. Jamie Connelly and Paul O'Day also served on the Dinner Committee. Special wines of the type favored by the nation's third President were also served. I had now also become the ad hoc Club historian, and was asked to deliver a presentation about the history of the Club. It was a wonderful evening.

On September 15, 1993, we held one of the more unique events in Club history. Representative Howard Coble of North Carolina, a long time supporter of the Club, who served many years later as Honorary Chair, invited racing icon Richard Petty to be honored by the Club on the Hill. Petty didn't know anything about the Club, but apparently was touched by the invitation and a very nice luncheon was held. Ted Bronson, another Club member, was a big racing fan and also helped organize the event, as I recall. Petty left his race car on display out in front of the House Office Building; it was a funny looking car, with only one seat. Anyway, I didn't know shinola about racing, but since I was Executive Vice President got to sit next to Richard Petty during the luncheon. He was a very nice man and we had a good time. I remember what he said in his sort-of-formal remarks. He had been driving around the Hill and people would say about those walking on the street, "There's Senator So and So, and that's Congressman Frick and there's Representative Frack." Petty said he was impressed, but he asked was it really true that Members of Congress just wandered around the streets all day long? He got a big laugh out of that.

We had missed the 1992 Citizen of the Year, so we were pleased to resume that honored tradition the next year by honoring Congressman Jack Brooks of Texas, Chairman of the House Judiciary Committee. Brooks had been a member of the Club since 1961 and had fond stories about it. It was about that time that the new Administration put in place new ethics rules, and Members of Congress were no longer permitted to be given a membership in a club at reduced dues. At the time, Members of Congress only paid $50 annually in dues, as I've mentioned. I think most of them probably paid it, and we had maybe 30 or 40 Congressional Members at the time. After that ethics rule was adopted, we cleared a new arrangement with the ethics committees of both the House and Senate, which permitted us to call Members of Congress who agreed "Friends of the Club." We also could have a Congressional Board of Advisors. In 1993, our Advisors included Jack Brooks, Bill Brewster, Ben Cardin, Howard Coble, Bill Emerson, Dante Fascell, Jimmy Hayes, Blanche Lambert (to be Senator Lincoln after her marriage), Gene Taylor, Jamie Whitten, and Don Young. Many of these Congressmen remain supportive of the Club to this day. Gene Taylor drove his motorboat all the way down the Potomac River from Washington, DC one year and arrived in the pitch black, never having been to the Island before. Club Manager Colleen Wise and Darrell were waiting out in the River with signal lights to guide him to the Island. That's some service!

I believe that 1993 was when we first met Nancy Cole. Avid Club member and man in a thousand places around town, Jamie Connelly, knew of Nancy from some prior connections. She had worked with the Kennedys and was a big Democratic event organizer. Nancy hails from Kentucky, and doesn't like to miss the Derby. Jamie and I met with Nancy in her office back then to see if we could "synergize." I guess we did, since Nancy has been working with the Club, putting on our wonderful events ever since. She can organize the State of the Union Reception, the Wild Game Reception, or Citizen of the Year Dinner with her hands tied behind her back. Prior to Nancy, the Club had worked extensively with Leslie Hayes, wife of then Congressman Jimmy Hayes from Louisiana. Leslie was a great organizer as well, and put together many of the events in the 1980's.

We also initiated a Congressional Breakfast series in 1993. We scheduled hour long informal breakfasts with a number of Members of Congress and charged $50 per person. These were very intimate affairs held on the Hill, where the Member would talk off the record about developments on the Hill. About eight to ten Club members would attend. A number of Members of Congress helped support these events by contributing their time, including Ben Cardin, Bill Emerson, and Bill Brewster among others.

We also had another unique event on April 13, 1994 celebrating Thomas Jefferson's real birthday. We had arranged for Bill Barker, who played a very convincing Thomas Jefferson (about six feet two and long red hair; it was scary), to appear at the reception held in the U.S. Capitol. We also honored four Members of Congress who were retiring that year after over three decades of service: Bob Michel, Jake Pickel, Bill Ford, and Don Edwards. Bill, aka, T.J., gave a wonderful presentation in costume. He has worked the Williamsburg gig for years.

In the fall of 1994, we honored Senator Robert Byrd with the Club's Citizen of the Year Award. Byrd was President Pro Tempore of the Senate and Chairman of the Appropriations Committee. I have been fortunate to attend most of these events and was honored to meet Senator Byrd. What sticks in my mind about this event was the invocation given by Father Bill George, S.J. I didn't really know Father George then, but he was ubiquitous on the Hill. He was a lobbyist for Georgetown University and ministered to many Members of Congress. Later I was to get to know Father better when he was President of Georgetown Preparatory School and I was President of the Alumni Association. He thought the alumni were all trying to kill his land development deal and shut us out of the process. It wasn't fun, but other than that, I really like him.

Anyway, he delivered a very moving invocation for Senator Byrd's dinner. I have his notes from the event and here is about what he said: "Lord God, we are ever grateful for your gift of the Chesapeake Bay and the special Island we call Jefferson. As the prophet wrote, 'To everything there is a season.' When the sounds of the Bay change to the honks and quacks of waterfowl, we sense the harmony your changes in nature reveal. As we honor your son, Robert, we realize how diverse your beauty must be, because in the rugged mountains of West Virginia the change is announced in the wonderful multi-colored coat of the forest. We know these are but glimmers of your beauty in heaven. Thank you. Bless our conversation and friendship tonight, and we ask you to bless this food we are about to receive." Nice, huh?

The Club also helped sponsor a "Salute to Jefferson Wine Tasting" on May 17, 1995 in the Rayburn House Office Building, along with the National Association of Beverage Importers, Wine & Spirits Wholesalers of America, the National Wine Coalition, and the Vinifera Wine Growers Associations. We had a lot of great wine that night. I also remember going with Doug Metz to the Jefferson Memorial on Thomas Jefferson's birthday on April 13 one of those years and reading a proclamation in honor of T.J. from the Club. We even had a permit from the National Capitol Police or Park Service, whichever has jurisdiction. Doug wanted to offer a toast and had brought some grape juice (I don't think our permit allowed alcoholic beverages) that we poured into wine glasses. The Park Police didn't like that and wouldn't let us take a picture, which they explained was because they didn't want people using the Memorial as some sort of a commercial for grape juice or wine. Fortunately, we were not sent to jail or anything like that.

We had more Family Picnics and also some Congressional staff picnics in 1995. Rep. Bill Brewster took his staff to the Island for a day of relaxing, fishing, swimming, and eating, and so did Steny Hoyer. Steny also has been a long time supporter of the Club. He received the Millard E. Tydings Award at the Crab Feast one year. There is a picture in the Bar at the Clubhouse of me in a crazy blue, one-of-a-kind JIC hat presenting the Award to Steny. The Award had also been presented in the past to Louis Goldstein and in 1995 was bestowed upon Lt. Governor Kathleen Kennedy Townsend. Rep. Don Young of Alaska attended the Crab Feast that year and presented the award to Kathleen. Young received the Citizen of the Year Award that year, too. Senator Paul Sarbanes was honored with the Millard Tydings Award another year, and Steny showed up to help honor him.

One of the stalwart Club members over the years, particularly with respect to the Club's "political" side, has been Jim Desmond. He works as a lobbyist for Lockheed Martin, and it seems like he knows everyone in Congress intimately. He has personally been responsible for securing many of our Citizens of the Year. He served as Vice President of Washington Programs for perhaps ten years, until 2006. We owe Jim a lot.

In 1996, the one thing that stands out in my mind was the Citizen of the Year Dinner. Bill Emerson has been a member of the Club when he worked with TRW in Washington. I remember meeting with him in the late 1970's about Club stuff. He was a good member and a great guy. He was elected to Congress from the 8th District of Missouri in 1980, and served for 16 years. Bill had cancer, and the Club wanted to honor him. We named him Citizen of the Year and he was to receive the award on June 19. A week or so beforehand, we heard Bill had taken a turn for the worse, but decided to go ahead with the event. I remember standing around the evening of the dinner, and the rumor was that Bill had gotten significantly worse. He didn't make it to the dinner, and passed away three days later on June 22. His wife JoAnn and four daughters came to the dinner, nonetheless, in a real show of courage and dedication, but it was not a happy evening. JoAnn now holds that seat from Missouri. There was a bridge in Missouri dedicated to Bill in 2003.

After I surrendered the Executive Vice President position in 1997, Charlie Cromwell and I persuaded Pat Presley to take on the role, and the Board changed the title to President. Pat was a wonderful fellow and friend of the Club. I don't remember who brought him into the Club, but I do remember meeting him at the Island before becoming aware of his prowess on the Hill. Pat was a cousin of the King, and had that intriguing Southern drawl. We talked at the Island one day, and Pat wasn't wearing shoes even though it had been a little rainy and muddy. He was an Island kind of a guy. He also was a government relations executive to the BP America company. He took on the President role with relish, and was the key architect of the 1997 Citizen of the Year Dinner for Trent Lott. It was a smashing success, with over 400 people in attendance. We sold a bazillion tables and made a lot of money; one of the best ever.

The next year, John Dingell was Citizen of the Year, and he delivered a wide ranging discussion of Thomas Jefferson. The following year, in 1999, Pat's brainstorm was to honor both John Breaux and Thad Cochran in a demonstration of bipartisanship. The theme was a "return to civility." The event was another success, but the Club's efforts at bipartisanship and civility unfortunately have not seemed to be very successful on the national level.

Pat was also very successful at bringing in corporate sponsors. We had attempted to start such a program earlier, but Pat was the one who drove the bus home. In 1999, BP America, Chevron, and Philip Morris were Jefferson sponsors at $7500 per year. This sponsorship program (with three sponsorship levels has been another life-saver for the Club, and some of the recent sponsors have included the Altria Group, Bellsouth, Kellogg, Brown & Root, Texaco, BNFL Inc., Deloitte & Touche, Dow Chemical, Dow Agroscience, Harris Corp., Lockheed Martin, Norfolk Southern, the National Rifle Association, Yamaha Outboard Engines, and others.

I also need to report that, in November 1998, Dante Fascell passed away. He was an amazing person and great supporter of the Club. We wondered what we could do to honor him. He had loved to eat crabs on the porch in front of the Clubhouse, as Jeff Rosen recalled. So, in a ceremony at the Crab Feast the next year, we dedicated that porch to him in a very nice ceremony. I was asked to say a few words and, frankly, began choking up. Dante had so many close friends, but he had just been really special to me and to the Club. Father Bill George was at the Crab Feast as a guest of Jim Desmond. He picked up the slack and said some nice words about Dante and his dedication to the Club. Next time you're on the porch, check out the brass plaque we put on the wall.

Another catastrophe struck in June of 1998. A tornado smashed into the Clubhouse and obliterated the north wing. From the Presidential Suite to room number 8 at the north end, there was basically nothing left. Debris was hurled down the lawn nearly as far as the Farmhouse. Fortunately, again, no one was injured. Vice President of Island Operations Jon Swindle reacted quickly and organized a number of volunteers. Justin McInerny braved the rain with Jon to weatherproof the open structures, and an interim Club Manager, Chris Hicks, ferried workers back and forth to help with the clean up effort. John Kern was the ultimate key to the operation, soliciting bids and managing the reconstruction. A stroke of good luck enhanced the timely clean up and reconstruction.

Jim Gunn, owner of Costal Design, the firm that had completed our previous seawall/rip rap projects, was completing a project nearby on the River and brought in his crew and heavy equipment, which made quick work of the clean up. He also transported the bulk of the new building materials that were quickly compiled by John. Mike Killelea used his considerable clout with suppliers to purchase and have about fifty tons of material delivered to the Club dock in a period of 24 hours. That's a lot of material! Jim Gunn's crew also dug a huge pit at the former dump site at the south end of the Island and filled it with the debris from the demolished north wing. When the weather conditions were right, the debris was burned and filled back in, thus eliminating the very costly process of removing it from the Island.

There is now no one who knows the nitty-gritty of the facility like John Kern. John basically commuted two hours each way from his home in Bethesda each day until the work was completed several month later. John was responsible for completing extensive and frustrating negotiations with the county to obtain the permits needed to accomplish the reconstruction. I had been able to find the old architectural drawings for the Clubhouse, which apparently helped expedite the process. John consulted with local architects and competitive bids were solicited from bonded and insured contractors. With the insurance proceeds, the north end was fixed back up better than ever. The rooms in the north wing now clearly outshine the south end (although frankly I still like the old end better, just for sentimental reasons). In addition, John was able to manage the insurance money so well, and with donating his services as general contactor and his hands on carpentry, he was also able to achieve at the same time a new kitchen, roof, carpeting, Kabota tractor, boat and motor, new beds, linens, and reduce the Club debt significantly. Never before have female-type visitors to the Island felt so comfortable about the modern kitchen as the one we have now. Colleen keeps the whole place ship-shape and it is really beautiful. Of course, here husband Darrell, who basically grew up in and around the Island, is a tremendously competent, talented, and friendly guy. My kids all worship Darrell, I think in particular because he always has a toothpick wedged in his teeth.

Earl Comstock became President in 2001 and served for two years. Earl had worked on the Hill for Senator Ted Stevens of Alaska and was able to obtain the Senator as Citizen of the Year in 2002, following Rep. Billy Tauzin in 2001. Senator Jim Inhofe, Chairman of the Senate Committee on Environment and Public Works was Citizen of the Year in 2003, and had been a member of the Club years back when he was in the House of Representatives. Earl's initial tie with the Island was through his wife, Anne, who was General McInerney's daughter. The General has been a loyal member for years and often brings large contingents of retired military friends to the Island for parties.

Kirsten Rowe was Executive Director of an association and loyal member, and took on the President's position in 2003. She helped secure Chairman Joe Barton and Rep. Duncan Hunter as Citizens of the Year in 2004 and 2005, respectively. I think it was during Kirsten's reign that we first got the Club a website! Check out www.jeffersonislandsclub.org!

As the Club moves into its 75th anniversary year, Mike Mitchell has assumed the mantle of Presidency. He had been with the Club many years, is an avid hunter and Island user, as well as a lobbyist in Washington. The Citizens of the Year in 2006 are Senators Pete Domenici and Jeff Bingaman, Chairman and Ranking Member, respectively, of the Senate Committee on Energy and Natural Resources. I like the bipartisan theme. A new format was tried out, with a reception, rather than a dinner. The price tag seemed a little steep for me personally at $1000 per head, but the more successful the better in terms of keeping the Club alive.

One of the Club's long-time friends on the Hill is Rep. Howard Coble from North Carolina. He has served as Honorary Chair of the Club for many years. He is always at Club events and loves the oysters at the State of the Union and Wild Game Receptions, particularly the oyster stew. Recently, Rep. Colin Peterson of Minnesota has been the co-Chair with Mr. Coble. Colin is an excellent musician, and his band has played at a number of Club events on the Hill.

You know, there are probably many other stories and additional facts that I could have written about in this book. But I've forgotten more stories than I can remember, and I just got tired of going through all those boxes. Of course, many records have been lost, too. So, this is not a complete history, but it's the best I can do for now. Maybe for the 100th anniversary of the Club in 2031, if I'm "still on two," I'll try to add some more things from those old boxes and hopefully folks will tell me some new stories.

Nonetheless, we'll end our history with a slightly revised chapter from the first book, the purpose of which is to make you feel like you're actually on the Island, maybe even love the old gal like I do. Check it out.

An All-Season Visit to the Island

The Island unveils different faces during each season. Those who only visit in the summer, for example, miss the scenes of winter: the swans, the ice and the bitter yet invigorating northwest wind. Let's indulge for a few moments in an imaginary visit to the Island. A walk for all seasons.

As we glide across the Sound from the mainland on the Seahawk, the water itself differs with the seasons. In the heat of August, the River is still, "ca'm" as the locals say. In the hottest summer sun, the green and dark brown water might be covered with algal scum in some places. It's saltier in the summer too, but most salty in fall. The air of summer is so heavy you can cut it with a knife. Humid.

In winter, the water is clear blue. The air slaps cold in your face and chilling dampness permeates your bones. The tide would most likely be low in winter, blown down and out of the River and Bay by the prevailing nor' westers. In January or February many years past, we might have to walk over on the ice. If it wasn't solid enough, we just wouldn't go. Several days of a strong northwest wind have been known to blow all the water away, leaving only puddles in the deep spots of the sound, nearby creeks and streams. We could just walk then, like Moses crossing the Red Sea.

Northeasterly storms bring high tides, almost covering the docks. Rain and ocean water blown up the River raise the sea level several feet above normal. This is a dangerous situation for boats, because logs and driftwood lift off the beaches and float half-submerged, like icebergs waiting for passing ships.

If we are riding over at night, the moon will determine whether we drive through blackest black or bask in bright light. The moon also affects the tides, which have greater velocity and are more extreme, high and low, when the moon is full.

We land at the main dock on St. Catherine's Island. The House Cove is a perfect harbor, protecting the Club boats from severe winds. It is only about 6-8 feet deep in the middle. The bottom is mud. Pure, slimy, black muck. Perfect for eel and widgeon grass and crabs, too. The shores are sandy and mostly covered by sharp thick grass and reeds.

This dock was originally constructed by Joe and Bernie Wise. Each pole was worked in by hand. Drive it, wiggle it, turn it, jump on it. Hard work. Yet their dock remained solid for nearly twenty years.

As we walk onto the Island toward the Clubhouse, the lawn stretches out before us. In the summer, people relax at the pool or play frisbee, horseshoes, or softball. Let's walk to the beach towards Captain William's Point. Joe Wise used to keep a flock of geese penned on the northwest side of the point, to attract others in during hunting season.

We look out over the Potomac and realize how vast it is. Nearly seven miles across to the Nomini Cliffs of Virginia, it impresses us with its power. The Potomac River watershed has a total drainage area of some 9.4 million acres. The upper Potomac basin includes the area around Front Royal and Waynesboro, Virginia, northwest through West Virginia, Cumberland, Maryland and reaches as far north as Chambersburg, Pennsylvania. It is the longest and broadest estuary entering the Chesapeake Bay. Directly in front of us are Coode's Flat (named after the infamous John Coode) and Kettle-Bottom Shoals. These shoals are formed of rocklike stalagmites, jutting up from the river bed. These shoals proved to be formidable obstacles to British sailing ships reaching toward Washington in the War of 1812, before the channels were marked.

The overall health of our River is questionable. This historic Bay tributary, once so bountiful, is struggling to survive. Bernie Wise's father once told him, "Son, I may not live to see it and you might not either, but one of these days, there's going to be nothing in this River but high and low water."

Let Frederick Tilp explain why he asked, "Must the River Die?" in his book on the Potomac River. He said: "Today, our Nation's Number One River is in its agonizing death throes, not by natural processes, but because of sewage, industrial chemicals, detergents, top soil, petroleum products and sludge and the myriad slops and substances which man discards while booming along the greatest wave of population growth and industrial progress since the river took form before history began."

It's hard to believe that the great sturgeon used to fly into the air within view of our nation's capital. The channel of the Potomac near Washington was 7 fathoms deep only 200 years ago; now it's but 3 fathoms. Of course, some may say that the River is better than it was. But consider how bad it had become. In the late 19th century, the Potomac was called "The River of Garbage" in local newspapers.

Frederick Tilp, again: "More than three thousand acres of marsh lands, swamps, clear water springs, canals, fish filled streams and wildlife country in the

Washington area have been filled with raw garbage, dead animals, manure, hides, street sweepings, refuse and coal ashes… During and after the Civil War, garbage and dead animals were delivered by wagon to the waterfront in Washington and loaded into dump scows to be towed down river by tugs. A dump scow is a square-end flat-bottom vessel, so fitted as to permit lowering the bottom compartment, dumping the animal and garbage load into the River. Dumping grounds were originally off Wide Water, Virginia as requested by watermen who hoped to attract more blue crabs to the river's upper reaches. Frequently, there were more garbage and dead animals than the fattened crabs could consume, resulting in shore lines being littered with rotting refuse and half-eaten carcasses."

In 1894, the Pubic Health Service declared the River unsafe for swimming, cooking, and bathing. In the late 1920s, water chestnut seaweed, imported from Europe as ornamental aquarium plants, found its way into the River and nearly smothered it. In the 1940s, an invasion of Eurasian water milfoil struck the River. The bluegreen algal blooms of the '60s, nourished by excessive amounts of nitrogen and phosphorous caused by sewage, strangled much of the waterway.

The power of the River also includes its resiliency, thank goodness. Generally, it has recovered from these attacks. But we must be cognizant of the dangers and careful in our treatment of this wonderful resource. Turbidity and sediment-loading of millions of tons per year caused by urban developments, highways, and construction continue to decrease light penetration and photosynthesis beneath the surface of the water. The numbers of oysters and crabs are at all time lows.

Here in the lower Potomac, however, the water is relatively clean. I think it's better than it was. You can swim safely. Take off your shoes and walk in the water toward the northwest point. A crab just darted by, see him? Claws raised up and running sideways as fast as he can go. Be sure not to step on him! Look, there is a school of minnows, darting away from your every step. Yes, the River still lives, despite man's efforts to kill it.

Now, look to the west! The sun is setting and it's glorious. Bright colors fill the sky. The winter sunsets are even more brilliant than summer. If we wait long enough, the moon will set, too. More subtle than the sun, the moon often slips below the horizon in a glow of orange, or pink, or purple. It is worth the wait or the early rise with camera and tripod poised.

Returning to the Clubhouse, we go inside. The foyer greets us and we can't avoid signing the thick register on the entry table. Lots of names in there. They tell an interesting story. Congressman Pete Jarman's name shows up a lot in the early years, so does Senator A. Owsley Stanley. There's a description of the first lowering of the duck at midnight on New Year's Eve, now an honored tradition. Our eyes are drawn to the River we see through the door to the porch. It looks like you could just dive in from there.

The mahogany dining table to the left is huge. It used to be too tall, and now it's too short, but it is still solid. The scenes on the end paneled wall of the filled up to the Farmhouse was painted by Betsy Glassie, a famous artist. There is wood furniture everywhere; it's cozy. Pictures of former Club luminaries adorn the walls. In the living room area, Thomas Jefferson's image hangs over the fireplace, across from Franklin Roosevelt. A small statue of a donkey sits on the carpet. Children ride on it and use the rotating ear as an accelerator. I distinctly remember when I got too big to easily sit on it.

The first television I remember was brought down in about 1976. At one time there was only a metal pole outside with an antenna; you had to go out and turn the pole to get better reception. Now, there's satellite TV. The card table has seen many games and lots of cigars. There has never been a knob on the door to the restroom, but only a hook. If you could look up into the ceiling over the toilet, you'd see a water holding tank that provides the water pressure for the Clubhouse.

We decide to walk down Pennsylvania Avenue, named after an obscure street in Washington, D.C. The pine and cedar trees sprout up everywhere. The honeysuckle covers everything and the fragrance is heavenly. Bayberry bushes proliferate and titillate the nose with refreshing aroma. As we walk, we reach for a handful of anise; green licorice. You can taste the smell.

Haywood recalls, "As a kid, I used to think of the Island almost like a continent; it seemed huge, because there was seashore, forest, bogs, these deer trails that would lead to sort of secret rooms with moss floors under pines, and even the dump, where I remember seeing maggots for the first time, which just floored me. Nature!"

Pennsylvania Avenue has been in use as long as I can remember. It leads to Chevy Chase Circle, which overlooks the Narrows to Colton Point. Just before we arrive at this Circle, however, we come upon Lake Pierdon. This lake was at most a pond, and in the dry summer it was hardly more than a muddy hole in the ground. Now, it's being covered with vegetation and trees. The seawall construction crew dug up this pond for backfill for the wall. On the other side of the pond, tall pines and cedars provide cool shade in the summer. I used to ride back there with Sea Biscuit Bob Boy, watching out for the old, rusted barbed wire that used to lie on the ground in some places; I think it's gone now. Milkweed and some brilliant purple pod-like plants grow under the tree canopy. Lime-green ferns puncture the needle covered ground and soft, velvety moss creeps from one spot to the next.

This is where I first spotted a golden orb spider! On a walk one day, a brilliant golden-yellow flash turned my head. This large, nearly three-inch spider wears velvet black leggings and a white and bright yellow gold abdominal cape. It is beautiful! And calm and peaceful resting in the center of a silver web.

There are many other interesting insects to be found on the Island. (Some even find you!) I've seen a spotted bright red and black velvet ant a couple times, usually at the pool area. About one and one half inches long, it is really a wingless wasp. A variety of flutterbys abound; some spice brushed swallow tail black butterflies, little white butterflies (for lack of a better term), orange tipped butterflies or pieridae, and the popular monarch-type. This orange and black butterfly looks almost exactly like a monarch, but is somewhat smaller. I've noticed them over the years and they seemed to congregate near the milkweed pods near the Farmhouse and on the outskirts of the lawn. I don't think there are many left.

Of course, we have our bees and wasps, sweat bees, and mud dobbers. A plethora of fly varieties visit ever so often, usually when there's a land breeze. Of course, who can forget the dreaded green-headed fly, which attacks swimmers or loungers with scissor-like jaws. They take a bite and always come back for more, but usually can be smitten by even the less quick souls. The damselflies (helicopters) are not really flies. They are elongated winged creatures that fly around in pairs when mating. The female dips her abdomen in the water and drops off the eggs. The purple and blues of their transparent wings shimmer as they hover and dart around the shore.

A crazy little bug I know you've seen is the whirly-gig beetle, which runs around on top of the water. A scavenger at heart, his legs act like oars with little foot pods that don't break the surface of the water. The dragonfly is a territorial insect that stakes out an area and main-tains its sovereignty. The stately preying mantis may be seen from time to time, poised to snatch an unsuspecting bug.

Our walk continues down to what we call Honeymoon cove. This sandy, crescent beach is beautiful at night, with the moon rising from the east and waves pushed by a south wind lapping at the shore. To the right, cat tails and other plants grow. Erosion has taken its toll; there used to be wooden steps from Chevy Chase Circle down to the water. Now, you'd have to climb up or down hand over hand. Once on the beach, we go north toward Hawes Bar, although now you have to wade in the water to get there. Notice the greenish fruit hanging from the gray-barked persimmon trees. The persimmon fruit is not edible until the first frost, when it becomes sweet and juicy. But, please, don't taste it during the summer, no matter how luscious it looks. It is the epitome of "pucker" and "dry-mouth." Yech!

In the summer, we've all noticed those zippy tiger beetles that jump around on the sand. They are predators, tiger striped, that eat flies and mosquitoes. What is fascinating are young tiger beetle larvae, which live underground. These little larvae hear and feel other insects walking above them on the sand, pop out of their hole, attack the bugs (small ones, I'm sure) and drag them back into their holes. They even have little hooks on their backs so they can't be dragged out of their holes by their victims. Amazing.

Hawes Bar has grown and shrunk by a couple hundred feet in the last few years. The sea takes from one area and gives back to another, for a while. I don't think the Island ultimately has a chance with global warming and rising sea levels. Might as well enjoy it while it lasts. The water near the bar is shallow on the east side and fairly deep off the west. As a matter of fact, on the right tide, you can wade nearly fifty feet to the east without the water going above your knees.

Continuing our hike, we return by way of Boy Scout Trail. We soon pass the low, swampy area (being careful not to disturb the Swampwampus) and, in late June, find ourselves picking blackberries. These blackberries are extremely juicy and sweet. As we near the Farmhouse, we see tall locust trees. There used to be among them one plum and two pear trees. The pear trees bore fruit into the 1980s, but the plum tree was not as productive. The three trees used to blossom beautifully, but they fell into the water several years ago. In fact, Boy Scout Trail along the north side of the Island is threatened, and much of Truman Bluffs has fallen into the River. When walking the Trail a few years ago, you couldn't hardly see the water. Now, the bank is not far from your feet.

A small patch of daffodils always used to burst forth in the spring in front of the Farmhouse. The land here has not eroded too much, but there wasn't much to give. Despite the deposit of some rip rap along the bank, the old septic tank has now been uncovered by erosion. This point of land is much less exposed to the prevailing winds than on the River side, but don't be surprised if the Farmhouse topples in one of these days. It will just break my heart.

Looking across the Cove, we see several great blue herons poking in the shallow water for soft crabs. Last time I sat down to count these gorgeous creatures, I saw about 19 in a few minutes. Seagulls party over on the rip rap rocks surrounding what's left of Captain William's Point, and go for a fly whenever a boat glides by. In the winter, geese, ducks, and swan claim the Cove, next covered by the ice. In spring, we watch mallards teach their young to swim. Occasionally, an egret returns. Once in a while, a glossy ibis. Hopefully, they will come back soon.

We walk down the lawn from the Farmhouse to the Clubhouse. The old skeet range constructed by Joe Wise is no longer, although you can see the slab of concrete with his name etched in. A cozy new area has been cleared out for shooting clay pigeons. A number of members have hearing aids due to the lack of proper ear protection during all those years of hunting. Now, everyone wears ear plugs or other protection.

At night, depending on the moon, or lack thereof, you can see as well as day or miss your hand in front of your face. It's so dark sometimes you feel like you're walking off the Island. A loud "snort" means that the deer, out for a late night graze, didn't see or hear you coming. But, oh those stars. The city sky doesn't know what stars are; can't even compare. I remember lying on my back on the lawn as a child with my father, gazing up at the Milky Way and looking for shooting stars. The perfection of the Universe is there to see, if we will only look. And the peace that is everything calms my soul particularly well on this oddly shaped body of land that I've loved all my life.

In 2004, I was married to Julie Littell on the Island. It was June 19 (Juneteenth, as the African-American community calls it, because that was when the slaves in Texas were finally told they were free in 1865, two years after the Emancipation Proclamation). The Island returned its love to us on that day. It was glori-
ous weather. We had moved the old platform that one of Liz Linkin's children had been married on back in the 1980's to underneath the cedar and pine trees that Jimmy Oliver cleared out years ago and where we now hammer crustaceans at the annual Crab Feast. It's a beautiful site, knocking crabs and looking out over the Potomac, always with a breeze. Since we got married there, I've called it the St. Catherine's Island Chapel and Crab Shack. The wind stood up that day, and the skies remained clear. Our family and friends joined us for a nice ceremony. Special musician friends Andra Faye and Chris Jones, Grant Dermody, and Allen Holmes played during the ceremony. One of the highlights was Resa Gibbs playing a "secret" song with my son Max Glassie; they wouldn't tell us what it was until they played it. My son Jay and daughter Anne both did readings. My sister Claire and her family came, my mother was there, my brother Haywood and brother Don, and lots of other family. After the ceremony, folks played music, ate crabs and the delicious meal Colleen had arranged through Thompson's Seafood, swam in the pool, and walked around the Island. Who says you can't love a piece of land? I do.

In 2006, the 75th anniversary of the Jefferson Islands Club, we look forward to a bright future. The facilities are in excellent shape, although I just heard that Hurricane Ernesto knocked off the roof of part of the north wing of the Clubhouse (again) and erosion took a huge chunk out of the land near the old Farmhouse. Due to the combined efforts of many great people, our Island has prospered and will continue to prosper. Problems remain, mostly financial, but the spirit of the founding fathers lives on. After all, there still is a "Club House with suitable surroundings and comforts where members may assemble, discuss and promote Jeffersonian philosophies…" If you listen carefully, you may hear Harry Truman playing the piano.

JEFFERSON ISLANDS CLUB, INCORPORATED
· 1931 ·

Other tools for peace from PeacEvolutions LLC

PEACE AND FORGIVENESS by Jefferson Glassie [ISBN 0-9753837-0-1, 112 pages, $14.95] and DOUBLE AUDIO CD read by the author [ISBN 0-9753837-1-X, $14.95]. This life is our perfection, says the author. Who could imagine any heaven more perfect than this earth, with butterflies, snowflakes, and mountain tops? Though we are all peace and love, man has fears that cause war, anger, hate, and everything that isn't love. Letting go of fear – forgiving - brings peace. If we learn this, we can change the world.

POEMS OF PEACE AND FORGIVENESS by Jefferson Glassie [ISBN 0-9753837-2-8, 72 pages, $12.95], with photographs by the author. This book captures the concepts from Glassie's book, Peace and Forgiveness. These beautiful poems explain there's no right or wrong, no evil or sin, in the Universe. Everything that's not love is just based on fear. Glassie teaches the lessons of forgiveness that can lead to peace of mind, and peace in our society. We are all one, in perfection.

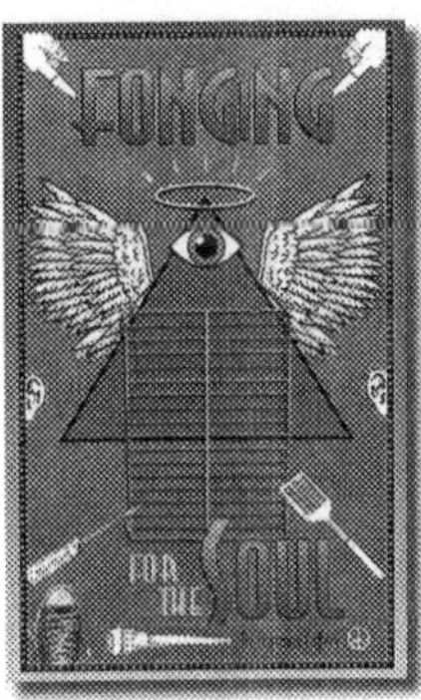

FONGING FOR THE SOUL by Erasmus Caffery [ISBN 0-9753837-3-6, 78 pages, $14.95]. Gathering with others, tapping on an oven rack attached to strings tied to fingers that are stuck in your ears, listening to primal sounds. Fonging brings us to together in laughter, and is much more sane than war. This book explains how to fong. It's very simple and you can do it with anyone. By understanding the simultaneous silliness and splendor of life, we learn to create a better and more peaceful world through inanity. With many helpful illustrations, because you'll need them.

SONGS OF PEACE AND FORGIVENESS [ISBN 0-9753837-4-4, $16.98] featuring original and public domain songs by Gaye Adegbalola, Scott Ainslie, Roddy Barnes, Eleanor Ellis (on a Bill Ellis song), Andra Faye and the Mighty Good Men, Grant Dermody and Frank Fotusky, Allen Holmes and Alison Radcliffe, Kelley Hunt (on a Jim Ritchey song), Ray Kaminsky, Mark Kinniburgh, MSG – The Acoustic Blues Trio, Jesse Palidofsky, and Alex Radus. The most unique blues CD you've ever heard. It will make your heart soar. Proceeds go to help preserve the famous "Barbershop" in Washington, DC run by the Archie Edwards Blues Heritage Foundation, winner of The Blues Foundation's 2005 Keeping The Blues Alive (KBA) Award.

peacEvolutions LLC **Order Form**

Fax orders to (301) 263-9280 with completed order form.

Email orders by logging on to www.peace-evolutions.com

Telephone orders by calling (301) 263-9282.

Postal orders may be sent to   Peace Evolutions, LLC
P.O. Box 458-31
Glen Echo, MD 20812-0458

Please send the following:

Peace and Forgiveness, book	$14.95 each	quantity: ______
Peace and Forgiveness, audio CD	$14.95 each	quantity: ______
Poems of Peace and Forgiveness, book	$12.95 each	quantity: ______
Fonging for the Soul	$14.95 each	quantity: ______
Songs of Peace and Forgiveness	$16.98 each	quantity: ______
My Love Affair with an Island	$20.00 each	quantity: ______

We will honor all requests for full refund on returned items. Please send more free information on:

❏ presentations   ❏ other publications and information

Name: ____

Address: ____

City: _________________________________ State: ____ Zip: _________________

Telephone: ____

Email address: ____

Sales tax: Please add 5.00% for products shipped to Maryland addresses.

Shipping and handling:

United States: $5.00 for first book/CD and $2.00 for each additional item.

International: $7.00 for first book and $5.00 for each additional item.

Payment:

❏ Check or   Credit Card ❏ Visa ❏ Master Card ❏ Discover

Card number: ______________________________________ Exp. Date:_____________

Name on Card: ____